Rhetoric, Knowledge and the Public Sphere

STUDIES IN LANGUAGE, CULTURE AND SOCIETY

Edited by Łucja Biel, Andrzej Kątny and Piotr Ruszkiewicz

VOLUME 8

Agnieszka Kampka /
Katarzyna Molek-Kozakowska (eds.)

Rhetoric, Knowledge and the Public Sphere

Bibliographic Information published by the Deutsche Nationalbibliothek
The Deutsche Nationalbibliothek lists this publication in
the Deutsche Nationalbibliografie; detailed bibliographic
data is available in the internet at http://dnb.d-nb.de.

This work was supported by the Rhetoric Society of Poland
in accordance with contract 892/P-DUN/2015.

Library of Congress Cataloging-in-Publication Data
Names: Kampka, Agnieszka, 1976- editor. | Molek-Kozakowska, Katarzyna, editor.
Title: Rhetoric, knowledge and the public sphere / Agnieszka Kampka ;
  Katarzyna Molek-Kozakowska (eds.)
Description: Frankfurt am Main ; New York : Peter Lang, [2016] | Series:
  Studies in Language, Culture and Society ; Volume 8
Identifiers: LCCN 2016018686| ISBN 9783631666333 (Print) | ISBN 9783653059502
  (E-Book)
Subjects: LCSH: Communication models. | Rhetoric--Social aspects. |
  Information society--Social aspects. | Knowledge economy--Social aspects.
  | Discourse analysis--Social aspects. | Critical discourse analysis. |
  Speech acts (Linguistics)
Classification: LCC P93.55 .R53 2016 | DDC 808--dc23 LC record available at
https://lccn.loc.gov/2016018686

ISSN 2195-7479
ISBN 978-3-631-66633-3 (Print)
E-ISBN 978-3-653-05950-2 (E-Book)
DOI 10.3726/978-3-653-05950-2

© Peter Lang GmbH
Internationaler Verlag der Wissenschaften
Frankfurt am Main 2016
All rights reserved.
Peter Lang Edition is an Imprint of Peter Lang GmbH.

Peter Lang – Frankfurt am Main · Bern · Bruxelles · New York ·
Oxford · Warszawa · Wien

All parts of this publication are protected by copyright. Any
utilisation outside the strict limits of the copyright law, without
the permission of the publisher, is forbidden and liable to
prosecution. This applies in particular to reproductions,
translations, microfilming, and storage and processing in
electronic retrieval systems.

This publication has been peer reviewed.

www.peterlang.com

Contents

Acknowledgements 7

Agnieszka Kampka, Katarzyna Molek-Kozakowska
Rhetoric and the public sphere: Making a case for a knowledge society 9

Part One: Visualization as a strategy in knowledge representation

Cezar M. Ornatowski
Knowledge and surveillance society 27

Christine Isager
A poor show of knowing: the horror and comedy of
unsuccessful writers on film 43

Marcus Gottschling
Lend me your eyes: Creating immediate understanding through Prezi 57

Part Two: Rhetorical and argumentative resources in the public sphere

Martijn Wackers, Jaap de Jong and Bas Andeweg
Structure strategies for a memorable speech: the use of rhetorical
retention techniques by scholars and politicians 75

Louise Schou Therkildsen
Becoming a citizen: Knowledge and identity in
European textbooks for citizenship tests 93

David Isaksen
From calutrons to Congress: The democratic challenge of
specialized knowledge 109

Part Three: National varieties of rhetorical action

Gabriela Scripnic
Emotion-invoking strategies in the presentation of Roşia Montană
Project in the Romanian public sphere 131

Hilde van Belle
Polemics and paradoxes in the media:
The case of the Dutch TV-show *Pauw* 149

Ludmilla A'Beckett
Stigmatizing female oppositionists in Russia:
Stances toward comparisons with Joan of Arc 167

Part Four: Rhetoric, pedagogy and production of knowledge for democratic citizenship

Maureen Daly Goggin
Preparing students for the emergent knowledge society:
Rethinking learning and pedagogy in rhetoric 189

Ove Bergersen
Kindergartens and the civic art of rhetoric:
Citizens, character and knowledge 209

Anne E. Porter
'Responsibilizing' the youth: The rhetoric of civic participation
in the World Bank's 2009 climate change essay competition 223

Contributors 239

List of figures 243

Index 245

Acknowledgements

This monograph, *Rhetoric, Knowledge and the Public Sphere* edited by Agnieszka Kampka and Katarzyna Molek-Kozakowska, as well as its sister volume, *Rhetoric, Discourse and Knowledge* edited by Maria Załęska and Urszula Okulska, has been prepared under the auspices and with the financial support of the Rhetoric Society of Poland.

The publication of these monographs gives us an opportunity to thank the invited contributors for sharing their inspiring findings and insightful arguments, the reviewers for their efforts and engagement and our collaborators who offered their advice on shaping the manuscripts. Last, but not least, we are grateful to the Peter Lang team for enabling this project.

Agnieszka Kampka

Warsaw University of Life Sciences-SGGW

Katarzyna Molek-Kozakowska

Opole University

Rhetoric and the public sphere: Making a case for a knowledge society

1. Introduction

The phrase "the knowledge society" often functions as a metaphor that attempts to grasp either the current socio-economic situation or the society's future orientation. On the one hand, a knowledge society can be defined as a set of conditions in which knowledge – understood as our abilities to access, process, analyze, store and manage information – becomes the main element of the social capital. Many institutions and individuals now seem devoted to fostering that kind of knowledge-intensive social arrangement. However, the so-called knowledge societies are also marked for many new and unresolved problems, divisions and obstacles, which need to be confronted to enable their future development.

Optimists say that new technologies and scientific solutions will give us new means of communicating high quality knowledge more democratically, as epitomized for example by wikinomics. (Tapscott, Don/ Williams, Anthony D.: *Wikinomics. How Mass Collaboration Changes Everything*. Portfolio: London 2006) Pessimists, on the other hand, point to such issues as climate change, depletion of resources, and great migrations in order to claim that neither technology nor science has helped us to solve any of those crises. In fact, there are a few possible scenarios of dealing with each of the above issues, and none of them is based on unquestioned facts, calculations and diagnoses. In such situations, policy-makers have to argue for their cases and persuade people to their causes. (Majone, Giandomenico: *Evidence, Argument and Persuasion in the Policy Process*. Yale University Press: Chelsea 1992) The political process now depends on how skillful communicators are in establishing their version of what is known to be publicly acceptable. Arguably, the role of rhetoric as a tool of persuasion in the public sphere has never been as important. As a result, rhetorical analysis has gained a new momentum: both in terms of studying argument-building mechanisms and in terms of demystifying argument-presentation devices. The studies collected in this volume testify to this increase in the significance of rhetorical construction of knowledge in the contemporary public sphere.

The notion of rhetoric espoused here is not of some historical scholarly tradition with no relevance today. Neither is rhetoric seen as an auxiliary, primarily style-oriented sub-discipline of language or literary studies. We see it as a current and valid field of inquiry in its own right, where scholarship concentrates on how the means, conventions and forms of knowledge transmission actually impinge on the nature of knowledge produced in the process. We assume that rhetoric is explored whenever some intentionally persuasive message is explored.

In yet another sense of rhetoric, this volume has been inspired by some reflections as to whether the label "knowledge societies" is equivalent to "knowledgeable societies," particularly as one realizes that the dominating vision of a knowledge society is associated more with specialization and expertise than with emancipation and equity. This situation brings us to an understanding of rhetoric as a pedagogical orientation as well.

In the knowledge society it is often assumed that the so-called hard sciences are to reveal objective facts about the natural and social worlds and thus facilitate the civilizational advancement. In this context, natural sciences, medicine, engineering, even economics and social sciences have been praised for having contributed to the society's knowledge pool, whereas the humanities have been increasingly treated as mere arts. The former are considered to be a-rhetorical, the latter as all-rhetorical. Our position is, however, that without developing rhetorical scholarship with a pedagogical edge, knowledge societies (in which there is much knowledge) will not become knowledgeable societies (in which citizens know much). (cf. Molek-Kozakowska, Katarzyna: "A Knowledge Society or a Knowledgeable Society? The Role of the Humanities in the Fostering of Knowledge through Critical Literacy." *Polish Journal of Philosophy* 2010, pp. 33–46)

2. The public sphere and its mediated multimodal affordances

The public sphere is the physical or virtual space where meaning can be articulated and negotiated in the process of deliberation. (Koller, Veronika/ Wodak, Ruth: "Introduction: Shifting Boundaries and Emergent Public Spheres." In: Koller, Veronika/ Wodak, Ruth (eds.): *Handbook of Communication in the Public Sphere*. De Gruyter Mouton: Berlin et al. 2010, pp. 1–17) Indeed, the public sphere tends to be seen as a complex constellation of multimodal discursive encounters that are at least partly rhetorical in nature, as they are channeled towards persuading partners in deliberation. (cf. Habermas, Jürgen: *The Structural Transformations of the Public Sphere.* Cambridge University Press: Cambridge 1989; Habermas, Jürgen: *The Theory of Communicative Action.* Vol. 1: *Reason and the Rationalization of Society.* Heinemann: London 1984; Elster, Jon (ed.): *Deliberative Democracy.* Cambridge University Press: Cambridge 1998; Dryzek, John: *Deliberative Democracy and Beyond: Liberals, Critics, Contestations.* Oxford University Press: Oxford 2002; Chambers, Simone: "Rhetoric and the Public Sphere: Has Deliberative Democracy Abandoned Mass Democracy?" *Political Theory,* Vol. 37 (3) 2009, pp. 323–350)

Public deliberation involves various rhetorical activities in which citizens are invited to participate by either actively voicing opinions or passively following and considering arguments. Although there are many obstacles to open deliberation, including access, education or engagement, ideally, deliberation should be instantiated to identify and resolve differences of opinions, stances or political solutions. According to Fairclough and Fairclough, for example, "arguments are based on different but often reasonable values and value hierarchies (normative priorities), which often turn out to be hard or impossible to reconcile, and political deliberation has to find ways of dealing with these differences." (Fairclough, Isabela/ Fairclough, Norman: *Political Discourse Analysis.* Routledge: London 2012, p. 21) The claim in this collection also is that the nature of the public sphere is fundamentally rhetorical and that knowledge shaped as a result of that process is a product of strategic choices in communication.

And yet Habermasian concept of deliberation, which focuses on predominantly rational debates in ideal communicative situations, seems to have underestimated the plurality of current forms of democratic participation in the public sphere. According to Fraser (Fraser, Nancy: "Rethinking the Public Sphere: A Contribution to the Critique of Actually Existing Democracy." *Social Text* 25/26 1990, pp. 56–80) sharing a common culture and a value system is no longer a prerequisite for a public sphere to thrive. (cf. Fraser 1990, p. 57) Public deliberation is no longer about the rational rules of how opinions and arguments are expressed, but rather about the very process of their making and articulating in a competitive, mediatized "marketplace of ideas," in which some arguments find resonance and later get implemented as regulations.

The participation in the public sphere is also a multimodal endeavor. Various signifiers and meaning-making codes tend to be drawn to articulate one's position: from street protests to internet virals and hacking attacks, from elaborate and costly campaigns to mere boycotts. The mediated public sphere is designed for multiple audiences that are highly networked and increasingly media-savvy. However, saturated with global media content, or easily digitalized and transmitted formats, public spheres tend to be overloaded with short messages, perishable communications and superficial relationships that may create an illusion of dialogue. (Dahlgren, Peter: *Media and Political Engagement. Citizens, Communication and Democracy*, Cambridge University Press: New York 2009) New media genres and technologies (below-the-line comments, homepages, social media, online presentations, videos) have enabled new voices to be heard, but also to be marginalized and disempowered. (cf. A'Beckett, van Belle, this volume) The rise of the visual culture has had its reflection on the public sphere with the new forms of activity reaching new segments of the populace, but also commercializing some of the domains of public life. The multimodal affordances of the public sphere allow for new forms of expression for active citizen groups, but have potential for engendering apathy, cynicism and "narcotizing dysfunction" for the public at large. (McKee, Alan: *The Public Sphere: An Introduction*. Cambridge University Press: Cambridge 2005) It seems that the public sphere has never been so complex and diverse, and as difficult to grasp in its entirety as it is today.

It is worth stressing that both language and imagery can be used and re-used for impact, influence and argument. Hardly any press conference, scientific lecture, political debate, official announcement, even if primarily verbal, is devoid of significant visual props and illustrations. Images (including communicators' appearances) may be persuasive by building ethos and logos, particularly when arguments presented as simulations, maps and figures are made to seem self-evident. (cf. Gottschling, Ornatowski, this volume) However, in the visual culture, images are also increasingly used for pathos: from generating sympathy and concern to dramatizing the issue and ridiculing the political opponent. (cf. Scripnic, Porter, van Belle, Isager, this volume) The multimodal is not restricted to individual pictures, icons and images, however. Multimodality does act as a mental shortcut, a visualization of the social, or a catalyst for public activity, but, in its broader understanding, also as a framing device mandated by the mediated public sphere. It seems that Web 2.0, with its netoric, has embraced the multimodal as the fundamental mode of proof, the prerequisite for deliberative rhetorical situation and for the dynamics of meaning-making interaction:

> While classical rhetoric teaches how the hierarchy of arrangement, the structuration of ideas and the casual sequence of premises make a speech and exert influence on the audience, netoric show how divergent elements are joined by associational logic in a paratactic connection and carry meaning. While rhetoric in the traditional view was a conserver of the culture, netoric can be considered as a displayer of constant change. While rhetoric could be regarded by Kennedy as a mental energy sparked by an emotional reaction to a situation in which an individual feels threatened, netoric in turn can be thought of as a digital capacity that is operationalized in situation when the individual wants to feel connected in meaningful interaction. (Aczél, Petra: "Netoric". In: van Belle, Hilde et al.

(eds.) *Verbal and Visual Rhetoric in a Media World*. Leiden University Press: Amsterdam 2013, pp. 307–323, here p. 321)

The point is that the contemporary public sphere allows multiple voices, opinions and interests to be articulated, but with less and less regard to indexing their social importance, moral value or aptness. Ideally, in large societies independent and free media institutions could filter and organize these messages for the public opinion to deliberate upon. But it would be a truism to note that nowadays many mediated representations, arguments and debates are subjected to media agendas, not public agendas. In most cases, the mediator's rhetoric can additionally modify the claims, redefine premises and reshape knowledge provided by representatives of non-elite interest groups (cf. van Belle, A'Beckett, this volume). Thus because neither the elites nor corporate media are likely to provide their full assistance in public deliberation, citizens have to seek their own rhetorical tools for filtering information, building knowledge and participating in public debates (cf. Isaksen, Bergersen, Goggin, this volume).

If, as claimed by some scholars, being a citizen is no longer a given, then one is to perform one's citizenship discursively and communicatively. (cf. Kock, Christian/ Villadsen, Lisa (eds.): *Rhetorical Citizenship and Public Deliberation*. Pennsylvania State University Press: University Park, PA 2012) To be identified as a citizen, as a member of a larger polity or community, one needs to align their expression, knowledge and practice with others. (cf. Hauser, Gerard A.: *Vernacular Voices. The Rhetoric of Publics and Public Spheres*, The University of South Carolina Press: Columbia 2008) By acquiring the knowledge and practice of articulating this citizenship, one is in the process of becoming a citizen (cf. Therkildsen, Porter, this volume). As a result, this volume sees the public sphere as an arena of multimodal articulations that ought to be studied "from below," as theoretical accounts of contemporary public communication rarely do justice to its practical and expressive complexity.

3. Public sphere and rhetoric

As most information is mediated and public knowledge is shaped in a process of articulation and deliberation, rhetorical tools are routinely resorted to in cases when contested interests or ideologies are presented, validated or refuted. Although deliberation rarely proceeds smoothly and the outcomes of public debates do not always lead to political or social consensus (cf. Scripnic, Isaksen, this volume), this collection assumes the fundamentally rhetorical nature of the public sphere in which institutions and interest groups may take a stance and represent knowledge in such a way as to argue for or against given solutions.

The "rhetorical turn" in current social studies, according to Schiappa and Hamm, is due to the fact that rhetoric takes up some fundamental issues: "Humans must communicate to survive and such communication always takes place under contingent circumstances." (Schiappa, Edward/ Hamm, Jim: "Rhetorical Questions." In: Worthington, Ian (ed.): *A Companion to Greek Rhetoric*. Blackwell Publishing: Malden, MA et al. 2007, p. 5) Being knowledgeable in the field of rhetoric helps change the material circumstances of existence by means of collective action and by exerting an influence on individuals. (cf. Goggin, Bergersen, this volume) A specific language needs to be developed to enable the process of influencing others and imbue it with ideological or moral significance. A Polish sociologist Stanisław Ossowski notes that rhetoric as a verbal technology of persuasion may not have changed much since antiquity, except for the use of microphones and media. (Ossowski, Stanisław: *O osobliwościach nauk społecznych*. Wydawnictwo Naukowe PWN: Warszawa 2001, p. 209)

The orator's rhetoric has the longest history of scholarship. The Socratean tradition teaches us how to use language and questions to uncover the truth and achieve self-improvement (if not perfection) in reasoning. The sophistic tradition instructs us how to present our arguments to defend our position and appeal to our audiences. Aristotelean rhetoric helps us to reconcile various interests and mindsets and to offer solutions in the course of discussion and with reference to commonly shared values, not with forceful measures. Classical rhetoric is also referred to in this volume, but with respect to newest technologies of mediating knowledge (cf. Wackers et al., Gottschling, Bergersen, this volume). But if we take rhetoric as somewhat larger than oratory, as a theory of human communication in the public sphere (Schiappa/ Hamm 2007, p. 6), we should explore the various interfaces between persuasion, democracy and situated language use and their implications. (cf. A'Beckett, Therkildsen, Porter, this volume)

For example, in the current political context, leaders in democratic societies are obliged to justify their decisions and legitimize their policies. They need to persuade the increasingly fragmented societies to their positions and priorities. (Kane, John/ Patapan, Haig: *The Democratic Leader. How Democracy Defines, Empowers and Limits its Leaders*. Oxford University Press: Oxford 2012) But while studying political rhetoric, one can note that sometimes such verbal legitimization is based on emotional appeals, logical fallacies and eristic devices, which displace factual arguments and logical reasoning. (cf. Scripnic, Porter, Isaksen, this volume) Since the rhetorical advice is to adjust the expression to the needs and expectations of the audiences, opinion leaders are bound to apply the situational, pictorial and verbal tricks all too frequently. (Norval, Aletta J.: *Aversive Democracy. Inheritance and Originality in the Democratic Tradition.* Cambridge University Press: Cambridge 2007, p. 64)

Some scholars would say that according to the rules of informal reasoning, solutions tend to be accepted and implemented if there are practical reasons for them that overweigh counterarguments articulated during the discussion. (cf. Walton, Douglas: *Practical Reasoning: Goal-driven, Knowledge-based, Action-guiding Argumentation.* Rowman and Littlefield: Savage 1990) For example, a claim in favor of a given political solution requires rational and moral premises which are subjected to evaluation procedures that are compatible with democratic practice. A claim against a solution also requires sufficient premises, which may additionally include counterarguments that take the validity and persuasiveness away from the opposite claim. It is through strategic presentation of arguments and counterarguments that knowledge can be built in a society. In consequence, rhetoric can be viewed as aiming for effectiveness in argumentation in the public sphere, considering the existence of multiple audiences with different, possibly incompatible, commitments, vales and ideologies. (*cf.* Perelman, Chaim/ Olbrechts-Tyteca, Lucie: *The New Rhetoric: A Treatise on Argumentation.* University of Notre Dame Press: Notre Dame 1969) While argumentation is about evaluating the soundness and strength of reasoning, rhetoric is about how the argument is to be communicated to convince the public, how it can be turned into socially accepted fact or common sense. (cf. Potter, Ornatowski, Bergersen, this volume)

Indeed, rhetoric and argumentation are combined in the concept of strategic maneuvering (Eemeren, Frans H. van/ Houtlosser, Peter: "Strategic Maneuvering in Argumentative Discourse." *Discourse Studies* 1 (4), 1999, pp. 479–497; Eemeren, Frans H. van: *Strategic Maneuvering in Argumentative Discourse.* John Benjamins: Amsterdam 2010), which, far from representing the so-called empty rhetoric, sophistic argument or eristic trick, involves a concern for effectiveness on par with reasonableness. Rhetorical scholars have both a right and a duty to explore how knowledge is shaped in the public sphere and to identify rhetorically-charged representations, false arguments and maneuvers that could obscure the interests and intentions of the communicators. (cf. van Belle, Scripnic, A'Beckett, this volume) This collection contributes to this endeavor by highlighting such cases or exploring whole domains in which social knowledge has been constructed with rhetorical means, be they data-gathering, authority discourses, institutional communication, mediated messages, film representations, educational materials or promotional websites.

4. Rhetorical criticism and pedagogy

Today, calling an argument a "rhetorical" one is usually interpreted as an attempt at demystifying some kind of manipulation. This is a result of rhetoric acquiring a bad reputation for helping the manipulators manipulate even more effectively. This moral dilemma has accompanied rhetoric scholars since Aristotle, who sees rhetoric's main redeeming potential as a form of pedagogy (cf. Bergersen, Goggin, this volume). Having that in mind, rhetoricians have put much effort into fostering rhetorical criticism and rhetorical education as part of citizenship (cf. Therkildsen, Porter, this volume). When equipped with rhetorical skills, people can articulate their positions more effectively and chose to be persuaded (or not) by public communicators. According to Condor, Tileaga and Billig, by paying attention to the fine details of argumentation, they can evaluate how communicators mobilize rhetorical resources to support ideological ends, and which lines of argument are foregrounded. However, to be productive, rhetorical criticism must be contextualized, as communicators use language and other symbolic resources flexibly and creatively to construct patterns of argument, and to undermine the constructed claims of their opponents. (Condor, Susan/ Tileaga, Cristian/ Billig, Michael: "Political rhetoric." In: Huddy, L./ Sears, D.O./ Levy, J.S. (eds.): *Oxford Handbook of Political Psychology*. Oxford University Press: Oxford 2013, p. 300)

In the knowledge society, arguments from science and authority seem to be particularly common and insidious. (Turner, Stephen: "What is the Problem with Experts?". *Social Studies of Science* 31, 2001, pp. 123–149) The ways in which expertise may mask ideology merits deeper analysis, as scientists' authority, as well as experts' data, figures and estimates may have hidden political and economic underpinnings. (cf. Isaksen, Scripnic, this volume) More than a few scholars have demonstrated that scientific discourses are fundamentally rhetorical constructions of what is worth studying, which models and methods to use and how to frame the implications of results and feed them back into theoretical considerations. (for a review see, e.g., Załęska, Maria: *Retorica della Linguistica. Scienza, Struttura, Scrittura*. Peter Lang: Frankfurt a. Main et al. 2014) Knowing how specialists use rhetoric and unmasking the rhetorical processes where they are not expected to have been employed is one of the tasks of this volume too. (cf. van Belle, Hilde: "Introduction: Rhetorical Perspectives." In: van Belle, Hilde et al. (eds.): *Verbal and Visual Rhetoric in a Media World*. Leiden University Press: Amsterdam 2013, pp. 9–33) The descriptive and pedagogical aspects of knowledge transmission within the domain of science are explored in the sister volume to this monograph *Rhetoric, Discourse and Knowledge* edited by Maria Załęska and Urszula Okulska. (Załęska, Maria/ Okulska, Urszula (eds.): *Rhetoric, Discourse and Knowledge*. Peter Lang: Frankfurt a.M. et al. 2016)

Indeed, much of our everyday knowledge and common sense are the results of socially constructed meanings, identities and relationships. (Tindale, Christopher W.: "The Words of Other People: The Fundamental Role of Testimony in Rhetorical Argumentation". In: van Belle, Hilde et al. (eds.): *Verbal and Visual Rhetoric in a Media World*. Leiden University Press: Amsterdam 2013, pp. 41–59) When making personal and citizen decisions, we follow common sense (Aristotle's *phronesis*, Thomas Aquinas' *prudentia*), even though our trust in our reasonableness is being undermined by elites. (cf. Garsten, Bryan: *Saving Persuasion. A Defense of Rhetoric and Judgment*. Harvard University Press: Cambridge et al. 2006, p. 8) This is precisely where rhetorical criticism links with rhetorical pedagogy that consists in how to be able to see the positions of others, to make our positions known, to seek consensus if possible, to persuade others to accept the validity of our purposes. (cf. Goggin, this volume) Rhetorical pedagogy should be a part of civic, democratic education based on shared rules of involvement in deliberation and enabled by new forms of communication in the public sphere. For Garsten (2006, p. 210), there is no other organization or institution which could be better able to discuss and resolve public issues in a fairer, wiser way than civic rhetorical activity. To be able to engage in this process and empower ourselves as citizens, we have to acquire the rhetorical tools which give us the possibility to understand the others' arguments and emotions to help them understand our causes.

5. This volume

The contributions in this collection are grouped in four parts which discuss (1) visualization as a strategy in knowledge representation; (2) rhetorical and argumentative resources in the public sphere; (3) national varieties of rhetorical action; and (4) rhetoric, pedagogy and production of knowledge for democratic citizenship. The common thread in all of them is the attention not only to *what kind of knowledge* is produced in the given domain or discourse but also to *what rhetorical means* this is done with.

"Knowledge and surveillance society" by **Cezar M. Ornatowski** focuses on visualization and resulting strategic representations of collective knowledge produced through surveillance. He reminds us that today the job of "intelligence analysts, law enforcement professionals, public health officials, economic forecasters, market analysts, policy makers, as well as scientists and other researchers" is to engage in collecting large quantities of digital data on a wide range of issues and activities and to use "computational modeling, simulation, and prediction" in their research. Claiming that surveillance is the core of both political economy of knowledge and rhetoric of knowledge, Ornatowski traces the transition from data through visualization to knowledge. He illustrates his point with such examples as Geofeedia or Open Street Map projects, as well as other applications in which big data can be correlated, overlaid to identify regularities, visualized through mapping and strategically interpreted to represent "knowledge." The author's tentative conclusion seems to be that continuous technology- and data-driven surveillance enables not only various innovative forms of knowledge display, but also refinement of that knowledge and its application to naturalize and reinforce social control.

Christine Isager develops the theme of "knowledge workers as objects of cultural representation" in popular film. She studies two writers in the movies by Kubrick and Allen and sees them as abstractions or reductions of knowledge workers with completely unspecified tasks ("a writing project" that their surroundings must respect). Writers as knowledge workers have a fragile framework for these tasks that they themselves must administrate, structure and legitimize and which ends up being revealed as a terrible failure, since their projects have developed into mere bluff, mere shows of knowing. This is an indication that film media tend to humiliate writing/knowledge work in the abstract form as pretentious but remind us how much we trust the experts' sense of judgment. Although trust is necessary for projects to succeed in this world, it is sometimes completely betrayed (which is horrific in Kubrick's depiction and comical in Allen's depiction).

Marcus Gottschling's chapter "Lend me your eyes: Creating immediate understanding through Prezi" demonstrates how visualization is incorporated into argumentation with the goal of a creation of a vivid and sudden insight (*evidentia*), which then leads to persuasion: the change of opinion and behavior of the audience. We are reminded of the functionality and importance of visualizations in presentations in universities and schools, with the growth in use of presentation software such as PowerPoint, Prezi or Keynote. The author draws on classical and modern rhetorical concepts from Aristotle to Burke and appropriates them for the study of the contexts of visual communication. He provides us with an argument that certain visual maneuvers (as in Prezi's panning and zooming navigation) have a capacity to facilitate certain processes of knowledge building, or even to legitimize certain understandings of reality by making it appear as self-evident. Pointing to a range of studies into how learning is facilitated through visual presentations, the author urges us to look at the rhetorical layer of presentations and certain effects (such as the aha-moment) some maneuvers could be catalyzing.

Martijn Wackers, Jaap de Jong and Bas Andeweg in their study on "Structure strategies for a memorable speech: how scholars and politicians transfer knowledge with rhetorical retention techniques" consider the role of rhetorical devices that can be used by professional communicators, notably scholars and politicians, to enhance the retention of information provided to the public in speeches and presentations. Drawing on the overview of 80 English-language and Dutch-language textbooks on public speaking, the authors identify the most often repeated advice for "making a speech memorable." But is that theory implemented in practice? The authors conducted an explorative rhetorical analysis to determine the distribution of two types of structural retention techniques: local techniques (e.g., explicit transitions and question figures) and techniques that are used once in a speech to shape a presentation on a higher hierarchical level. The findings include the fact that it is more typical for the scientists to use techniques that emphasize the structure of a presentation in a didactical, explicit way. Politicians use the more implicit techniques (e.g., of referring in conclusion to initial claims and statements) more often. A comparison of preferred strategies for building knowledge through ensuring more retention can lead to experiments that lend more insight into the effects of various retention techniques and the relation between rhetoric and memory theory.

Louise Schou Therkildsen provides us with a comprehensive analysis of how two European states (Denmark and Austria) attempt to educate applicants for citizenship ("Becoming a citizen: Knowledge and identity in European textbooks for citizenship tests"). By charting some metaphors, narratives, anecdotes and linguistic markers found in official booklets for applicants, the author deconstructs the dominant discursive strategies of projecting national identities and citizen responsibilities. The rhetorically charged construction of citizenship becomes evident when we are given a chance to compare the two ways of "writing up" the "obligatory" information for citizenship applicants in the respective brochures. Therkildsen points out which materials/fragments contain more "essentailizing mechanisms" that might alienate applicants, and concludes about the paradoxical nature of all citizenship textbooks, which inescapably (albeit to different degrees) have to essentialize national identities in the context of increasingly diffuse, globalized and multicultural social arrangements.

In "From calutrons to Congress: The democratic challenge of specialized knowledge" **David Isaksen** revisits a historical case of prominent American scientists and intellectuals attempting to acquaint the post-WWII public with the implications of the discoveries and developments in nuclear weaponry within the Manhattan Project. Comparing various rhetorical strategies used in the writings, the author demonstrates the efficacy (and the failure) of some types of argumentation for the purposes of nuclear science literacy. From formal specialized descriptions, to subjective and emotional appeals, to visual propaganda, the challenge remains on how to empower the society in making informed policy decisions about which technologies to approve. The conclusion is, however, that if scientists will not risk giving up some of their prestige in engaging in grass-roots popularization and polemical attempts, "knowledge societies" in which specialized knowledge is democratized will not arise.

The chapter by **Gabriela Scripnic** "Emotion-invoking strategies in the presentation of Roşia Montană Project in the Romanian public sphere" provides a detailed rhetorical and linguistic analysis of a sample of promotional materials produced to garner Romanians' support for a controversial commercial gold mining project at Rosa Montana. The author focuses on the emotion-stimulating devices employed in the project's official website, which, overriding environmental and community concerns, focuses on engendering the feelings of righteousness and satisfaction involved in envisioning prosperity. By contrast, to promote the investment, pro-development commercials seem to exploit the undercurrents of anxiety and misery present in rural Romania. Scripnic contextualizes her analysis within the modified version of Habermasian public sphere, where, due to media intervention and cultural transformation, the emotional and the private tend to dominate the rational and the public.

In her chapter devoted to "Polemics and paradoxes in the media: The case of the Dutch TV-show *Pauw*" **Hilde van Belle** elucidates the role and characteristics of dissensus. Understood as an alter-ego to the rational deliberation and solution-seeking, the genre of polemics is claimed to be at the core of a democratic public sphere. It exposes interests that are mutually exclusive and ideological positions that are irreconcilable. This situation makes rhetoric-laden polemic discourse worth studying critically. Van Belle's case study of a Dutch political talk-show *Pauw* reveals how the moderator is able to stage a polemic in order to discredit his guest by a range of rhetorical strategies: repositioning of footing, yes/no rather than open questions, quote-jiggling and paradoxes. The study sheds new light on how the news media, with their conflict-driven agendas, could be using polemics to sustain hegemonic rather than truly democratic public communications.

Ludmilla A'Beckett explores the rhetoric of "Stigmatizing female oppositionists in Russia: Stances toward comparisons with Joan of Arc". Her paper is concerned with the dissuading rhetoric which creates bad publicity about Russian and Ukrainian female public figures and the political causes they advocate. In the examples analyzed, the naming "Joan of Arc" has been utilised as a tool of stigmatisation. This analysis of strategies of persuasion that engage the audience by negative identity construction adopts some methods of cognitive linguistics and discourse analysis. The analytical techniques used include appraisal theory and discourse dynamics framework for metaphor. The author's results reveal that the defamation of female public figures can be achieved through (1) exaggerating problematic characteristics, (2) demonstrating authorial distance from positive comparisons, (3) ironic juxtapositions, and (4) evoking cultural prejudices toward strong-willed, independent and self-confident women.

In "Preparing students for the emergent knowledge society: Rethinking learning and pedagogy in rhetoric" by **Maureen Daly Goggin**, we find much more than a pedagogical overview of present challenges to higher education institutions confronted with the changing paradigms of knowledge production. The author points out that in the knowledge-based economy, more jobs will require lifelong learning, critical reflection and complex communication and presentation skills. Thus, courses in rhetoric and writing should actually gain in significance and popularity. After tracing some paradigm shifts in American pedagogy and comparing the main metaphors of learning, Goggin proceeds to demonstrate the advantages of the educational innovations recently implemented at Arizona State University in the form of a practical rhetoric-centered major in Studies in Writing, Inquiry, Rhetoric and Literacies (SWIRL). The main aim of the program seems to be analysis of and reflection on rhetorical situations that are relevant in the social world, as well as fostering students' creativity, self-reliance and savviness with respect to multimodally presented materials. The exemplary materials of students' assignments and projects show how educators could confront the current pedagogical challenges.

Ove Bergersen, in his chapter on "Kindergartens and the civic art of rhetoric: Citizens, character and knowledge," introduces the concept of rhetorical citizenship, highlighting the role of rhetorical knowledge, skill and practice in the context of politics, ethics and society. Following Eugene Garver's reading of Aristotle, Bergersen positions the citizen as the centerpiece of such interactions as democratic participation, community-building and rationality-driven deliberation. Then, by taking the notion of rhetorical citizenship to the educational context, Bergersen demonstrates how such documents as, for example, kindergarten prospectuses can function as sites of negotiation and deliberation about the values and practices of the society. His analysis shows that the description of kindergarten mission and philosophy, or curriculum and regulations can be read as indicative of strategic ways of community-building, moral character formation and knowledge/reason development. Altogether, such texts may help (or not) to develop what Aristotle termed as phronesis – an ingredient in rhetorical citizenship.

"'Responsibilizing' the youth: The rhetoric of civic participation in the World Bank's 2009 climate change essay competition" by **Anne E. Porter** takes up the issue of youth civic engagement through essay contests. First, the author maps the relation between civic engagement, rhetoric and the youth pointing to the problems of democratic empowerment in the context of neoliberal economy. She reviews research related to the efficacy of top-down youth empowerment initiatives. Next, she presents the evolving rhetoric of the World Bank as an institution claiming to foster the ideas of knowledge society, while also proclaiming financial and economic assistance. In this vein, the World Bank-sponsored youth-oriented online essay competition on how climate change can be addressed by the youth themselves is critically analyzed (both the framing documents and the essays themselves). The analysis traces some "responsibilizing" strategies in the texts through which youth are projected as accountable for confronting the issue and "saddled with" remedying the consequences of climate change. Acknowledging the discontinuities in the World Bank rhetoric, Porter calls for critical rhetorical attention to various texts reproducing dominant discourses of powerful institutions, which, while claiming to democratize knowledge, may actually privilege neoliberal ideologies.

References

Aczél, Petra: "Netoric". In: van Belle, Hilde et al. (eds.) *Verbal and Visual Rhetoric in a Media World*. Leiden University Press: Amsterdam 2013, pp. 307–323.

Chambers, Simone: "Rhetoric and the Public Sphere: Has Deliberative Democracy Abandoned Mass Democracy?" *Political Theory*, Vol. 37 (3), 2009, pp. 323–350.

Condor, Susan/ Tileaga, Cristian/ Billig, Michael: "Political Rhetoric." In: Huddy, L./ Sears, D.O./ Levy, J.S. (eds.): *Oxford Handbook of Political Psychology*. Oxford University Press: Oxford 2013, pp. 262–300.

Dahlgren, Peter: *Media and Political Engagement. Citizens, Communication and Democracy*, Cambridge University Press: New York 2009.

Dryzek, John: *Deliberative Democracy and Beyond: Liberals, Critics, Contestations*. Oxford University Press: Oxford 2002.

Eemeren, Frans H. van: *Strategic Maneuvering in Argumentative Discourse*. John Benjamins: Amsterdam 2010.

Eemeren, Frans H. van/ Houtlosser, Peter: "Strategic Maneuvering in Argumentative Discourse." *Discourse Studies* 1 (4), 1999, pp. 479–497.

Elster, Jon (ed.): *Deliberative Democracy*. Cambridge: University Press Cambridge 1998.

Fairclough, Isabela/ Fairclough, Norman: *Political Discourse Analysis*. Routledge: London 2012.

Fraser, Nancy: "Rethinking the Public Sphere: A Contribution to the Critique of Actually Existing Democracy." *Social Text.* 25/26, 1990, pp. 56–80.

Garsten, Bryan: *Saving Persuasion. A Defense of Rhetoric and Judgment.* Harvard University Press: Cambridge et al. 2006.

Habermas, Jürgen: *The Structural Transformations of the Public Sphere.* Cambridge University Press: Cambridge 1989.

Habermas, Jürgen: *The Theory of Communicative Action.* Vol. 1: *Reason and the Rationalization of Society.* Heinemann: London 1984.

Hauser, Gerard A.: *Vernacular Voices. The Rhetoric of Publics and Public Spheres,* The University of South Carolina Press: Columbia 2008.

Kane, John/ Patapan, Haig: *The Democratic Leader. How Democracy Defines, Empowers & Limits Its Leaders.* Oxford University Press: Oxford 2012.

Kock, Christian/ Villadsen, Lisa (eds.): *Rhetorical Citizenship and Public Deliberation.* Pennsylvania State University Press: University Park, PA 2012.

Koller, Veronika/ Wodak, Ruth: "Introduction: Shifting Boundaries and Emergent Public Spheres". In: Koller, Veronika/ Wodak, Ruth (eds.): *Handbook of Communication in the Public Sphere.* De Gruyter Mouton: Berlin et al. 2010, pp. 1–17.

Majone, Giandomenico: *Evidence, Argument and Persuasion in the Policy Process.* Yale University Press: Chelsea 1992.

McKee, Alan: *The Public Sphere: An Introduction.* Cambridge University Press: Cambridge 2005.

Molek-Kozakowska, Katarzyna: "A Knowledge Society or a Knowledgeable Society? The Role of the Humanities in the Fostering of Knowledge through Critical Literacy." *Polish Journal of Philosophy* 2010, pp. 33–46.

Norval, Aletta J.: *Aversive Democracy. Inheritance and Originality in the Democratic Tradition.* Cambridge University Press: Cambridge 2007.

Ossowski, Stanisław: *O osobliwościach nauk społecznych* [About the specificity of social sciences]. Wydawnictwo Naukowe PWN: Warszawa 2001.

Perelman, Chaim/ Olbrechts-Tyteca, Lucie: *The New Rhetoric: A Treatise on Argumentation.* University of Notre Dame Press: Notre Dame 1969.

Schiappa, Edward/ Hamm, Jim: "Rhetorical Questions". In: Worthington, Ian (ed.): *A Companion to Greek Rhetoric.* Blackwell Publishing: Malden, MA et al. 2007, pp. 3–15.

Tapscott, Don/ Williams, Anthony D.: *Wikinomics. How Mass Collaboration Changes Everything.* Portfolio: London 2006.

Tindale, Christopher W.: "The Words of Other People: The Fundamental Role of Testimony in Rhetorical Argumentation". In: van Belle, Hilde et al. (eds.): *Verbal and Visual Rhetoric in a Media World.* Leiden University Press: Amsterdam 2013, pp. 41–59.

Turner, Stephen: "What is the Problem with Experts?". *Social Studies of Science* 31, 2001, pp. 123–149.

Van Belle, Hilde: "Introduction: Rhetorical Perspectives". In: van Belle, Hilde et al. (eds.) *Verbal and Visual Rhetoric in a Media World.* Leiden University Press: Amsterdam 2013, pp. 9–33.

Walton, Douglas: *Practical Reasoning: Goal-driven, Knowledge-based, Action-guiding Argumentation.* Rowman and Littlefield: Savage 1990.

Załęska, Maria: *Retorica della Linguistica. Scienza, Struttura, Scrittura.* Peter Lang: Frankfurt a. Main et al. 2014.

Załęska, Maria/ Okulska, Urszula (eds.): *Rhetoric, Discourse and Knowledge.* Peter Lang: Frankfurt a.M. et al. 2016.

Part One:
Visualization as a strategy in knowledge representation

Cezar M. Ornatowski

San Diego State University

Knowledge and surveillance society

1. Introduction

"If you need to be convinced that you're living in a science-fiction world," Bruce Schneier points out in a recent book, "look at your cell phone."

> Your cell phone tracks where you live and where you work. It tracks where you like to spend your weekends and evenings. It tracks how often you go to church (and which church), and how much time you spend in a bar; and whether you speed when you drive. It tracks – since it knows about all the other phones in your area – whom you spend time with, whom you met for lunch, and whom you sleep with. The accumulated data can probably paint a better picture of how you spend your time than you can, because it does not have to rely on human memory. (Schneier, Bruce: *Data and Goliath: The Hidden Battles to Collect Your Data and Control Your World*. Norton: New York 2015, p. 1–2)

Our computers also constantly gather data about us, including what we read, watch, and listen to, as well as what we think, insofar as our thoughts lead us to search the Internet: "On the Internet, surveillance is ubiquitous. All of us are being watched, all the time, and the data is being stored forever." (Schneier 2015, p. 32) "We are living in a golden age of surveillance." (Schneier 2015, p. 4)

Already in 2001, David Lyon described contemporary society as "surveillance society" in which everyday life is subject to "purposeful tracking, tagging, listening, watching, recording or verification." (Lyon, David: *Surveillance Society: Monitoring Everyday Life*. Open University Press: Buckingham, UK 2001, p. 1) Information societies, Lyon asserted, are *ipso facto* surveillance societies.

My focus in the present discussion, however, is not surveillance as an activity of monitoring something or someone – and emphatically not as one limited to "spying" or to Big Brother "listening in." Roger Clarke coined the term "dataveillance" for the narrower sense of surveillance as a "systematic monitoring of people's actions or communications through the application of information technology." (quoted in Lyon 2001, p. 143) Here, I treat dataveillance as one aspect of a more comprehensive *epistemic phenomenon*, where new knowledge arises at the intersection of electronic communication, tracking, and recording technologies; massive data-gathering and storage capacities (Big Data); and innovative computation and visualization techniques. In this view, surveillance is a *process of knowledge creation* that integrates *technologies of data gathering* with *techniques of data manipulation* and specific *forms of visual display*. The latter usually takes the shape of "maps", with "geography" (along with conceptual analogues such as "landscape") as the overarching metaphor for knowledge that connects physical, social, and cognitive "spaces". Although surveillance as an epistemic project is not a new, or even a modern, development, surveillance as a comprehensive, technologically leveraged process of knowledge creation based on pervasive dataveillance may indeed represent a novel institution of knowledge.

2. Surveillance: An epistemic view

The *Oxford English Dictionary* defines "surveillance" as a "watch or guard kept over a person" (esp. a suspected person) as well as spying, supervision, or supervision for the purpose of direction or control. "Survey" (etymologically implied in "surveillance") is defined as "the act of *viewing*, examining, or inspecting in detail, esp. for some specific purpose"; examining, inspecting, scrutinizing, or exploring; looking from, or as if from, a *great height* or *commanding position*,[1] as well as constructing "a *map*, plan, or detailed *description*" (emphases added). Surveillance instruments such as the plane table, alidade, or theodolite create a map in a cartographic sense.

In *Discipline and Punish*, Foucault connects "surveillance" to "review" and to modern forms of power and authority when he describes seventeenth-century French town procedures during the plague: "Everyone locked up in his cage, everyone at his window, answering to his name and showing himself when asked – it is the great *review* of the living and the dead." (Foucault, Michel: *Discipline and Punish: The Birth of the Prison*. Vintage: New York 1979, p. 196, emphasis added) "Review" includes data about each inhabitant: their "place" in terms of residence, movements, role, physical condition – thus their "location" within the community. Foucault connects such "review" to the disciplinary project (the term has epistemic – as in "disciplines" of knowledge – as well as axiological connotations): the disorder and confusion of the plague is "met by order"; "against the plague, which is a mixture, discipline brings into play its power, which is one of *analysis*." (Foucault 1979, p. 197, emphasis added) For Foucault, "surveillance" thus becomes a metonym for observation, segmentation, distribution, analysis, and control – activities

---

1 At Hampton Court palace, which once belonged to Cardinal Wolsey and later to King Henry VIII, little figures peer down from the rafters at the courtiers in the hall below. They inspired the term "eavesdropper", warning those below that everything they say can be overheard and used against them.

Foucault connects to the "political dream" of a "disciplined society": the "utopia of the perfectly governed city." (1979, p. 198)

In its relationship to knowledge, and rhetoric, surveillance is not a modern development. Philippe-Joseph Salazar traces surveillance back to ancient Greece. "Aristotle knew of ... surveillance," Salazar notes:

> In Ancient Greek the word "theory" refers to "observation", and specifically a "théoros" was an observer sent abroad overtly (as an ambassador) or covertly to observe how rival cities functioned .... Political "theory" was born of this comparative study of foreign policies, gathered through intelligence, in order to enable Athens to understand better her commercial adversaries (hence, "intelligence"), to respond swiftly to military challenges, and to develop rhetorical tools for strategic communication as a supplement for military action .... - this is the unspoken core of the *Rhetoric* .... (Salazar, Philippe-Joseph: "Surveillance in the Electronic Age: A Rhetorical Critique." *Cosmopolis: A Journal of Cosmopolitics/Revue de Cosmopolitique* 2 2015, p. 3)

Salazar relates surveillance to secrecy (as both secret knowledge and knowledge of secrets) and locates it within the "triage of *decretum/excretum/secretum*," thus within the rhetorically constructed and historically constituted *political economy of secrecy*. In fact, Salazar observes that periodic outbursts of public outrage at revelations of official "surveillance" (e.g., WikiLeaks, the Snowden affair) actually conceal the fact that surveillance has become a core component of "modern bio politics," whose fundamental assumptions (such as the need for individual and collective security guaranteed by appropriate authority) in effect presuppose surveillance, yet are never questioned in principle.

In contrast, I treat surveillance as a *technique of knowledge creation* and locate it at the core of the contemporary *political economy of knowledge*, just as monitors, cameras, sensors, and chips constitute core components of 21st century technologies, from cars to credit cards and smart phones.[2]

Jacques Ellul defines "technique" as "the translation into action of man's concern to master things by means of reason, to account for what is subconscious, to make quantitative what is qualitative, to make clear and precise the outlines of nature, *take hold of chaos and put order into it*." (Ellul, Jacques: *The Technological Society*. Vintage: New York 1964, p. 43, emphasis added) Today, "chaos" is not the plague, as described by Foucault, but such phenomena as the destabilization of traditional forms of power and control, the *de facto* dissolution of borders, mass human migrations, novel (asymmetrical) forms of conflict (esp. terrorism), as

---

2   By 2030, the billions of sensors embedded in automobiles, pacemakers, elevators, all sorts of appliances, even trees, will have the ability to communicate with each other, adding untold volumes of information to the creation of knowledge (Schneier).

well as the overwhelming tsunami[3] of data (Big Data) generated by proliferating communication, monitoring, and sensing technologies. These developments pose novel challenges to the need for order, understanding, predictability, security, as well as the need to "master things by means of reason."[4] Technique, Ellul points out, implies *purpose* and *method*.

Surveillance – both as dataveillance (monitoring, tracking, and recording) and as knowledge creation – is *purpose-driven* in principle. Underlying it is the expressed need, in practically every realm of human affairs – from education to business, science, commerce, international relations, public health, and warfare – for data-driven, actionable, ultimately *strategic*, knowledge. This need is supported by developments in technology. Maturing mobile technology and smart phone devices enable intelligence analysts, law enforcement professionals, public health officials, economic forecasters, market analysts, policy makers, or scientists to collect data on a wide range of activities and digital behaviors and engage in research involving computational modeling, simulation, and prediction. Today, anybody can overlay Google Maps with different sorts of data using Keyhole Markup Language (KML) files (KML files can be created for anything that one wants to put on a map), creating different kinds of applied intelligence: business intelligence, strategic intelligence, firefighting intelligence, and so on.

Method is implicit both in the monitoring, tracking, and recording devices, search algorithms, or imaging software, as well as in intellectual operations, from the design of data mining algorithms to interpretation of emerging information and design of visualizations that serve knowledge "discovery." There is a growing recognition of the importance of spatial and temporal dynamic relationships (known as the "spatial turn") in explaining processes relevant to human behaviors,

---

3   Expression used by Christopher Southan and Graham Cameron in "Beyond the Tsunami: Developing the Infrastructure to Deal with Life Sciences Data." In: Hey, Tony/ Tansley, Stewart/ Tolle, Kristin (eds.): *The Fourth Paradigm: Data-Intensive Scientific Discovery*. Microsoft Research: Redmond, WA 2009, pp. 117–123.

4   In his Foreword to the *Atlas of Knowledge*, James Burke suggests that "[a]ccurate prediction in now more essential than ever." (Börner, Katy: *Atlas of Knowledge: Anyone Can Map*. The MIT Press: Cambridge, MA 2015, p. viii) Similarly, William Bogard emphasizes the centrality of speed and emphasis on prediction in societies dependent on surveillance, from prediction of purchasing behaviors to political or criminal behaviors. (Bogard, William: *The Simulation of Surveillance: Hypercontrol in Telematic Societies*. Cambridge University Press: Cambridge, UK 1996) McNeely and Wolverton point out that knowledge has always been driven by practical needs and exigencies, including prominently novel forms of warfare. (McNeely, Ian F./ Wolverton, Lisa: *Reinventing Knowledge: From Alexandria to the Internet*. Norton: New York 2008)

social activities, communication, public health, intellectual trends, and other social processes. In this endeavor, the "map" emerges as the major form of representation of information that involves dynamic, spatial and temporal relationships between different kinds of phenomena.

3. Knowledge creation process in surveillance

Knowledge creation in surveillance proceeds from *data gathering* through *computing operations* to *visualization* and on to *new knowledge*. Sources of data include HUMINT (human intelligence), GEOINT (geospatial intelligence), MASINT (measurement and signature intelligence), OSINT (open-source intelligence), SIGNIN (signals intelligence, derived from interception of signals), TECHINT (technical intelligence), CYBINT/DNINT (cyber/digital network intelligence), FININT (financial intelligence, from financial transactions), IMINT (imagery intelligence, of objects reproduced electronically or by optical means), COMINT (communications intelligence), and MEDINT (medical intelligence).[5] Data is also obtained from open sources such as planefinder.net, shipfinder.co, marinetraffic.com, activefiremaps.fs.fed.us, or mined from the Internet.(cf. Ornatowski, Cezar M./ Pottathil, Akshay: "Digital Communications Surveillance." *African Yearbook of Rhetoric* 2 (3) 2012, pp. 13–22) Subscription services such as Geofeedia give access to social media communications (current and going back in time) emanating from a given location or area, revealing the location as a communication "landscape" defined by networks of contacts and influence (analysts even speak of "winds" of influence). Anything that is geospatial can be, and usually is, tracked and recorded.

Knowledge comes not so much from data as from *correlating* different kinds of data. Correlation is done by overlaying data on other data, as well as on a map. Knowledge arises from the perception of *relationships* and *patterns* within the data. In the knowledge creation process, the visual-computational environment is designed in ways that combines non-geographic information with maps and other graphics that allow patterns and attribute relationships to be explored in order to facilitate knowledge construction. This construction is ultimately mediated through *visualization* – the key stage is the knowledge creation process. At this stage, multiple graphic views of the data are created in order to stimulate the *visual thinking process*. (Koua, Etien L./ Kraak, Menno-Jan: "An Integrated Exploratory Geovisualization Environment Based on Self-Organizing Map." In: Argawal, Pragya / Skupin,

---

5   http://www.intelligence.gov/mission/data-gathering.html.

Andre (eds.): *Self-Organizing Maps: Applications in Geographic Information Science.* Wiley: Chichester, West Sussex, UK 2008, pp. 45–66) Visualization is considered "a very powerful strategy for getting high-level human intelligence involved … since human vision is extremely effective when it comes to recognizing patterns, relationships, trends, and anomalies." (Yan, Jun/Thill, Jean-Claude: "Visual Exploration of Spatial Interaction Data with Self-Organizing Maps." In: Argawal, Pragya/ Skupin, Andre (eds.): *Self-Organizing Maps: Applications in Geographic Information Science.* Wiley: Chichester, West Sussex, UK 2008, p. 69)

As an example of what a visualization looks like, consider the "thematic map" below entitled "In Terms of Geography". "In Terms of Geography" represents one possible visual rendering of the "space" of knowledge in the discipline of Geography today.

Fig. 2.1: André Skupin. "In Terms of Geography". 2005 (Courtesy of André Skupin, San Diego State University, San Diego, CA. Reproduced by permission of the author)[6]

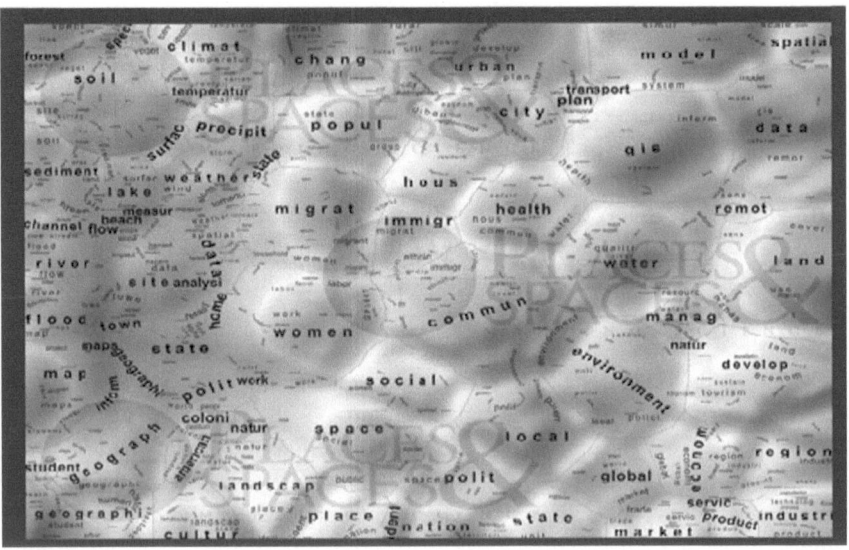

---

6   "In Terms of Geography" resides in the Center for Information Convergence and Strategy at San Diego State University. It can also be found in Börner, Katy: *Atlas of Science: Visualizing What We Know.* MIT Press: Cambridge, MA 2010, pp. 102–3) as well as at http://scimaps.org/mapdetail/in_terms_of_geograph_92.

"In Terms of Geography" is based on content coverage of Geography research between 1993 and 2002. It was generated from more than 22,000 abstracts submitted to the annual meetings of the Association of American Geographers. Data culled from the abstracts has been overlaid on a topographic "base map" that provides a geometric base and underlying "logic" for the display. "Mountains" represent areas of higher topical focus, with word stems serving as labels for major areas of geographical study. "Valleys" represent areas of less topical focus; they may be seen as information "sediments" from the surrounding mountains, heavily influenced by topics indicated on the mountains. The arrangement of mountains and valleys replicates the major global subdivisions of the Geographic knowledge domain. (explanation after Börner, Katy: *Atlas of Science: Visualizing What We Know*. MIT Press: Cambridge, MA 2010, p. 102)

"In Terms of Geography" is an example of a "map of science".[7] Such maps serve as "visual interfaces to immense amounts of data" that would normally overwhelm the senses. (Börner 2010, p. ix) Through such maps, according to Katy Börner, "we can begin to see all that we know as landscape – *viewed as if from above or from a great distance.*" (2010, p. ix, emphasis added)

Interestingly, visualizations, especially ones related to science and knowledge, (such as "In Terms of Geography") are regarded as personal creations and are often signed and exhibited as if they were works of art. Such implicit attributions of "artistic" quality pose the question of their ultimate status, questions that recall early debates about photography: a new mode of knowing, an art, or both?[8] The question opens its own rhetorical issues, especially in regard to visualizations in science.

4. Surveillance and the rhetoric of knowledge

Through devices, software, and algorithms for monitoring, listening, mining, tracking, recording, and storing masses of everyday data, as well as computer operations and visualizations that make it possible to perceive and understand

---

7   More of such maps, as well as a history of mapping as creation of knowledge, may be found in Katy Börner, *Atlas of Science* and Katy Börner, *Atlas of Knowledge*, as well as in the online exhibit "Places & Spaces: Mapping Science" at http://scimaps.org. Examples of visualizations of other sorts of data (not related to science) may be found in Agarwal, Pragya/ Skupin, Andre, eds.: *Self-Organizing Maps: Applications in Geographic Information Science*. Wiley: New York 2008.

8   Cf. Susan Sontag: "Photographic Evangels." In David Rieff (ed.): *Essays of the 1960s & 70s*. New York: The Library of America 2013.

complex and otherwise invisible relationships between phenomena often distant in time and space, surveillance in effect extends the human senses and perception and changes what and how we "see" (not only in terms of vision and sensory data, but also as enlarging the general capacity for perception, as in "I see how A relates to B) and what and how we "know".

The relationship between seeing and knowing constitutes one of the major foci of rhetorical approaches to knowledge. Bruno Latour emphasizes the centrality of practices of "inscription" to knowledge making. (see Latour, Bruno: *Science in Action: How To Follow Scientists and Engineers Through Society*. Harvard University Press: Cambridge, MA 1987) In their classic study of the making of knowledge in a scientific laboratory, Bruno Latour and Steve Woolgar saw conversion of data into various forms of inscription (printouts, records, notes, formulas) and then into a variety of texts (presentations, papers, proposals) as the dominant mode of doing science and the major activity of scientists. (Latour, Bruno/ Woolgar, Steve: *Laboratory Life: The Social Construction of Scientific Facts*. Sage: Beverly Hills, CA. 1979)

Historically, changes in ways of seeing have usually been associated with different ways of knowing. Claude Levi-Strauss has suggested that "[f]or Renaissance artists, painting was perhaps an instrument of knowledge." (quoted in Berger, John: *Ways of Seeing*. BBC and Penguin: London 1972, p. 86) Photography, Susan Sontag notes, "gave a tremendous boost to the cognitive claims of sight, because – through close-up or remote sensing – it so greatly enlarged the realm of the visible." (Sontag, Susan: "Photographic Evangels." In Rieff, David (ed.): *Essays of the 1960s & 70s*. New York: The Library of America: New York 2013, p. 608) The epistemic claims for photography emphasized that "photography provides a unique system of disclosures: that it shows us reality as we had *not* seen it before." (Sontag 2013, p. 611) Surveillance, both through visualizations as well as in terms of its perceptional scope and capacity for retaining information (Big Data), certainly shows us reality as we had not, and could never have, seen it before. In fact, Big Data obtained through ubiquitous surveillance gives a new sense to Berenice Abbott's contention, advanced originally in regard to photography, that "[t]oday, we are confronted with reality on the vastest scale mankind has known." (quoted in Sontag, 2013, p. 608)

Latour and Woolgar regard inscription as "not so much a method of transferring information as a material operation of creating order." (Latour/ Woolgar 1979, p. 245) Scientific knowledge, they conclude, is about creation of order out of disorder (recall Ellul's characterization of technique as *taking hold of chaos and putting order into it*). "Inscription" therefore includes not only forms of notation and text, but also *techniques* (Latour and Woolgar's term) of data recording implicit in devices as well as forms of symbolization.

In surveillance, "inscription" is implicit in the entire process of monitoring, recording, and storing data as well as its analysis, manipulation, and visualization. Knowledge emerges out of computing operations conducted on 3-dimensional space defined as such by dynamic interaction (which implies also time) of entities that supplies the initial data. The entities interacting in the "space" (which may be physical or conceptual/notional) may be of different kinds: people, vehicles, organizations, forces, symbols, or ideas. In creating visualizations, this multidimensional, dynamic "space of interaction" (Geographic Information Systems term) is reduced to a two-dimensional representation (a process referred to as "dimensionality reduction")[9] yet retains some (ultimately symbolic) relationship to the "terrain" – similarly to maps in a topographic sense, which also leave much of reality out but become useful precisely because they select (out of the "chaos" of "reality") only what is significant in terms of the map-maker's and putative user's purpose. In surveillance, as in maps in a cartographic sense, the creation of order out of disorder is ultimately connected to refinement of forms of display.

In his reflections on maps and mapping, David Turnbull argues that "our experience of the world and our representations of it are mutually interdependent, so there is a sense in which the two are inseparable"; "[o]ur experience and our representations are formative of each other and are separable only analytically." (Turnbull, David: *Maps Are Territories: Science as an Atlas*. The University of Chicago Press: Chicago 1993, p. 61) That is what is meant by the slogan "the map is the territory." (Turnbull 1993, p. 10) "[M]aps are like theories," Turnbull argues, because they "embody or express a cognitive schema," while theories "embody sets of assumptions about how reality is ordered." (1993, p. 48) One can think of a cognitive schema as the "complex of unconscious assumptions about the ordering of reality which structures our experience of it." (Turnbull 1993, p. 48) The supposed "disengagement" offered by maps is one of the aspects of "theory" or theoretical understanding; Turnbull quotes Joseph Rouse to the effect that "[t]heoretical understanding is supposed to disengage us." (quoted in Turnbull 1993, p. 15) Maps and theories also share a characteristic that is "the very condition for the possibility of knowledge or experience – connectivity." (Turnbull 1993,

---

9 The goal of the knowledge-creation through visualization technique known as Self-Organizing Maps is to replicate in a two-dimensional output space major topological structures existing in an n-dimensional input space. However, technologies for 3-dimensional visualization are currently being perfected.

p. 61) "Science is an atlas," Turnbull concludes, "because the essence of maps and theories is connectivity." (1993, p. 62)

Surveillance transforms reality, especially human reality, into an "atlas" as it extends over increasingly wider "territories" of experience (science itself is among its latest frontiers).[10] Maps, like "knowledge," are aspects of "forms of life," which Steven Shapin and Simon Schaffer define as "the existing scheme of things, the invisible, conventional and self-evident 'patterns of doing things and of organizing men to practical ends.'" (Shapin, Steven/ Shaffer, Simon: *Leviathan and the Air-Pump: Hobbes, Boyle, and the Experimental Life*. Princeton UP: Princeton, NJ 1985, p. 15; quoted in Turnbull, p. 10)

"Organizing men to practical ends" is a fundamentally *strategic* project, just as "viewing things as if from a great height or distance" (Börner) represents a strategic vision. Surveillance thus implies a specific attitude toward and relationship to reality: a strategic one. Knowledge-creation through surveillance is typically need and task driven, just as a map in a cartographic sense implies a specific purpose (hence there may be different maps of the "same" terrain, represented, for example, by the different "layers" in Open Street Map[11]: "standard," "cycle," "transportation," "humanitarian"). Surveillance represents a "strategization" of knowledge, where strategy means "interest-guided action," utilitarian, "purposive-rational" action "oriented to the actor's success." (Habermas, Jürgen: *Communication and the Evolution of Society*. Beacon: Boston, MA 1979, p. 41) As the section "Science and Technology From Above" in the *Atlas of Knowledge* declares:

> In the physical world maps help us to navigate and locate where we need to be. Online services calculate the time and costs of different transportation modes. Data overlays on maps are used to communicate weather prediction, helping us decide when to take an umbrella, when to travel, and even when to harvest crops.
>
> In the online world, maps of topical spaces reveal the extent and structure of our collective knowledge, depict bursts of activity, and help us identify pathways of ideas and innovations. *Maps can also help us identify promising areas that may likely yield a high return when we invest our time, effort, resources, and compassion in them.* (Börner, 2015, p. 2, emphasis added)

---

10 David Lyon observes that surveillance practices have been moving steadily from targeted scrutiny of 'populations' and individuals to mass monitoring in search of actionable intelligence. (Lyon, David: "Surveillance, Snowden, and Big Data: Capacities, Consequences, Critique." *Big Data and Society*. Web)

11 Cf. openstreetmap.org.

Knowledge created through surveillance is also strategic in the sense defined by Michel de Certeau: as representing a "calculus (or the manipulation) of relations of force which becomes possible whenever a subject of will and power (a business enterprise, an army, a city, a scientific institution) can be isolated." (Certeau, Michel de: "On the Oppositional Practices of Everyday Life." *Social Text* 3 1980, p. 5) Today, one can add to the list a terrorist, an extremist group, a criminal organization, or for that matter any individual, group, or entity, even an abstract one such as "science" and "knowledge."

The search for knowledge through surveillance is often, in fact, driven by purposes that are strategic even in cases of what appear as mainly humanitarian endeavors, such as disaster relief, where military purposes often coexist with provision of aid or humanitarian protection. Few things today remain innocent of larger geo-political designs. The strategic character of knowledge crated through surveillance is reflected, for instance, in the name of the new research facility at San Diego State University devoted to knowledge discovery in a wide variety of areas, both public and private: Center for Information Convergence and Strategy.[12]

Strategy, as Machiavelli already noted, has more to do with usefulness than with truth. In this also surveillance resembles and approaches rhetoric itself, esp. in its sophistic incarnations. De Certeau, in fact, considers Aristotle's *Rhetoric* itself strategic due to its purposive, targeted, and systematic character as a *techne*: invention of means, (both "technical" and "artistic") based on observation (*theory*), to a given end.

The strategic character of surveillance as knowledge creation raises the matter of what Charles Bazerman calls "accountability": the way a text connects to the world which it purports to represent. (Bazerman, Charles: *Shaping Written Knowledge: The Genre and Activity of the Experimental Article in Science*. The University of Wisconsin Press: Madison, WI. 1988) Various kinds of texts (scientific, legal, literary, philosophical) use different strategies of accountability and thus are beholden in different ways and to different degrees to the "real" they presume to embody and represent. Such bodying forth of "reality" is a product of a certain set of strategies of representation and connection, strategies that are a fundamental element of knowledge making. Accountability concerns such questions as "How does a world of events get reduced to the virtual world of words (or, we might add in the present context, images)? What are the procedures for this reduction?

---

12 To get a sense of the range of subjects, products, and institutions involved in the knowledge creation project I here refer to as "surveillance", visit http://www.esri.com/events/user-conference.

What are the motives and assumptions implicit in the procedure? And what are the accountabilities that limit statements, ensuring the influence of the evidence of the world on human conception?" (Bazerman 1988, p. 62) In the context of surveillance, "accountability" raises both specific epistemological issues as well as ethical and political ones.

Jim Grey, as reported by Hey et al., has argued that "data-intensive computing" represents a "fourth paradigm" in science. (Hey, Tony/ Tansley, Simon/ Tolle, Kristin: "Jim Grey on eScience: A Transformed Scientific Method. In: Hey, Tony/ Tansley, Simon/ Tolle, Kristin (eds.): *The Fourth Paradigm: Data-Intensive Scientific Discovery*. Microsoft Research: Redmond, WA 2009, pp. xix–xxxiii, p. xix) Grey calls this "fourth paradigm" "eScience" and claims that it unifies theory, experiment, and simulation." (Hey/Tansley/Tolle 2009, p. xix) Rob Kitchin suggests that Big Data presents "the possibility of a new research paradigm across multiple disciplines." (Kitchin, Rob: "Big Data, New Epistemologies and Paradigm Shifts." *Big Data and Society*, April-June 2014, p. 3, Web) "Big Data analytics enables an entirely new epistemological approach for making sense of the world," Kitchin claims; "rather than testing a theory by analyzing relevant data, new data analytics seek to gain insights 'born from the data.'" (2014, p. 2) "There is little doubt," he concludes:

> that the development of Big Data and new data analytics offers the possibility of reframing the epistemology of science, social science and humanities, and such a reframing is already actively taking place across disciplines. Big Data and new data analytics enable new approaches to data generation and analyses to be implemented that make it possible to ask and answer questions in new ways. (Kitchin 2014, p. 10)

David Lyon notes, however, that Big Data "intensifies certain surveillance trends associated with information technologies and networks." (Lyon, David: "Surveillance, Snowden, and Big Data: Capacities, Consequences, Critique." *Big Data and Society*, July-December 2014, p. 2, Web) One such trend is the shift of surveillance practices from targeted scrutiny of "populations" and individuals to mass monitoring in search of actionable intelligence. (Lyon 2014, p. 2) He also notes the growing emphasis on prediction (which he refers to as "future orientation"); this future orientation "is likely to exacerbate the severance of surveillance [and perhaps also knowledge] from history and memory", while "the assiduous quest for pattern-discovery will justify unprecedented access to data." (2014, p. 6) "In the context of neo-liberal governance this anticipation is likely to place more weight on surveillance for managing consequences rather than research on understanding causes of social problems such as crime and disorder." (Lyon 2014, p. 6) In addition, "enthusiasm for Big Data 'solutions' may lead to the inappropriate transfer of techniques from one field to another." (Lyon 2014, p. 6) Finally, Bauman and

Lyon note the separation of knowledge from morality and ethics in the context of Big Data and surveillance. (Bauman, Zygmunt/ Lyon, David: *Liquid Surveillance: A Conversation*. Polity: Cambridge, UK 2013)

Viewing surveillance as adumbrated in this paper, as a novel *process of knowledge creation* that integrates *technologies of data gathering* with *techniques of data manipulation* and specific *forms of visual display*, helps bring together an entire spectrum of issues that in fact belong together as part and parcel of the same phenomenon: epistemic issues raised in discussions of Big Data; epistemic and rhetorical issues implicit in visualizations, mapping, and geography as dominant metaphor for knowledge; as well as ethical and political issues attendant on ubiquitous and often intrusive monitoring, tracking, and recording (dataveillance).

Surveillance in effect builds a virtual reality that is then taken back to affect the real world. A simple example are the "avatars" created by everyday *dataveillance* about each of us based on our shopping and spending behaviors, reading, watching, or Internet surfing habits, movements, or contact networks. It is these avatars that increasingly constitute the basis for decisions regarding our credit worthiness, political loyalties (in the case of a passport, visa, or residence application), or employment. In surveillance, computer screens in effect provide windows on the outside world[13] through which a 21st-century *théoros* (scientist, researcher, or a security agency) observes and "knows" the world. The ultimate assumption is that – as the slogan for Microsoft HoloLens has it – "When you change the way you see the world, you can change the world you see."[14]

5. Conclusion: Surveillance as a new institution of knowledge

Historically, changes in representations of time and space have been at the foundation of the evolution of conceptions of "knowledge." (McNeely, Ian F./Wolverton, Lisa: *Reinventing Knowledge: From Alexandria to the Internet*. Norton: New York 2008) In their history of knowledge creation in the Western world, McNeely and Wolverton argue that "'the West' itself is better defined by its institutions for organizing knowledge than as a set of cultural values or a region of the globe." (2008, p. xiv) "Ideas," they suggest, "can communicate their effect only through the institutions that organize them." (2008, p. xvii) Among the elements that

---

13 Dr. Eric Frost, "Open-Source Digital Mapping and Visualization Workshop," San Diego State University Visualization Center, April 8, 2015. The Situation Room in the White House, used for intelligence briefings and strategic decision-making, has *"knowledge* boards" on the wall, on which satellite and other surveillance data are projected.
14 https://www.microsoft.com/microsoft-hololens/en-us, accessed June 9, 2015.

constitute an "institution" of knowledge are ways of recording, communicating, distributing, and storing information (as well as the kind of "information" that is considered relevant for producing knowledge); symbols, images, and objects that constitute "knowledge"; provisions for overcoming the limitations of space and time; decisions about privacy and publicity; as well as core rationale for knowledge. There is also the raw material from which "knowledge" is fashioned and transformed by the institution into a "political, social, and cultural" force. (2008, p. xix) Traditionally, knowledge has also been "located," if not geographically than institutionally (e.g. in the monastery, the university, or the R&D laboratory): "The ways in which we organize intellectual activity remain crucial to how we create new knowledge an draw on it for moral an practical guidance in daily life." (2008, p. xx). Finally, "knowledge has always been about connecting people, not collecting information." (McNeely/ Wolverton, 2008, p. 271)

In all of the above respects, surveillance considered as creation of knowledge appears to be a new "institution" of knowledge. As such, it constitutes the epistemic core of the "communication revolution."

Since to create knowledge is to constitute a world, a different way of knowing in effect re-constitutes the world as we know it. Such as reconstitution is already underway. Knowledge based on surveillance facilitates decision-making in a wide range of areas both in the public and private domains, from economics to public health, education, science and technology policy, security and defense, and military and political strategy.

Acknowledgments

I wish to thank Dr. Eric Frost, Director of the Visualization Center at San Diego State University, and Dr. Andre Skupin, Co-Director of the Center for Information Convergence and Strategy at San Diego State University, for their guidance and help in the preparation of this paper.

References

Agarwal, Pragya/ Skupin, Andre (eds.): *Self-Organizing Maps: Applications in Geographic Information Science*. Wiley: New York 2008.

Bauman, Zygmunt/ Lyon, David: *Liquid Surveillance: A Conversation*. Polity: Cambridge, UK 2013.

Bazerman, Charles: *Shaping Written Knowledge: The Genre and Activity of the Experimental Article in Science*. The University of Wisconsin Press: Madison, WI. 1988.

Berger, John: *Ways of Seeing*. BBC and Penguin: London 1972.

Bogard, William: *The Simulation of Surveillance: Hypercontrol in Telematic Societies*. Cambridge University Press: Cambridge, UK 1996.

Börner, Katy: *Atlas of Science: Visualizing What We Know*. MIT Press: Cambridge, MA 2010.

Börner, Katy: *Atlas of Knowledge: Anyone Can Map*. The MIT Press: Cambridge, MA 2015.

Certeau, Michel de: "On the Oppositional Practices of Everyday Life". *Social Text* 3, 1980, pp. 3–43.

Clarke, Roger: "Information Technology and Dataveillance". *Communications of the ACM*, 31 (5), May 1988, pp. 498–512.

Ellul, Jacques: *The Technological Society*. Vintage: New York 1964.

Foucault, Michel: *Discipline and Punish: The Birth of the Prison*. Vintage: New York 1979.

Habermas, Jürgen: *Communication and the Evolution of Society*. Beacon: Boston, MA 1979.

Hey, Tony/ Tansley, Stewart/ Tolle, Kristin (eds.): *The Fourth Paradigm: Data-Intensive Scientific Discovery*. Microsoft Research: Redmond, WA 2009.

Kitchin, Rob: "Big Data, New Epistemologies and Paradigm Shifts". *Big Data and Society*, April-June 2014, from http://bds.sagepub.com/content/1/1/2053951714528481, accessed 22.11.2015.

Koua, Etien L./ Kraak, Menno-Jan: "An Integrated Exploratory Geovisualization Environment Based on Self-Organizing Map". In: Argawal, Pragya/ Skupin, Andre (eds.): *Self-Organizing Maps: Applications in Geographic Information Science*. Wiley: Chichester, West Sussex, UK 2008, pp. 45–66.

Latour, Bruno: *Science in Action: How To Follow Scientists and Engineers Through Society*. Harvard University Press: Cambridge, MA 1987.

Latour, Bruno/ Woolgar, Steve: *Laboratory Life: The Social Construction of Scientific Facts*. Sage: Beverly Hills, CA 1979.

Lyon, David: "Surveillance, Snowden, and Big Data: Capacities, Consequences, Critique". *Big Data and Society*, July-December 2014, from http://bds.sagepub.com/content/1/2/2053951714541861, accessed 20.11.2015.

Lyon, David: *Surveillance Society: Monitoring Everyday Life*. Open University Press: Buckingham, UK 2001.

McNeely, Ian F./ Wolverton, Lisa: *Reinventing Knowledge: From Alexandria to the Internet*. Norton: New York 2008.

Ornatowski, Cezar M./ Pottathil, Akshay: "Digital Communications Surveillance". *African Yearbook of Rhetoric* 2 (3), 2012, pp. 13–22 from http://www.african-rhetoric.org/book5.asp.

Rouse, Joseph: *Knowledge and Power: Toward a Political Philosophy of Science.* Cornell UP: Ithaca, NY 1987.

Salazar, Philippe-Joseph: "Surveillance in the Electronic Age: A Rhetorical Critique". *Cosmopolis: A Journal of Cosmopolitics/Revue de Cosmopolitique* 2, 2015, pp. 3–16 from http://www.cosmopolis-rev.org/2015-2-en.

Schneier, Bruce: *Data and Goliath: The Hidden Battles to Collect Your Data and Control Your World.* Norton: New York 2015.

Shapin, Steven/ Shaffer, Simon: *Leviathan and the Air-Pump: Hobbes, Boyle, and the Experimental Life.* Princeton UP: Princeton, NJ 1985.

Sontag, Susan: "Photographic Evangels". In: Reiff, David (ed.): *Essays of the 1960s & 70s.* New York: The Library of America: New York. 2013, pp. 608–634.

Southan, Christopher/ Cameron, Graham: "Beyond the Tsunami: Developing the Infrastructure to Deal With Life Sciences Data". In: Hey, Tony/ Tansley, Stewart/ Tolle, Kristin (eds.): *The Fourth Paradigm: Data-Intensive Scientific Discovery.* Microsoft Research: Redmond, WA 2009, pp. 117–123.

Turnbull, David: *Maps Are Territories: Science as an Atlas.* The University of Chicago Press: Chicago 1993.

Yan, Jun/Thill, Jean-Claude: "Visual Exploration of Spatial Interaction Data with Self-Organizing Maps". In: Argawal, Pragya/ Skupin, Andre (eds.): *Self-Organizing Maps: Applications in Geographic Information Science.* Wiley: Chichester, West Sussex, UK 2008, pp. 67–85.

Christine Isager

University of Copenhagen

A poor show of knowing: the horror and comedy of unsuccessful writers on film

1. Introduction

Popular film and television series at once reflect and inform the popular understanding of rhetorical practices. Cinematic portrayals of reporters, attorneys, coaches, or politicians who speak to motivate and move their audiences on film become tied up with our general understanding of rhetoric and its functions in society. In recent years, still more filmmakers have been exploring the cinematic potential of the intriguing, if really rather inconspicuous, rhetorical practice of *writing*. (cf. Buchanan, Judith (ed.): *The Writer on Film: Screening Literary Authorship*. Palgrave MacMillan: Houndmills 2013) The aspirations, compromises and successes of both historical and fictional characters who write with authority and resonance – or wish they did – have proved to have great popular appeal. Examples abound, and the gallery of characters span from prominent literary figures like Virginia Woolf (in *The Hours* from 2002) and Jane Austen (in *Becoming Jane*, 2007) over journalist and author Susan Orlean and screenwriter Charlie Kaufman (both portrayed in *Adaptation* from 2006) to completely fictional characters such as the professional letter writer Theodore (in *Her* from 2013) or troubled freelance careerists Hank Moody and Hannah Horvath (in television series *Californication*, 2007–2014 and *Girls*, 2012–), respectively.[1] Writing in these films is not typically considered as a way of imparting knowledge as such, which is an interesting point in itself. Writing is portrayed, instead, as a practice that holds promise of *rhetorical agency*, e.g., of affecting other people by way of the written word, while the writer possibly makes a living of this too.

This paper looks at two American movies that demonstratively deny their main characters knowledge, authority and resonance in each of their endeavors

---

[1] A Google search using the search term "movies about writers and writing" on 4th Dec 2015 establishes that this type of film is a widely recognized category of movies. Search results included "7 Must-See Movies about Writers | Indiewire", "IMDb: Top 80 Movies about Writers", "Best Films about Writers, Ranked | Flavorwire" and "100 Films About Writers/Writing – How many have you seen?".

to "write their own ticket": Jack Torrance (played by Jack Nicholson) in Stanley Kubrick's classic horror film *The Shining* (1980; adapted from Stephen King's novel from 1977) and Roy Channing (played by Josh Brolin) in Woody Allen's dramatic comedy *You Will Meet a Tall Dark Stranger* (2010). Both movies evoke the aesthetically and socially pleasing idea of the supposedly knowledgeable and creative writer at work to prepare an unspecified rhetorical intervention with society. This idea is evoked by way of effective visuals, only to collapse completely and prove to be exactly visual and no more: a mere show of knowing. More specifically, Kubrick and Allen depict book projects that are planned and carefully accommodated to specific social settings but eventually prove empty of knowledge and meaning – because of a mad, automated conduct in the case of Jack Torrance and a blatant act of plagiarism on the part of Roy Channing. As the positive expectations that the writers are met with are gradually undermined, the fragility of rhetorical agency becomes apparent and provides potent material for horror as well as for comedy.

The two particular film narratives reduce knowledge to a matter of marginal importance, as their respective main characters have become so desperate to perform that performance has become an end in itself. This situation makes knowledge a theme in these cinematic narratives by way of *praeteritio*: it is highlighted mainly by being bypassed. As a consequence of this, knowledge as such will not be a keyword in my analysis, but will be considered in relation to rhetorical agency, i.e., as a functional – or dysfunctional – aspect of rhetorical action. Therefore, before turning to the two films, I will introduce the concept of rhetorical agency, and I will present a formal feature of the particular theoretical discussion that has evolved around it. That discussion has been informed by an exceptionally rich imagery, as scholars have deployed elaborate metaphors and entire films to illustrate their particular understandings and make their points.

2. Rich imagery in rhetorical agency theory

The classical rhetorical tradition has both a practical and educational orientation which means that is has mainly been concerned with *good* speaking: How do we muster the best available means of persuasion, and how do we recognize and train the best orators? Yet, for all the education – the theory (*ars*), the steady practice (*usus*), and the imitation of good models (*imitatio*) – it is still relatively complex and somewhat mysterious as to what exactly makes rhetoric effective. What makes words count and function as social action? Over the last few decades, discussions of this topic have been centered on the concept of rhetorical agency (cf. Gunn, Joshua/ Cloud, Dana L.: "Agentic Orientation as Magical Voluntarism". *Communication Theory* 20, 2010, p. 52–57), and scholars have deployed a number of images and allegories in the theoretical discussion in an attempt to grasp the essence without sacrificing the complexity of the subject.

When Cheryl Geisler reported in *Rhetoric Society Quarterly* (*RSQ*) in 2004 from a conference debate about rhetorical agency, she defined the concept as the individual rhetor's "capability to act." ("How Ought We to Understand the Concept of Rhetorical Agency?: Report from the ARS." *Rhetoric Society Quarterly* 34 (3) 2004, pp. 9–17) In a humanist vein, she defended the concept against a postmodern critique, and her framing of the debate caused further discussion. In 2005, also in *RSQ*, Christian Lundberg and Joshua Gunn objected to Geisler's manner of referring to agency as a *possession* of the rhetor, i.e., as a resource that the individual rhetor may own and pass on to other people as if it were a strange substance or ectoplasm. (Lundberg, Christian/ Gunn, Joshua: "'Ouija Board, Are There any Communications?' Agency, Ontotheology, and the Death of Humanist Subject, or, Continuing the ARS Conversation." *Rhetoric Society Quarterly* 35 (4) 2005, pp. 88–90)

Instead, in a playful and polemic spirit, Lundberg and Gunn introduced the spiritualist image of the *ouija board* to illustrate their conception of rhetorical agency in a posthumanist vein. At the ouija board, also known as a "spirit board" or "talking board," the individual participant does not control social events. Participants are possessed, so to speak, by the social event and are uncertain about who or what causes the action. They are gathered around the board that typically has the letters of the alphabet, the numbers 0–10 as well as "Yes," "No," and "Good Bye" written on it. Each participant holds a finger on a planchette that moves and spells out answers to questions that participants pose to spirits invoked ("are there any communications?") during a séance. As Lundberg and Gunn describe it,

> the status and possibly even the existence of the agent who originates the action is undecidable ... [I]s my partner moving this thing? Am I moving it without even knowing it? Is it possible that some unseen spirit – a passed relative or worse, an evil genius – is moving the planchette (and therefore, us)? Although the somewhat admittedly perverse practice of talking to the dead is born of Kantian and Cartesian convictions, it nevertheless opens the question of an uncertain and unsettled subject position or disposition. (2005, p. 84–85)

As Lundberg and Gunn say here, this image illustrates, on the one hand, the silliness and "perversion" of human beings who trust themselves with unlimited communicative powers. On the other hand, the scenario as a whole offers an alternative and useful interpretation of agency: At the ouija board the social and material circumstances have power to "possess" people and enable agency in a way that makes any causal connection between a rhetor and social change hard to point out ("Is my ... ? Am I ... ? Is it possible that ... ?"), and this "undecidability" is exactly what Lundberg and Gunn make a case for. As a model for thinking about the nature of agency, this does not imply that rhetoric or agency is not worth studying and accounting for. On the contrary, the metaphor is presented as a challenge to the scholarly community to avoid facile, ideological explanations of the way rhetoric works in society and to embrace, instead, the complexity of social and material constraints on the symbolic action of individuals.

Carolyn Miller investigates the role of such constraints in an empirical vein in her article titled "What Can Automation Tell us about Agency?". (*Rhetoric Society Quarterly* 37 2007, pp. 137–157) In this article, Miller reports on an informal survey in which she asked 25 instructors in composition and public speaking about devices for automated writing assessment as well as about Auto-Speech-Easy™, "a revolutionary technology, which has benefited from major advancements in computer science and cognitive engineering" (2007, p. 139), and which is able to make automated assessments of student performances in public speaking. The concept for the latter technology, however, was fictional. It was made up for the occasion to provoke thought and enable Miller to "raise questions about the action and agentive capacity of the writer or speaker in the context of the presumably agentless motion of the mechanized audience." (2007, p. 140)

On the basis of her survey, Miller concludes that the idea of automated assessment is met with resistance because it effectively leaves students "in a rhetorical desert." (2007, p. 145) Agency, she argues, is "a property of the rhetorical event" (2007, p. 137) as rhetoric must be *performed*, be *addressed* to an audience and involve *interaction* in order to count as meaningful action. Interaction is:

> what creates the kinetic energy of performance and puts it to rhetorical use. Agency, then, is not only the property of an event, it is the property of a *relationship* between rhetor and audience. There are at least two subjects within a rhetorical situation, and it is their interaction, through attributions they make about each other and understand each other to be making, that we constitute as agency. (Miller 2007, p. 150)

Despite her emphasis on the mutual attribution of agency that energizes the rhetorical situation, Miller, in her discussion, consistently considers both oral and written communication. Even if "the writing situation mystifies us with the absence of the performed event" (Miller 2007, p. 146), a useful concept of agency would, observes Miller, "view *all* text as having a performative dimension." (2007, p. 146, italics added)

This point is important when we turn to the two movies in which the performance of writing is absent in very literal ways. Both Kubrick and Allen may be said to invert Miller's invention by portraying automation not of the audience, but of the rhetorical *performance* – by way of mechanical typing (Jack) and of stealing another person's manuscript (Roy). Insofar as the two writers are possessed by agency, they are possessed in dysfunctional ways.

From an elaborate metaphor or allegory (Lundberg and Gunn's séance), over an even more elaborate thought experiment (Miller's Auto-Speech-Easy™) that have informed discussions of rhetorical agency, I turn finally to *motion pictures* that became central to an ensuing theoretical debate. Sonja K. Foss, William J. C. Waters and Bernard J. Armada started it by studying a German film, Tom Tywker's *Run Lola Run* (*Lola Rennt*) from 1998, as a model for their concept of "agentic orientation." ("Toward a Theory of Agentic Orientation: Rhetoric and Agency in *Run Lola Run*." *Communication Theory* 17 2007, pp. 205–230) Tywker's film presents, in turn, three different versions of the same story about Lola (played by Franka Potente) who is given twenty minutes to raise 100,000 German Marks to save her boyfriend from being assassinated by the mafia. In the first rendering of her run through the city, Lola herself dies in the end; in the second version, her boyfriend dies; but in the third run, fairytale-like, Lola manages to raise the money, saving the day and both of their lives. Foss, Waters and Armada interpret the relative success of these "runs" in terms of three different attitudes or *agentic orientations* on Lola's part, i.e., three different manners of interpreting and acting upon structural constraints. During the first run, Lola orients herself as a *victim* of her circumstances; in the second run as a *supplicant* towards people around her, and then finally, the third time around, as a self-reliant *director* of her scene. The third orientation is presented as exemplary.

This provokes a (well-argued if remarkably harsh) response from Joshua Gunn and Dana Cloud, who refer to the concept of a director's agentic orientation as "magical voluntarism." (2010, pp. 50–78) As Gunn and Cloud point out, Lola's way of directing her scene includes decidedly unrhetorical moves as, for instance, pitching a scream at a casino at a level that somehow causes the roulette ball to fall in place at number 20 – where Lola has placed her money. As a model for rhetorical agency, such magical voluntarism, argue Gunn and Cloud, is overly reliant on constructivism and is characterized by "a belief in wish fulfillment through visualization and the imagination; and a commitment to radical individualism and autonomy." (2010, p. 71) The theory of Foss et al. would, they suggest, be better illustrated by a completely different popular movie, namely *The Secret* (2006, produced by Rhonda Byrne), a self-help classic that turns on the idea that human beings may attract wealth and good health by way of positive thinking. Like *The Secret,* the theory of agentic orientation "amplifies the powers of imagination in a manner that is said to transcend material conditions, including the laws of nature" (Gunn/ Cloud 2010, p. 71) and leads, in Gunn and Cloud's critique, to both "narcissistic complacency, regressive infantilism, and elitist arrogance." (2010, p. 52ff) The two argue, instead, for a more materialist and, in line with Carolyn Miller, *dialectical* understanding of agency (Gunn/ Cloud 2010, pp. 50, 55–56) which takes interaction as well as contingency and constraint seriously.

Linking rhetorical theory to popular film in this way strikes me as productive, as it connects rhetorical theory to cultural doxa in a very explicit manner. By virtue of being artistically scripted, films may, like the elaborate metaphor or the thought experiment, explore and reveal the cultural currency of particular interpretations of agency. What is more, by virtue of being *dramatized*, movies offer interpretations of agency that are situated in particular circumstances. Cinematic stories are typically less concerned with the rhetorical artifacts produced in the narrative and more with the perceived possibility conditions of rhetoric. In the case of the Kubrick and Allen movies, to which we now turn, these possibility conditions concern the potential agency of writing as evoked by the aesthetics and generalized ethos of "the writer."

3. The aesthetics of the writing space as a promise of agency

In both movies we follow a man who has temporarily adopted a lifestyle that promises to enable his agency as a writer and who is supported in these efforts by his wife, if only up to a point. In Stanley Kubrick's 1980 adaptation of Stephen King's *The Shining*, we follow the former schoolteacher and alcoholic Jack Torrance (Jack Nicholson), who is offered a job as caretaker of a big hotel in the Colorado Mountains while the hotel is closed down for the winter. During his job interview early in the film, Jack is warned that the snowy winter will bring on a "tremendous sense of isolation," to which Jack replies with confidence that "that just happens to be exactly what I'm looking for. I'm outlining a new writing project, and five months of peace is just what I want" (Kubrick, 5:27–5:46). He accepts the job and moves in with his wife and their young son, setting up his Adler typewriter with pencils and a stack of fresh paper alongside it on a huge, dark wooden desk in the center of a majestic lounge room with galleries and large windows; an iconically attractive setup for a writing project.

We soon learn, however, that the writing is slow. Jack responds to encouragement from his wife Wendy (Shelley Duvall) by engaging politely in conversation, but his remarks are delivered with raised eyebrows and in an overbearing, increasingly sarcastic tone to indicate that his writing troubles are not as easy to handle as she might think:

>   *Wendy*: [...] How about taking me for a walk after you finish your breakfast?
>   *Jack*: I suppose I ought to do some writing first
>   *Wendy*: Any ideas yet?
>   *Jack*: Lots of ideas, no good ones
>   *Wendy*: Well, something will come. It's just a matter of settling back into the habit of writing every day
>   *Jack*: Yep, that's all it is ... (Kubrick, 24:10–24:40)

In the following scene, the camera pans from a blank sheet of paper in Jack's typewriter to Jack playing ball up against a wall. The writing *is* slow, and Jack's sarcasm soon turns into unreasonable aggression. Jack is taking a deep breath and clearing his throat and, next, tearing up a piece of writing paper and hitting his forehead as he protects his writing space from Wendy's intrusion:

>   *Jack*: I'm *not* being grouchy, I just want to *finish* my work.
>   *Wendy*: Okay. I understand. I'll come back later on with a couple of sandwiches for you and ... maybe you'll let me read something then? (Kubrick, 30:20–30:37)

By offering to read along, Wendy sensibly offers Jack a sense of agency in Carolyn Miller's sense, a chance to address and interact, but this is plainly rejected as counterproductive:

>   *Jack*: Wendy, let me explain something to you. Whenever you come in here and interrupt me, you're breaking my concentration, you're *distracting* me, and it will then take me *time* to get back to where I was, understand?
>   *Wendy*: Yeah.
>   *Jack*: Fine. Now we're gonna make a new rule. Whenever I'm in here and you hear me *typing*, or whether you *don't* hear me typing, or what the *fuck* you hear me doing in here, when I am *in* here that means that I am working, *that* means don't come in. Now do you think you can handle that? (Kubrick, 30:38–31:20)

Jack clearly attempts to keep his wife at bay in order to maintain the impression that he is writing and doing an important piece of creative work. The nature of the scheduled writing project is not specified, but in one scene we see a scrapbook with newspaper clippings lying open next to Jack while he is working, so we get a very general hint that some sort of historical research forms the base of his work. We also get the impression that he is losing his sense of reality and proportion when their son is hurt under strange circumstances and Wendy suggests that they leave the hotel to see a doctor:

>   *Jack*: It is so fucking typical of you to create a problem like this when I finally have a chance to accomplish something. When I'm really into my work. I could really write my own ticket if I went back to Boulder now, couldn't I? Shoveling out driveways, work in a car wash – any of that appeal to you?

Wendy: Jack...
Jack: Wendy, I have let you fuck up my life so far, but I'm not going to let you fuck this up! (Kubrick, 1:01:25–1:01:54)

He speaks partly in stock phrases ("really into my work," "write my own ticket," "fuck up my life") which signals the oncoming breakdown of communication. Jack is possessed by other powers in a serious way – by spirits or by the hotel as such – as suggested by the twisted soundtrack and ominous crosscutting to events in the hotel that only Jack or his young son experience. It turns out that Jack's writing is completely automated. Jack has not been writing – processing knowledge or addressing anyone – he has been *typing* (as he himself accurately phrased it above) the same sentence over and over. His manuscript is carefully laid out, switching between conventional textual formats with what looks like indented quotes, dialogue, poetry, running prose, typos, except for repeating again and again the line: *All work and no play makes Jack a dull boy*. Wendy Torrance's discovery of her husband's meaningless and mechanized rhetoric (Kubrick, 1:14:33–1:17:20) is a legendary, horrifying highpoint of the film, after which their interaction develops into senseless arguments and, finally, bloody violence.[2] The particular proverb, *All work and no play*..., ironically confirms that a walk outside with his wife and son, who went, instead, on their own, before the snow came and they all became snowbound, would have been a good idea and prevented some of the madness of Jack's isolation.

In this manner, Jack Torrance is effectively lost in what Carolyn Miller referred to as a "rhetorical desert," with no skill or ambition left in terms of establishing rhetorical agency. No-one is even being addressed. In her development of Miller's conception of rhetorical agency as a mutual attribution, Elisabeth Hoff-Clausen has highlighted *trust* as precondition of making such attributions at all. (Hoff-Clausen, Elisabeth: "Retorisk handlekraft hviler på tillid" ["Rhetorical Agency: An Attribution Based on Trust"]. *Rhetorica Scandinavica* 54, 2010, pp. 49–66) She also argues that

> rhetorical exchanges are not just conditioned by the trustworthiness we ascribe to a speaker [i.e., *ethos*]. [...] When we attribute agency to others, speaking or listening to them, we entrust them with an opportunity to affect us and exert social influence (i.e.,

---

2   As previously pointed out in a blog post (Isager, Christine: "Skrækindjagende skriveprocesser" ["Horrifying Writing Processes"], *Videnskab.dk*, 21.03.2014, Web), a similar scene occurs in Lars von Trier's *Antichrist* (2009) where the husband (played by Willem Dafoe) intrudes on the wife's writing space to discover, as he leafs through her notes, that her academic prose has developed into still simpler sentences and still more clumsy and eventually unreadable handwriting.

we make ourselves vulnerable). We are not disposed to do so unless we trust *ourselves* […]; trust *the other party* involved in the event […]; and, to some basic degree, trust the societal institutions regulating the interaction. (Hoff-Clausen, Elisabeth: "Attributing Rhetorical Agency in a Crisis of Trust: Danske Bank's Act of Public Listening after the Credit Collapse". *Rhetoric Society Quarterly* 43 (5), 2013, pp. 425–448)

In Kubrick's portrayal of Jack Torrance, the writer does not trust himself enough to trust even his wife as a provisional substitute for a rhetorical audience. Societal institutions never enter into the picture except as abstract dynamics that constrain and alienate Jack and ultimately become irrelevant, because he remains isolated – in the snowbound mountain hotel, in his writing space, and in his own mind. In this manner, the dialectical or interactional nature of rhetorical agency and its foundation in trust is confirmed by way of negation. What the film adds to this is an understanding of the visual aesthetics of the writing space and the ethos of "the writer" in a generalized sense as effective, immediately appealing factors that indicate a *potential* for rhetorical agency. As Miller said, "the writing situation mystifies us with the absence of the performed event" (2007, p. 146). The fact that the writing situation also holds *promise* of performed events makes it apt material for film.

4. Plagiarism and the desperate rhetorical agent

In Woody Allen's *You Will Meet a Tall Dark Stranger* (2010), Roy Channing (Josh Brolin) is initially placed in an attractive writing space too: at a desk by a sash window in the bedroom of an old London apartment fitted with bookshelves and modern art. Roy lives there with his wife Sally (Naomi Watts), who works in an art gallery. Roy is struggling to finish a book manuscript to follow up on a first, moderately successful novel, and Sally, who is eager to move on with her career and have children, is losing patience. That is to say, trust attributed at the personal level weakens day by day. When the manuscript is finally done, and Roy's publisher has finally called back about it, Roy loses his self-trust and does not even attempt to keep up appearances:

> *Roy*: Well, that's it. They rejected my novel. They don't think it "comes off." "Not my best work." "Try harder." […] I *can't* try harder. That's *all* I have in me […]
> *Helena (Sally's mother)*: If writing is not in your future, medicine is a *noble* way to earn a living.
> *Roy*: Are you thick? I am never gonna be a doctor, okay? That boat sailed years ago, okay? You got it? Maybe I'll be a chauffeur or a messenger. So, your daughter married badly. Now can you get the hell out?
> *Sally*: How can you ask her to get out when *she* is the one paying the rent? (Allen, 52:21–53:46)

Like Jack, who evoked the idea of shoveling driveways or washing cars back in Boulder, Roy humiliates himself by his own standards (and not just those of his mother-in-law) by calling attention to his relatively unassuming alternatives to a writing career ("Maybe ... a chauffeur or a messenger"). The reality of the situation does seem to sink in with him in this scene, as he confirms that he trusts the judgment of the publishers as a societal institution with standards that he himself has failed to live up to: "[The publishers] are knowledgeable men, so I guess it *doesn't* come off. [...] I have to face it. I was a one-book fluke." (Allen, 54:02–54:09)

This point is where the narrative of Roy's writing project might have ended. Yet, in the comic spirit of Allen's film, Roy is reminded that, from a distance, he does not actually *look* like a fluke. His beautiful, guitar-playing neighbor, Dia (Freida Pinto), has confessed that she has been watching him write from her apartment across the street:

> *Roy*: You know I write?
> *Dia*: I see you too, you know.[...]
> *Roy*: [Y]ou don't bother me [by playing your guitar]. You inspire me.
> *Dia*: Perfect, I've always wanted to be someone's muse. (Allen, 35:03–35:17)

While Sally finally makes up her mind to ask for divorce, Dia has, as the cheerful voice-over lets us know, developed "strong romantic ideas about sharing *her* life with a writer" (Allen, 1:01:12–1:01:20). In order to live up to this attractive view of himself and his potential, Roy jumps at a chance to steal a full book manuscript from a talented friend who is killed (or so Roy is told) in a car accident. Roy has the stolen manuscript accepted for publication by the same publishing agent, Malcom Dodds (Alex MacQueen), who rejected his own manuscript.

Through this act of plagiarism, Roy puts on a show of skill and of knowing and receives a lot of praise for his (stolen) work at the expense of his (actual) previous work, which makes for great situational ironies:

> *Dodds*: We don't just *want* it [for publication], we are absolutely ecstatic! Everybody, I mean, literally everybody who has read it has been knocked out. Bill Cousin said to me, he said: "I can't believe the same man who wrote his last two books wrote this one." I mean, nothing you've done could prepare us for it! (Allen, 1:14:48–1:15:04)

Dia's father, who is presented as a literary connoisseur, also compliments Roy for his intimate knowledge of the material:

> *Father*: Your book is really riveting.
> *Roy*: Oh thank you, thanks.
> *Father*: You obviously must have spent a lot of time in Ireland and Scotland?
> *Roy*: Uh ... Some ... I, yeah, yeah, I did, I've done a lot of research, a *lot* of research.
> *Dia*: I thought you told me you've never been to Ireland?

> *Roy*: I've ... *Northern* Ireland ... but I've been to other places. I've been to Connemara ... is one of the places I've been ...
> *Father*: I loved so much the style of your writing, you know. Each word clicks along the page, and your characters are so, so original, almost startling! (Allen, 1:01:21–1:01:59)

The father's good taste and judgement add to the impression of Dia as a character who, at least until meeting Roy, represents a high level of commitment and cultivation of *genuine* skill and knowledge. This contrast is emphasized, for instance, when Roy asks her out for lunch on a whim, and she accepts, but asks for half an hour to finish her work first. Moreover, it turns out that, despite all the guitar-playing, she is not mainly a musician but plays a number of instruments while working to earn a Ph.D. in musicology.

The setup of Roy and Dia eyeing each other across the street and being equally fascinated by what they see, stresses the point that a genuine and a poor level of skill may appear equally persuasive at a distance. Yet, while Roy (and the audience of the movie) can actually hear that Dia plays well, Dia is in no position to see that Roy may not be able to live up to the aesthetics he has established around his writing life. With his mother-in-law paying the rent, he has not personally earned the lifestyle of their neighborhood, so to speak, and neither, as we know, has he written the "riveting" book which is based on a thorough knowledge of places that Roy himself has never visited.

The relations of trust that Roy has established on false grounds in relation to his love interest Dia, contrast with those with his friends and the publisher, which is stressed by the unbearable situational ironies and, again, failing communication (cf. Roy's faltering "Uh ...", "I've ... and desperate emphasis "a *lot* of research" in response to other people's straight and bona fide questions). Indeed, without the self-trust, what ultimately holds Roy up as a rhetorical agent is the trust invested in him by his surroundings. As we know from Miller and Hoff-Clausen, however, rhetorical agency is not a one-way phenomenon but, indeed, a mutual attribution based on trust. The delayed performance and privacy of Roy's writing process has bought him time to meet his own positive expectations as well as those of his spouse and surroundings. Yet, when his self-trust is finally gone ("I'm a one-book fluke"), the trust of others becomes constraining rather than enabling in terms of rhetorical agency. This pressure leads Roy to betray their trust which eventually stands to consume him completely as a rhetorical agent.

5. Séance

In the prologue to *You Will Meet a Tall Dark Stranger*, the voice-over narrator tells us that "Shakespeare said life was full of sound and fury and, in the end, signified nothing," and the film closes again with a reference to "our little tale of sound and fury signifying nothing. And one has to wonder, given all of life's uncertainty and pain, how do we get through it? Well, as Sally told Roy, sometimes the illusions work better than the medicine." This reference to illusions is made in reference to Helena, Sally's mother, who recovers from a personal crisis after her divorce from Sally's father by spending a number of encouraging sessions with (and her money on) a fortune teller and, next, becomes romantically involved with a spiritualist who runs an occult bookshop and gathers friends for séances. This process does no harm to Helena herself for the time being, but the fortune teller's financial advice, for instance, turns out to have great consequences for the lives of people around her. This particular motif brings us back to Lundberg and Gunn and their image of the ouija board. Both Stanley Kubrick and Woody Allen play with the contrast and overlap between social, material, and psychological circumstances that make it unclear who is acting on what, or what is acting on whom. In the case of Jack Torrance and Roy's mother-in-law, the brush with supernatural forces may be hallucinations (Jack) or illusions (Helena), but it still constrains their actions as well as the people around them in a highly material manner by creating alienation and tension – and horror and comedy. The pressure makes Jack and Roy resort to mechanical acts of "writing"; Jack and Roy create their own "rhetorical desert" ending up either dead, caught in deep snow (Jack), or living on in fear of exposure and complete humiliation (Roy).

6. Conclusion: The horror and comedy of signifying nothing

This study of Stanley Kubrick's horrific and Woody Allen's comic scenarios shows how the visual rhetoric of the two films highlights the aesthetic and social side of written rhetorical action. The films are able to make their immediate appeal and promise present for appreciation if only to produce, next, a strong sense of alienation in viewers, as the narratives unfold to expose the pretentious deceit of the particular writer. So, on the one hand, they confirm the dialectical understanding of rhetorical agency as interplay between individuals and their social and material circumstances. The films take note of "the particular circumstances and material specificity of a given event." (Gunn/ Cloud 2010, p. 73) The two directors do so by presenting a highly generalized, visually based narrative of "writing" and "the writer," displaying how social conventions, including the particular delay and temporary privacy and the aesthetics of writing itself, serve to nurture trust in the writer and his rhetorical agency. Indeed, both movies emphasize personal trust as a very concrete precondition for social trust. Moreover, they display how such trust may, of course, sometimes turn out to unwarranted, betrayed, or lost for any number of reasons, social or material and reduce, before our eyes, the potential of a writer's agency to a mad or vain illusion.

To summarize, the cinematic narratives are apt to portray writing as empty of agency: as a mere show of knowing. The potential rhetorical action, "the book," is ruthlessly stopped in both of these films before becoming rhetorical. Still, what the very comedy and horror of the scenarios suggest is that it *might* have worked under different circumstances, and that, for better or worse, the aesthetics of the writing space remains a source of positive social expectations that enables people to operate as promising rhetorical agents in society.

References

Allen, Woody: *You Will Meet a Tall Dark Stranger* [motion picture DVD]. Mediaproducción, S.L., Versátil Cinema, S.L. & Gravier Productions, Inc. and Scanbox Entertainment Denmark A/S, 2010.

Buchanan, Judith (ed.): *The Writer on Film: Screening Literary Authorship*. Palgrave Macmillan: Houndmills 2013.

Foss, Sonja K./ Waters, William J. C./ Armada, Bernard J.: "Toward a Theory of Agentic Orientation: Rhetoric and Agency in *Run Lola Run*." *Communication Theory* 17, 2007, pp. 205–230.

Gunn, Joshua/ Cloud, Dana: "Agentic Orientation as Magical Voluntarism." *Communication Theory* 20, 2010, pp. 30–78.

Geisler, Cheryl: "How Ought We to Understand the Concept of Rhetorical Agency?: Report from the ARS." *Rhetoric Society Quarterly* 34 (3), 2004, pp. 9–17.

Hoff-Clausen, Elisabeth: "Attributing Rhetorical Agency in a Crisis of Trust: Danske Bank's Act of Public Listening after the Credit Collapse." *Rhetoric Society Quarterly* 43 (5), 2013, pp. 425–448.

Hoff-Clausen, Elisabeth: "Retorisk handlekraft hviler på tillid" ["Rhetorical Agency: An Attribution Based on Trust"]. *Rhetorica Scandinavica* 54, 2010, pp. 49–66.

Isager, Christine: "Skrækindjagende skriveprocesser" ["Horrifying Writing Processes"], *Videnskab.dk*, 21.03.2014. Retrieved 02.12.2015, from http://videnskab.dk/blog/skraekindjagende-skriveprocesser.

Kubrick, Stanley: *The Shining* [motion picture DVD]. Warner Brothers, 1980.

Lundberg, Christian/ Gunn, Joshua: "'Ouija Board, Are There any Communications?' Agency, Ontotheology, and the Death of the Humanist Subject, or, Continuing the ARS Conversation." *Rhetoric Society Quarterly* 35 (4), 2005, pp. 83–106.

Miller, Carolyn: "What Can Automation Tell Us about Agency?" *Rhetoric Society Quarterly* 37 (2), 2007, pp. 137–157.

Marcus Gottschling

University of Tuebingen

Lend me your eyes: Creating immediate understanding through Prezi

1. Introduction

When thinking about the importance and relevance of visualizations in what is maybe the most popular form of speech in today's knowledge society, slideshow presentations, it can prove fruitful not to begin with the rise of the ubiquitous software PowerPoint or even the dawn of photography and film as reproducible representations of reality. Instead, how visualizations in oratory work can already be traced in a speech that was – in one form or the other – held over 2000 years ago and whose dramatization dates back to the end of the 16th century. In his history drama *Julius Caesar* from 1599, William Shakespeare lets Mark Antony begin his speech at Caesar's funeral with the carefully chosen words "Friends, romans, countrymen, lend me your ears." (Shakespeare, William: *Julius Caesar*. Ed. by T.S. Dorsch. The Arden Edition of the Works of William Shakespeare. Methuen: London 1955, 3.2.75) In the following speech, Mark Antony persuades his audience of Caesar's goodness and that the conspirators, although being "honorable men," were unjustified in killing him. What Shakespeare could have appended, however, was "lend me your eyes" – for Mark Antony not only uses speech in his eulogy but also visualization as a persuasive means to guide the audience's attention and opinion: Caesar's bloody cloak. Mark Antony makes the audience *see* the bloody cloak from his own perspective – mourning, bereaved of a true and just friend. By guiding the audience's attention towards it, Mark Antony succeeds in letting the cloak itself become visual evidence that Caesar's murder was unjustified – and helps turn around the people's opinion: the conspirators around Brutus and Cassius are discredited and have to flee Rome. By incorporating the cloak, Mark Antony's verbal strategy of mourning Caesar while criticizing the conspirators in an indirect way is given additional visual credibility. Mark Antony creates interplay of the visual and the verbal – by making the people *see* from his own point of view. In rhetorical terms, such use of visualization can be linked to what Kjeldsen calls visual argumentation as thick representation in rhetorical discourse. (Kjeldsen, Jens E.: "The Rhetoric of Thick Representation: How Pictures Render the Importance and Strength of an Argument Salient." *Argumentation* 29, 2015, pp. 197–215) Visualization is incorporated into argumentation with the goal of creating a vivid and sudden insight (*evidentia*) which then leads to persuasion: the change of opinion and behavior of the audience.

Over 400 years later, we have become used to this kind of visual argumentation in everyday experiences, because, in the form of the slideshow presentation, it has spread into all of the civic and thus rhetorical spheres of our lives, the economic (e.g. marketing pitches or presentations of results), the social (e.g. slideshows accompanying wedding speeches), and even the political (e.g. Barack Obama's State of the Union Addresses). Especially in the educational sphere, in universities and schools, we are reminded of the functionality and importance of visualizations in presentations every day, mostly through the use of presentation software such as PowerPoint or Keynote. (Kjeldsen, Jens E.: "The Rhetoric of PowerPoint". *Seminar. net – International Journal of Media, Technology and Lifelong Learning* 2 (1) 2006, pp. 1–16; Lobin, Henning: *Inszeniertes Reden auf der Medienbühne. Zur Linguistik und Rhetorik der wissenschaftlichen Präsentation*. Peter Lang: Frankfurt a.M. et al. 2009; Schnettler, Bernt/ Knoblauch, Hubert (eds.): *Powerpoint-Präsentationen. Neue Formen der gesellschaftlichen Kommunikation von Wissen*. UVK: Konstanz 2007) And inasmuch technological innovation and progress have widened the possibilities of using visualization in speech, the mode of operation in incorporating visualizations into speech has not changed since the days of Shakespeare: visualizations still lend credit to speech by the creation of *evidentia*. With the help of visualizations, presenters seek to create immediate understanding of their topics. In this chapter, I argue that in today's educational and scientific presentations, bringing the audience to lend their eyes to the speaker's perspective is one of the central goals of a presenter. Two examples from the presentation software *Prezi* will help illustrate this thought. Firstly, however, it has to be discussed why scientific and educational presentations can be understood as rhetorical acts.

2. The rhetoric of presentations

Fundamentally, how presenters are able to create immediate comprehension in presentational situations is linked to three questions: In what way can presentations be understood as rhetorically structured? Which strategies can we take from classical rhetorical theory? And how do we need to re-conceptualize them for our present day situation? In what sense, then, is a presentation a rhetorical situation? Both, presentational and rhetorical situations can be seen as goal-oriented, communicative actions. Scientific and educational presentations usually are defined as monologues, which are subject to certain temporal and spatial constraints. They have developed from lectures and instructive dialogues and still share the same goals: the transfer of information from speaker to audience. (Peters, Sybille: "Über Ablenkung in der Präsentation von Wissen. Freier Vortrag, Lichtbild-Vortrag, Powerpoint-Präsentation – ein Vergleich". In: Schnettler / Knoblauch, pp. 37–52) What lets them stand out against other forms of instructional speech is that they incorporate the use of media and presentational tools, both digital and analogue. The effects of digital presentation tools on scientific and educational presentations have been researched in recent years, although not to a definitive conclusion, drawing both praise and condemnation for presentation software. (Coy, Wolfgang/ Pias, Claus (eds.): *PowerPoint. Macht und Einfluss eines Präsentationsprogramms*. Fischer: Frankfurt a. M. 2009; Tufte, Edward R.: *Beautiful Evidence*. Graphics Press: Cheshire, CT 2006) More balanced rhetorical assessments by Kjeldsen (2006), Casteleyn (Casteleyn, Jordi: *New Media and the Rhetoric of Presentations*. Academia Press: Ghent 2013) and Pflüger (Pflüger, Jörg: "Auf den Punkt gebracht. Prolegomena zu einer Rhetorik der Präsentation". In: Coy/ Pias 2009, pp. 146–216) incorporate the 'ideological' effects of presentation media while at the same time account for the orator's responsibilities in delivering the information in a persuasive way, choosing "the right moment (kairos) to say what is pertinent and appropriate (aptum)." (Kjeldsen 2006, p. 14) So, in contrast to being understood just as a demonstration of facts via digital or analogue presentation tools, information has to undergo linguistic and rhetorical treatment in presentations. Presenters have to structure information in such ways that audience members can absorb and transform it, expanding their own knowledge in the process.

This process does not mean that knowledge dissemination cannot be the act of simply informing the audience about facts. However, in obtaining successful communication of information, the audience's attitude and motivation has to be taken into account: the absorption of information is often dependent on the acceptance and compatibility of existing structures of knowledge. Knowledge, as Nassehi (Nassehi, Armin: "Eingeborene unter Eingeborenen". In: Schimank, Uwe/ Schöneck, Nadine M. (eds.): *Gesellschaft begreifen. Einladung zur Soziologie*. Campus: Frankfurt a.M. 2009, pp. 169–177) puts it, is not an invariable item but re-/de-constructed by the individual and this construction depends on perception and cognition. Hence, presenters must structure their communication strategically and rhetorically: presentations have to be treated as rhetorical situations, as deliberate ways of "linguistically or symbolically creating salience." (Vatz, Richard E.: "The Myth of the Rhetorical Situation". *Philosophy and Rhetoric* 6 (3), 1973, pp. 154–161, p. 160) Through adapting to the audience's interests, through posing central questions about socio-scientific complexes as well as structuring their presentations, presenters can create their own kind of what Bitzer (Bitzer,

Lloyd F.: "The Rhetorical Situation". *Philosophy and Rhetoric* 1,1968, pp. 1–14) calls the exigence of a rhetorical situation. Thus, I argue that presenters act strategically when transferring knowledge through presentations, acting as orators in making the audience aware of the purpose of the actual increase of knowledge and that means construing knowledge, making it visible, tangible and understandable.

Such operations often rely on the presenter's capability to mark an additional value, showing and telling the audience what they themselves gain from listening to the explanations. Success then depends on the audience's acknowledgement of the accuracy, appropriateness and clarity of the presented information. This acknowledgement is often threatened by constraints of time and space that influence the speaker as well as the audience. Therefore, the synchronicity of showing and telling on the presenter's side and an immediate understanding on the audience's side are crucial to a successful dissemination of information and construction of knowledge. Such immediate understanding can be induced by the use of a rhetorical operation called *evidentia*. The rhetorical figure of *evidentia* was shaped in antiquity and it has to be adapted to today's modified rhetorical situation. In antiquity, *evidentia* was defined as the production of clarity or visuality through the use of words, as *pro ommaton poein* or *subiectio sub oculos*. Through a placement of words, "things are set before the eyes that signify actuality." (Aristotle. Transl. Freese, John, H.: *The "Art" of Rhetoric*. Harvard University Press: Cambridge, MA/ William Heinemann: London 1975b, 1411b) Therefore, *evidentia* is connected to visual perception as well as the mental imagination of a concept. If used correctly a new idea is conveyed and "something is learnt." (Aristotle 1975b, 1412a) Aristotle mentions two different techniques of achieving the *pro ommaton*: on the one hand, he describes what he calls *enérgeia*, which means going into detail and describing a concept or term so meticulously that through sheer description a mental image is created. The use of this technique in scientific presentations, however, can be problematic, as its constraints complicate the use of lengthy explanations or narration. The other evidential technique seems to be more promising: Aristotle describes *enérgeia* as a vivification of the absent, turning possibilities and concepts into actuality. *Evidentia* as *enérgeia* means that the vivification takes place simultaneously, so that the 'image' is understood in the same moment as it is evoked. Therefore the synchronized interplay between showing and understanding is the key to using presentations as rhetorical situations.

Since antiquity, creating *evidentia* through the use of *enérgeia* was first and foremost ascribed to the metaphor. It is not hard to see that in today's presentations the metaphor could indeed be able to deliver the synchronous and interplay of seeing and astonished understanding demanded by the presentational situation. According to Erard, "metaphors close the gap in people's ability to grasp something, or speed up what they're already on track to see". (Erard, Michael: "See through Words". *Aeon Magazine*. 9th June 2015. Web) But there is also a possible difficulty to the use of metaphors: metaphorical speech is figurative, it uses "pseudo-mistakes" to generate meaning and convey new ideas, as Erard argues. However, these pseudo-mistakes have to be decoded immediately and correctly to work as *evidentia*, a process that involves active intellectual commitment from the audience. An obscure metaphor that the audience cannot decode correctly or that takes time to get decoded seriously threatens the proper and immediate understanding and thus the transfer of knowledge itself. The use of metaphors therefore is in conflict with the principle of immediate understanding included in *evidentia*. That is why, according to Asmuth (Asmuth, Bernhard: "Der Beitrag der klassischen Rhetorik zum Thema Verständlichkeit". In: Beetz Manfred et al. (eds.): *Rhetorik*. Band 28: Rhetorik und Verständlichkeit. Niemeyer: Tübingen 2009, pp. 1–20), Aristotle himself criticized the use of metaphors in rhetorical and philosophical uses, instead opting for phrases that are clear with regard to content, but at the same time unusual.

Regarding their use in presentations, we can conclude that metaphors can function as illustrations, but these illustrations stay on a figurative, non-actual level and their understanding depends on a successful decoding of pseudo-mistakes. In such a way, metaphors can be described as auxiliary structures, profiting from the effectiveness of actual illustrations and visualizations. What we are dealing with in today's scientific and educational presentations, however, is a whole new set of tools and possibilities, especially since digital technology has made it easy and effortless to use actual visualizations. In presentations, instead of verbally evoking visuality through metaphors or detailed descriptions that transform themselves into mental images, presenters are able to simply utilize the means of the presentation and use pictures, graphs and diagrams – and, naturally, they tend use these means.

3. Visualization and contextualization

A wide range of scientific research shows that the visual dimension of self-evidence plays a central role in the construction and transfer of knowledge. In the humanities, concepts such as the 'iconic' or 'visual turn' or the recent interest in 'presence' relate to the importance of visuality and the visible in contrast to hermeneutics and reflexivity. (Gumbrecht, Hans Ulrich: *Production of Presence: What Meaning Cannot Convey*. Stanford University Press: Stanford 2004) Cognitive and educational psychology have shown that perception works faster than imagination and that learning is improved through the inclusion of pictures into explanations. Anderson argues that from a cognitive viewpoint, humans are almost as good mentally visualizing things as perceiving them. In a way, cognitive psychology confirms the rhetorical idea from antiquity that *evidentia* can be verbally produced and that it operates in a similar way as visual perception. However, *almost* is a key word here. According to Anderson, actual perception is processed more easily and faster than mental visualization: "If given a choice, people will almost always choose to process an actual picture of a situation rather than imagine it." (Anderson, John R.: *Cognitive Psychology and its Implications*. 2nd ed. Freeman: New York 1985, p. 121) Regarding its use in evidential techniques, visual perception is superior to mental representation. In addition, visual perception supports learning and knowledge reception. The *Cognitive Theory of Multimedia Learning* states that the audience profits from information that was conditioned multimodally: "People learn better from words and pictures than from words alone." (Mayer, Richard E.: *Multimedia Learning*. 2nd ed. Cambridge University Press: Cambridge, NY 2009, p. 1) The human brain processes words and pictures through different, separated channels and so can absorb, structure and process information separately through "active processing." (Mayer 2009, p. 63)

And not only from a psychological but also from a rhetorical viewpoint, including visualization in principle should make sense. In his *Metaphysics*, Aristotle states that we prefer seeing to everything else: "of all the senses sight best helps us to know things, and reveals many distinctions." (Aristotle. Transl. Tredenick, Hugh: *Metaphysics*. Harvard University Press: Cambridge, MA/ William Heinemann: London 1975a, 980a) Seeing then is not only the proverbial *believing*, but also *knowing*. As Lucaites and Hariman put it: "To 'see' is more than just to 'look' at or to 'gaze' upon; to see the world is to be in it and to be of it; it is to understand the world actively." (Lucaites, John L./ Hariman, Robert: "Beyond Literalism: Reality and Imagination in the Public Eye". In: Kramer, Olaf (ed.): *Media of Evidence/ Evidence of Media*. Southern Illinois University Press: Carbondale, IL 2016. forthcoming) Visualizations, relying on the human trust in sight, can be used to produce immediate understanding, working analogue to what Aristotle (1975b, 1413a) said about *enérgeia*: the more briefly a new idea can be expressed, the more striking it is. However, we should keep in mind one of the most important factors in the use of *evidentia*. According to Aristotle, the issue, which has to be placed before the very eyes, has to be appropriate for the audience. Accordingly, Campe (Campe, Rüdiger: "Aktualität des Bildes. Die Zeit rhetorischer Figuration". In: Boehm, Gottfried/ Brandstetter, Gabriele/ Müller, Achatz von (eds.): *Figur und Figuration. Studien zu Wahrnehmung und Wissen*. Fink: Paderborn: 2007, pp. 163–182) argued that the words – and, as we can add: pictures – used for creating *evidentia* should neither demand too little nor too much from the audience. That means, that on the one hand, creating *evidentia* for well-known facts is problematic because it might just bore the audience. On the other hand, using the technique of *evidentia* for information that has not been structured appropriately also will not result in the immediate production of immediate insight, because the audience cannot relate the new information to their existing knowledge.

The production of *evidentia* as a means of knowledge dissemination has for these reasons been mostly neglected in favor of other learning techniques. Only through the use of diascopy, photocopiers, overhead projectors, and, most lately, digital projectors in schools and universities, visualizations have become ubiquitous in educational and scientific discourse. One could even argue that only since the digital age, presentation as a genre has developed. Thanks to presentation media there is now the possibility of accompanying visualizations to oral speech, and thanks to that, presenters are able to create *evidentia* and construe immediate understanding directly on a visual level, skipping the intermediate step of mental representation. However, the effects of presentation media still depend on the performance of the presenter, because human perception is always mediated and processed. According to Schürmann (Schürmann, Eva: "Transitions from Seeing to Thinking. On the Relation of Perception, Worldview and World-disclosure". In: Sachs-Hombach, Klaus/ Totzke, Rainer (eds.): *Bilder, Sehen, Denken. Zum Verhältnis von begrifflich-philosophischen und empirisch-psychologischen Ansätzen in der bildwissenschaftlichen Forschung*, Herbert von Halem: Köln 2011, pp. 93–105), what humans do can be described as 'aspect-seeing' or 'seeing-as': seeing always includes subjective interpretation, being dependent on the perceiving subject and never free from its ideas and experiences. Again, this complicates the construction of immediate comprehension. At the very moment the presenter tries to produce *evidentia* through a visual example, he entrusts his audience to reach immediate comprehension through perception, which results in a loss of control on the presenter's side. It is important, then, for the presenter to minimize this loss of control through contextualization. One possibility of contextualization is verbal embedding, which simply means explaining what the audience is about to see.

Ideally, showing and embedding, visualization and contextualization complement each other in a process that gives the audience access to the presenter's interpretation of visual knowledge. From the presenter's perspective, the rhetorical production of *evidentia* must start with the multiple subjective perspectives of the audience members. Then, through verbal contextualization, the presenter can instruct the audience to lend their eyes, to adopt the presenter's point of view and so smoothen the production of *evidentia*. That is why we have become accustomed to such phrases as "let me show you…" or "as you can see…" in presentations. Such sentences are the guarding rails of *evidentia*, verbal deictic operations, which accompany the visualization and which are very useful to specifically lead the audience's interpretation of visual knowledge. However, there is a significant disadvantage to verbal contextualization regarding the synchronized interplay of *evidentia*: in his explanation of *enérgeia* Aristotle points out that vivification has the biggest impact when a moment of surprise or rupture is included. He even goes so far to advise the orator to mislead the listener when building up towards the moment of *evidentia*: "For it becomes more evident to him that he has learnt something, when the conclusion turns out contrary to his expectation." (Aristotle 1975b, 1412a) In announcing the creation of *evidentia* through contextualization, the presenter on the one hand secures the audience's interpretation. On the other hand, if what the audience should see has to be verbally pointed out, not only the effect of surprise is threatened but also the synchronicity of seeing and understanding and therefore successful knowledge dissemination.

To avoid such perils, the presenter can turn to more subtle ways of contextualization. Just as the production of *evidentia* does not have to be verbal, contextualization can also be transferred to the realm of visualization. One way to achieve this is to support the deictic operation of *evidentia* and thus to simply point at what is relevant for the understanding. There has been a long tradition of using pointers for visual guidelining, from Socrates' stick in the sand to wooden and telescopic pointers up until today's laser pointers. Visual contextualization, however, can also be transferred to the use of graphic organizers in presentation media. Graphic Organizers are visual structures like arrows, mind and concept maps or word clouds and also marking elements as color highlighting, underlining or circling. They work as nonlinguistic representations, replacing verbal instructions with a visual representation of "relationships among specific concepts in text by spatially arranging those concepts." (Casteleyn, p. 14) This form of nonlinguistic contextualization, according to Casteleyn, is most helpful, when learners themselves, construct graphic organizers to structure their knowledge. However, according to the CTML and the dual-coding theory, which argues "that knowledge can be stored both in a verbal and imaginary form, and the latter form is called 'nonlinguistic representations,'" also an audience witnessing a presentation should profit from the use of graphic organizers.[1] (Casteleyn, p. 70) For presenters acting

---

[1] Casteleyn, however, could not confirm this hypothesis with his studies. (Casteleyn 2013)

on the principles of rhetoric, this could mean that nonlinguistic contextualization through graphic organizers gives them a chance to minimize their verbal contextualization and thus the possibility to maximize the effect of immediacy by synchronized interplay between seeing and understanding.

4. Zoom and pan

Presentation software such as PowerPoint can be used to incorporate graphic organizers in order to structure knowledge and guide the audience's eyes to immediate understanding through visualizations. However, the most recent iterations of presentation software are also capable of enhancing the experience of graphic organizers by making them disappear, or rather: by making them invisible and turning them into spatial movement. This process can be best traced in the presentation software *Prezi*, which was first introduced in 2009. Operating on a seemingly infinite canvas rather than with slides of a fixed format, *Prezi* allows a somewhat immersive presentation experience, because the transition between 'frames', the so called 'path' resembles the movement of a camera – hovering over the canvas and piloting the audience through a non-linear progression of words, images etc. that have been placed on the canvas in various sizes and places. With this transition from fixed slides to an open canvas come two key functionalities of *Prezi* that are of great interest to the question regarding the use of *evidentia* in presentations. Those two functionalities, 'pan' and 'zoom', are spatialized graphic organizers, resulting from the camera movement between stages of the presentation, and are one of the most important factors of the popularity *Prezi* has gained.[2] In the meantime, other presentation applications such as PowerPoint have adapted panning and zooming as well, albeit to a significantly lesser extent.

With *Prezi*, panning and zooming become the backbone of the presentation – just as bullet points and transitions are the core of PowerPoint; in a *Prezi* presentation, whatever is presented is linked together by spatial contextualization, and with that, presenters are required or even forced to use them. It is because of this transition from slide to spatial movement, Casteleyn argues, "presentations embracing graphic organizers as a major communication technique, have returned to the limelight of academic research." (Casteleyn, p. 73) He links *Prezi*'s mode of operation to Burke's concept of circumference (Burke, Kenneth: *A Grammar of Motives*. Prentice-Hall: New York, NY 1945), the varying – widening or narrowing – scope that guides and influences the interpretation of the word or scene.

---

2   According to data from September 2015, Prezi surpassed one billion views and 60 million customers. https://prezi.com/press/announcements/#34, published 17.9.2015.

With *Prezi* that means "placing a word (or image, or phrase) in a certain pattern, enlarging or narrowing the scope, and correspondingly creating a nonlinguistic representation of the information presented." (Casteleyn, p. 73) From a rhetorical viewpoint then, the task at hand would be for presenters to use *Prezi's* inherent tendency to circumference through spatial contextualization in an appropriate, i.e. *evidentiary*, way. Two examples can show how such an appropriation of pan and zoom as techniques for producing *evidentia* can work. The first example is taken from the very popular series of presentation events 'TED', self-describing as featuring topics in Technology, Education, and Design, mostly through positive, informative and entertaining short presentations. Although they are not strictly grounded in an academic or educational background, TED-talks are an excellent possibility to study presentation techniques that are used in universities and schools. The second example is a *Prezi* presentation that has not been accompanied by a physical presenter, instead only relying on words, images and graphic organizers as well as pan and zoom. Although the argumentation in this paper regarding pan and zoom deals with the interplay of presenter and digital software, the second example will be used, as it is a prime possibility to analyze the ramifications of zoom.

Fig. 4.1–4.6: JR One Year of Turning the World Inside Out

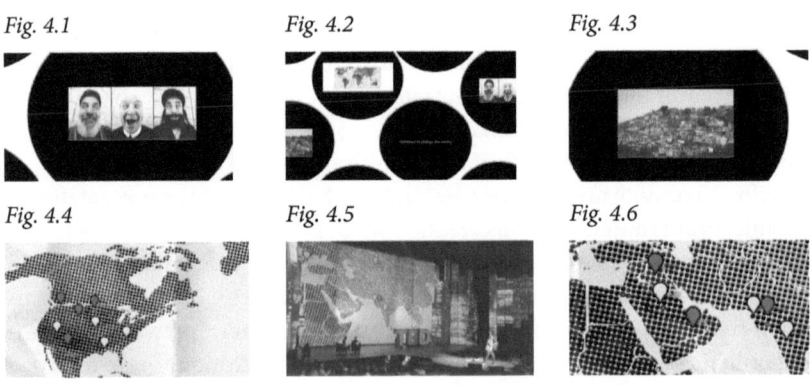

Fig. 4.1   Fig. 4.2   Fig. 4.3

Fig. 4.4   Fig. 4.5   Fig. 4.6

These pictures show small parts of the presentation "One Year of Turning the World Inside Out" held by French artist JR at a TED-event in 2012. In this presentation JR describes his goal as changing the world through art by shooting portraits of people in regions that are often troubled by poverty, local conflicts or dictatorship, scaling them up in meter high paper prints and flyposting them in to public locations in those places:

Lend me your eyes: Creating immediate understanding through Prezi

Twelve years ago, I was in the street writing my name to say, "I exist." Then I went to taking photos of people to paste them on the street to say, "They exist." From the suburbs of Paris to the wall of Israel and Palestine, the rooftops of Kenya to the favelas of Rio, paper and glue – as easy as that. (JR: *One Year of Turning the World Inside Out*, retrieved 17.9.2015, Web)

Figures 4.1 to 4.3 show the accompanying pan to JR's words "the wall of Israel and Palestine, the rooftops of Kenya," similar to the other panning motions used in this part of his presentation. These short distance pans between the different pictures in the black dots connect them to each other and to the artist's intention: to show that those people in dangerous regions "exist." Held together by spatial contextualization in a narrow circumference, the photographs relate to *his* claim of connecting the world. In the course of the presentation, JR describes the next step in his artistic program, inviting people to fly-post their own portraits to their public locations. Now, via long distance pans, different places all over the world are connected and, with the help of the visualization, the audience is able to visit them all. Figures 4.4 to 4.6 show how the scope is widened, all the little black dots containing the pictures together make a map of the world where JR has listed all the places that people have fly-posted portraits: Tunisia, Russia, Karachi (Pakistan), North Dakota (USA), Juarez (Mexico), Iran. Used in this way, panning not only helps to visualize dynamic movement and processes, at the same time the relation of concepts and ideas becomes visible. Over a short distance, a pan can show a tighter relation, in this example the ideas and work of one artist, whereas a long distance pan signalizes a looser connection between frames, signaled by people all over the world that took up the artist's idea and made art themselves.

In itself, panning is nothing that is bound to digital presentations exclusively; in fact, presenters use it verbally and visually every day. In his presentation on climate change, "An Inconvenient Truth," Al Gore has used the now world famous 'hockey stick graph' to relate the rise of the mean temperature to increasing CO_2 emissions. Being self-evident on its own (Schneider, Birgit: "Die Kurve als Evidenzerzeuger des klimatischen Wandels am Beispiel des 'Hockey-Stick-Graphen'". In: Harrasser, Karin/ Lethen, Helmut/ Timm, Elisabeth (eds.): *Sehnsucht nach Evidenz*. Transcript: Bielefeld 2009, pp. 41–55), what rendered the visualization of the hockey stick graph salient was Gore's use of a scissor lift, elevating him right to the top of the chart, about 3–5 meters above ground. Using the lift, Gore achieved a panning and thus guiding of the audience's eyes, following him upward, to show them, what he wanted them to *see* and thus: know. Through this surprising ascent, the gravity of our ever-increasing CO_2 emission became immediately self-evident. The power of guiding the audience's eyes to let them *see* is as a consequence bound to regulating the circumference of the audience's focus. Using panning as spatial contextualization in digital presentations can help to shape the 'active processing' of this circumference.

This mode of operation becomes even clearer when we look at the other spatial contextualization in *Prezi*: zoom. Zooming contextualizes the circumference of a concept or idea by visualizing its embedding in hierarchical structures and claims of validity. By zooming in, the emerging detail signals to be part of a bigger complex, zooming out, the viewer gets the sense of a distancing, the wider frame, and the bigger picture, witnessing connections and concepts that seem far away but none the less related.

Fig. 4.7–4.12: Putting Time in Perspective by 'Prezi Jedi'

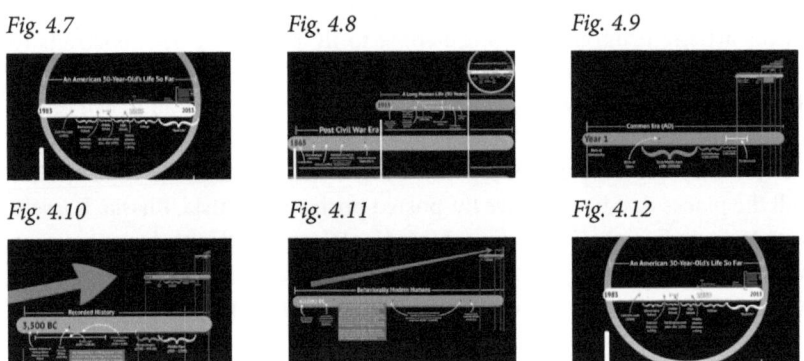

In this *Prezi*, which won the award for Best Prezi Presentation 2013 in the category of Zoom, the design agency 'Prezi Jedi' is *Putting Time in Perspective*, relating the life of a 30-year-old American (Fig. 4.7) to other human timespans, from a long human life (90 years), post-civil-war era (beginning 1865, Fig. 4.8), US history (1776), European colonization of the Americas (1492), common era (year one, Fig. 4.9), recorded history (3500 BC, Fig. 4.10), to the age of behaviorally modern humans (60,000 BC, Fig. 4.11). Every new and wider step is reached through zooming-out, showing a new circumference of human life in relation to the previous step. When relating to human history in general, highlighted by the arrow serving as another graphic organizer (Fig. 4.10, 4.11), the lifespan of a 30-year-old is nothing more than a tiny spot, nearly unrecognizable for the naked eye and as such lacking any importance. By zooming back in to the first step (Fig. 4.12), the life of a 30-year-old, this lifespan is literally put back into perspective visually, and with that, the viewers are reminded of their own lives and their perspectives on history and themselves. Here, zoom first opens up perspective, widening the circumference of human history, before, through zooming-in, narrowing it back down. It is this last zoom that creates not only a surprise, but also lets the audience see – and therefore know – their relation to human life in general. What this finding means for presentations is that with the help of zoom, presenters are able to focus attention or broaden it and so with that keep the audience close to the presenters' point of view.

The efficacy of pan and zoom, and generally speaking, the efficacy of *evidentia* as a whole, depends on the audience's trust towards the presenter. By lending their eyes to the presenter, they entrust their primary tool of retrieving information and building knowledge. As with all forms of creating *evidentia*, spatial contextualization also has an obvious threat to its effectiveness and thus to the audience's trust: according to CTML, the overuse of visualizations can lead to a cognitive overload of the visual channel with the audience members. (Mayer, Richard E./ Moreno, Roxana: "Nine Ways to Reduce Cognitive Load in Multimedia Learning". *Educational Psychologist* 38 (1), 2003, pp. 43–52) An abundance of visuals can eclipse the content and the increase in knowledge cannot be transferred. Also, especially in relation to the use of pan and zoom in *Prezi*, audience members can experience motion sickness through circling and twisting movement, fast switches from zooming in to zooming out etc., for which Apostel (Apostel, Shawn: *Avoiding Prezilepsy: Organization Strategies to Reduce Motion Sickness Caused by Prezi*, Web) has coined the term *Prezilepsy*. Although the cases of motion sickness are mostly based on anecdotal evidence, *Prezi* as a company as well as educational institutes are acknowledging it as a fact: *Prezi* co-founder Peter Halacsy (Halacsy, Peter: *Motion Sickness*, Web) addressed the problem of motion sickness as early as 2009 and the Sheridan Center for Teaching and Learning at Brown University (The Sheridan Center for Teaching and Learning: *8 Reasons Why Prezi is not Recommended for Teaching*, Web) lists motion sickness as one of the reasons for not recommending *Prezi* for teaching. However, the ability to pan and zoom as a means of structuring knowledge can be used without creating motion sickness when used sparingly and directly connected to content and argumentation. (Potter, Ned: *How to Stop Your Prezi Making People Feeling Sick*, Web)

5. Conclusion

Again, then, it is the presenter who is responsible for success or failure of a presentation that uses the technique of *evidentia*. What a presenter can do with pan and zoom is to regulate the audience's attention, transferring his own point of view into presentation media and therefore linking the visualization to the presenter's own interpretation of a picture or graph. The presenter's task is to choose visualization and contextualization appropriately. It is up to him or her to structure knowledge and make it clear to the audience what they can gain by lending not only their ears, but also their eyes. In fact, what the presenter can do is guide the audience's gaze, binding it to his own interpretation, and use the audience's trust of lending their eyes to disseminate knowledge. Creating *evidentia* through presentation media must then be understood as a careful woven interplay of words and pictures that can lead to the surprising moments of immediate comprehension in presentations.

References

Anderson, John R.: *Cognitive Psychology and its Implications*. 2nd ed. Freeman: New York, NY 1985.

Apostel, Shawn: *Avoiding Prezilepsy: Organization Strategies to Reduce Motion Sickness Caused by Prezi*, retrieved 26.12.2015, from https://prezi.com/-a3q9q7qxn2a/avoiding-prezilepsy-organization-strategies-to-reduce-motion-sickness-caused-by-prezis/.

Aristotle. Transl. Freese, John Henry: *The "Art" of Rhetoric*. Harvard University Press: Cambridge, MA/ William Heinemann: London 1975.

Aristotle. Transl. Tredenick, Hugh: *Metaphysics*. Harvard University Press: Cambridge, MA/ William Heinemann: London 1975.

Asmuth, Bernhard: "Der Beitrag der klassischen Rhetorik zum Thema Verständlichkeit". In: Beetz Manfred et al. (eds.): *Rhetorik*. Band 28: Rhetorik und Verständlichkeit. Niemeyer: Tübingen 2009, pp. 1–20.

Beetz Manfred et al. (eds.): *Rhetorik*. Band 28: Rhetorik und Verständlichkeit. Niemeyer: Tübingen 2009.

Bellmann, Johannes/ Müller, Thomas (eds.): *Wissen, was wirkt. Kritik evidenzbasierter Pädagogik*. VS: Wiesbaden 2011.

Bitzer, Lloyd F.: "The Rhetorical Situation". *Philosophy and Rhetoric* 1, 1968, pp. 1–14.

Boehm, Gottfried/ Brandstetter, Gabriele/ Müller, Achatz von (eds.): *Figur und Figuration. Studien zu Wahrnehmung und Wissen*. Fink: Paderborn 2007.

Burke, Kenneth: *A Grammar of Motives*. Prentice-Hall: New York, NY 1945.

Campe, Rüdiger: "Aktualität des Bildes. Die Zeit rhetorischer Figuration". In: Boehm, Gottfried/ Brandstetter, Gabriele/ Müller, Achatz von (eds.): *Figur und Figuration. Studien zu Wahrnehmung und Wissen*. Fink: Paderborn 2007, pp. 163–182.

Casteleyn, Jordi: *New Media and the Rhetoric of Presentations*. Academia Press: Ghent 2013.

Coy, Wolfgang/ Pias, Claus (eds.): *PowerPoint. Macht und Einfluss eines Präsentationsprogramms.* Fischer: Frankfurt a.M. 2009.

Erard, Michael: "See through Words". *Aeon Magazine.* 9th June 2015, retrieved 17.9.2015, from aeon.co/magazine/culture/how-to-design-a-metaphor.

Gumbrecht, Hans Ulrich: *Production of Presence: What Meaning Cannot Convey.* Stanford University Press: Stanford, CA 2004.

Halacsy, Peter: *Motion Sickness*, retrieved 26.12.2015, from https://getsatisfaction.com/prezi/topics/motion_sickness.

Harrasser, Karin/ Lethen, Helmut/ Timm, Elisabeth (eds.): *Sehnsucht nach Evidenz.* Transcript: Bielefeld 2009.

JR: *One Year of Turning the World Inside Out*, retrieved 17.9.2015, from https://www.ted.com/talks/jr_one_year_of_turning_the_world_inside_out.

Kjeldsen, Jens E.: "The Rhetoric of Thick Representation: How Pictures Render the Importance and Strength of an Argument Salient". *Argumentation* 29, 2015, pp. 197–215.

Kjeldsen, Jens E.: "The Rhetoric of PowerPoint". *Seminar.net – International Journal of Media, Technology and Lifelong Learning* 2 (1) 2006, pp. 1–16.

Kramer, Olaf (ed.): *Media of Evidence/ Evidence of Media.* Southern Illinois University Press: Carbondale, IL 2016 (forthcoming).

Lobin, Henning: *Inszeniertes Reden auf der Medienbühne. Zur Linguistik und Rhetorik der wissenschaftlichen Präsentation.* Peter Lang: Frankfurt et al. 2009.

Lucaites, John L./ Hariman, Robert: "Beyond Literalism: Reality and Imagination in the Public Eye". Kramer, Olaf (ed.): *Media of Evidence/ Evidence of Media.* Southern Illinois University Press: Carbondale, IL 2016 (forthcoming).

Mayer, Richard E.: *Multimedia Learning.* 2nd ed. Cambridge University Press: Cambridge, NY 2009.

Mayer, Richard E./ Moreno, Roxana: "Nine Ways to Reduce Cognitive Load in Multimedia Learning". *Educational Psychologist* 38 (1), 2003, pp. 43–52.

Nassehi, Armin: "Eingeborene unter Eingeborenen". In: Schimank, Uwe/ Schöneck, Nadine M. (eds.): *Gesellschaft begreifen. Einladung zur Soziologie.* Campus: Frankfurt a.M. 2009, pp. 169–177.

Peters, Sybille: "Über Ablenkung in der Präsentation von Wissen. Freier Vortrag, Lichtbild-Vortrag, Powerpoint-Präsentation – ein Vergleich". In: Schnettler, Bernt/ Knoblauch, Hubert (eds.): *Powerpoint-Präsentationen. Neue Formen der gesellschaftlichen Kommunikation von Wissen.* UVK: Konstanz 2007, pp. 37–52.

Pflüger, Jörg: "Auf den Punkt gebracht. Prolegomena zu einer Rhetorik der Präsentation". In: Coy, Wolfgang/ Pias, Claus (eds.): *PowerPoint. Macht und Einfluss eines Präsentationsprogramms.* Fischer: Frankfurt a.M. 2009, pp. 146–216.

Potter, Ned: *How to Stop Your Prezi Making People Feeling Sick*, retrieved 26.12.2015, from https://prezi.com/c0lzoedtstfp/how-to-stop-your-prezi-making-people-feel-sick/.

Prezi Jedi: *Putting Time into Perspective*, retrieved 17.9.2015, from https://prezi.com/veychlhwrdgz/putting-time-in-perspective/.

Sachs-Hombach, Klaus/ Totzke, Rainer (eds.): *Bilder, Sehen, Denken. Zum Verhältnis von begrifflich-philosophischen und empirisch-psychologischen Ansätzen in der bildwissenschaftlichen Forschung*, Herbert von Halem: Köln 2011.

Schimank, Uwe/ Schöneck, Nadine M. (eds.): *Gesellschaft begreifen. Einladung zur Soziologie*. Campus: Frankfurt a.M. 2009.

Schneider, Birgit: "Die Kurve als Evidenzerzeuger des klimatischen Wandels am Beispiel des 'Hockey-Stick-Graphen'". In: Harrasser, Karin/ Lethen, Helmut/ Timm, Elisabeth (eds.): *Sehnsucht nach Evidenz*. Transcript: Bielefeld 2009, pp. 41–55.

Schnettler, Bernt/ Knoblauch, Hubert (eds.): *Powerpoint-Präsentationen. Neue Formen der gesellschaftlichen Kommunikation von Wissen*. UVK: Konstanz 2007.

Schürmann, Eva: "Transitions from Seeing to Thinking. On the Relation of Perception, Worldview and World-disclosure". In: Sachs-Hombach, Klaus/ Totzke, Rainer (eds.): *Bilder, Sehen, Denken. Zum Verhältnis von begrifflich-philosophischen und empirisch-psychologischen Ansätzen in der bildwissenschaftlichen Forschung*, Herbert von Halem: Köln 2011, pp. 93–105.

Shakespeare, William: *Julius Caesar*. Ed. by T.S. Dorsch. The Arden Edition of the Works of William Shakespeare. Methuen: London. 1955.

The Sheridan Center for Teaching and Learning: *8 Reasons Why Prezi is not Recommended for Teaching*, retrieved 26.12.2015, from http://www.brown.edu/about/administration/sheridan-center/teaching-learning/course-design/learning-technology/prezi.

Tufte, Edward R.: *Beautiful Evidence*. Graphics Press: Cheshire, CT 2006.

Vatz, Richard E.: "The Myth of the Rhetorical Situation". *Philosophy and Rhetoric* 6 (3) 1973, pp. 154–161.

Part Two:
Rhetorical and argumentative resources in the public sphere

Martijn Wackers

Delft University of Technology

Jaap de Jong

Leiden University

Bas Andeweg

Delft University of Technology

Structure strategies for a memorable speech: the use of rhetorical retention techniques by scholars and politicians

1. Introduction

If Aristotle would have been able to travel to the 21st century and observe rhetorical practices, he would see some similarities with his day and age: people still try to inform and persuade each other in many different situations, often using a speech or presentation as a vehicle in doing so. He would probably also be struck by differences. Access to presentations and speeches is not confined to those present at the actual event anymore, but presentations are often almost instantly available to many people around the world. For example, TED talks, intended to make knowledge and ideas widely accessible, are among the most viewed online videos. Scholars perform in online courses and travel around the world as speaking professionals to exchange their research with peers at conferences, using electronic media to support their stories. And although parliamentary speeches seemingly correspond to their counterparts in Aristotle's lifetime, they too are subject to almost immediate media coverage. This situation makes politicians professional speakers, as public speaking is an important part of their daily jobs.

In other words, Aristotle would see presentations playing an important role in today's knowledge society: "a society with access to knowledge and learning to everyone" as an ultimate stage. (Lytras, Miltiades C./ Sicilia, Miguel Angel: "The Knowledge Society: A Manifesto for Knowledge and Learning." *International Journal Knowledge and Learning* 1 (1/2), 2005, p. 4) According to Knoblauch, from a knowledge society perspective "the presentation as event is a process in which knowledge is seen to be exchanged between people and organizations." (Knoblauch, Hubert: *PowerPoint, Communication and the Knowledge Society*. Cambridge University Press: Cambridge 2013, p. 9) The importance of communication in the knowledge society is reflected by the development of communicative skills being earmarked as one of the learning priorities for the 21st century. (Anderson, Ronald E.: "Implications of the Information and Knowledge Society for Education." In: Voogt, Joke/ Knezek, Gerald (eds.): *International Handbook of Information Technology in Primary and Secondary Education*. Springer 2008, pp. 5–22)

For both speaker and audience a successful exchange of knowledge is an important goal of a presentation. A speaker would therefore aim for the audience to retain the main message or key points of the talk. In his textbook on presentation skills, memory expert Wagenaar even emphasizes that making sure the audience will remember the main message is the speaker's first and foremost purpose: "You have to be prepared to go to great lengths to achieve this, even if it means standing on your head on stage! I have stood on my head once." [translation MW] (Wagenaar, Willem: *Het houden van een presentatie*. [Giving a presentation]. (Studeren). NRC Handelsblad: Rotterdam 1996, p. 7)

"Make your message memorable" sounds easy enough. However, memory research shows the process of *information retention* is not that straightforward. Only few of the sensory stimuli people experience find their way to the long term memory. The way information is processed or interpreted at first determines for a large part whether it will be stored for a longer period and can be retrieved after a while. Since Atkinson and Shiffrin's memory model (Atkinson, R.C./ Shiffrin, R.M: "Human Memory: A Proposed System and Its Control Processes." In: Spence, Kenneth W./ Spence, Janet T. (eds.): *The Psychology of Learning and Motivation: Advances in Research and Theory*. Vol. 2. Academic Press: New York 1968), these processes of storage and retrieval play an important role in memory theory. (Baddeley, Alan/ Eysenck, Michael W./ Anderson, Michael C: *Memory*. Psychology Press: Hove 2009) *Attention* is an important condition for the ability to store information. Subsequently, the way information is 'encoded' defines how well it can be stored. For this storage to be successful, it can be of vital importance how the information is structured (*organization*), whether an image or picture is present or can be created (*visualization*), and how well the information can be linked to existing knowledge (*elaboration*). (Baddeley et al. 2009)

This article by no means intends to provide an exhaustive overview of memory research, but the theory is used here to obtain insight into how the retention process works when a presentation or a speech is given. A speaker aiming at achieving information retention will try to transfer the information in such a way that the main message will be stored in the long term memory of the listeners. The question is: which tools should be picked from the rhetorical toolbox to achieve information retention? Remarkably, not that many studies have focused on retention in the specific communicative situation of a presentation or speech. Results of studies aiming at an increase in information retention by the audience during or after a presentation by tracing rhetorical choices the speaker makes paint a varied picture. Some rhetorical techniques seem to influence information retention positively, albeit in a specific context. Announcing the concluding part of the talk will lead to an increase of information retention (Andeweg, Bas/ Jong, Jaap de/ Wackers, Martijn: "'The End is Near'. Effects of Announcing the Closure of a Speech." In: *Proceedings of the Professional Communication Conference IPCC. IEEE International*: Montreal 2008) a huministic element in a lecture is better remembered (Kaplan, Robert M./ Pascoe, Gregory C.: "Humorous Lectures and Humorous Examples: Some Effects upon Comprehension and Retention". *Journal of Educational Psychology*, 69 (1), 1977, pp. 61–65) and concise sentences used as titles on PowerPoint slides are more effective regarding retention than single words or short phrases. (Alley, Michael et al.: "How the Design of Headlines in Presentation Slides Affects Audience Retention". *Technical Communication* 53 (2), 2006, pp. 225–234) On the contrary, in an experiment by Andeweg and De Haan the use of explicit transition sentences did not cause an increase in information retention. (Andeweg, Bas/ De Haan, Corrie: "Overgangszinnen in een Powerpointpresentatie". [Transition sentences in a PowerPoint presentation]. In: Spooren Wilbert/ Onrust, Margreet/ Sanders, José (eds.) *Studies in taalbeheersing 3*. Van Gorcum: Assen 2009, pp. 17–29)

Because results are limited and diverse, inexperienced speakers preparing for a presentation so far mainly lean on ideas and advice they find in numerous public speaking textbooks, or examples of (experienced) colleagues or renowned personalities. An overview of the public speaking advice on retention and an inventory of the typical use of (advised) retention techniques by different groups of speakers, could offer starting points for more specific and focused research into retention effects of rhetorical techniques and strategies. This study's main question therefore is:

What rhetorical techniques are advised to influence the audience's retention of information and what is the typical use of these techniques in presentations of speaking professionals (scholars) and professional speakers (politicians)?

In this study[1] we confine ourselves to a number of structural and organizational techniques to which some influence on information retention is attributed, for practical reasons later explained. Section 2 deals with the first part of the main question and gives an overview of advice and techniques public speaking advisors link to information retention. An analysis of 80 English-language and Dutch-language public speaking textbooks has enabled some generalizations. Sections 3 and 4 then cover the second part of the main question: first we address the method for analyzing a corpus of research presentations and political speeches. Then we discuss the quantitative results and examples of typical uses of specific rhetorical retention techniques by speaking professionals (scholars) and professional speakers (politicians).

2. Retention advice in public speaking textbooks

Modern public speaking textbooks are an almost inexhaustible source of rhetorical advice for a speaker. Is there a clear-cut 'retention recipe' a speaker can apply, according to the textbook writers? To map out the modern retention advice, public speaking textbooks were analyzed. This section provides insight into the composition and analysis of this corpus (2.1) and the most frequently mentioned retention advice (2.2).

2.1 Composition and analysis corpus modern public speaking textbooks

80 public speaking textbooks were composed and analyzed[2]. The main objective was to select the most 'influential' English-language and Dutch-language public speaking textbooks of the last three decades. 'Influential' here is considered as the books being reprinted and available in as many libraries as possible. For each year in the period 1980–2009 one book has been selected, thereby reflecting the publications about public speaking advice in the last 30 years.

To obtain a representative collection based on the criteria 'reprinted' and 'availability,' WorldCat – the largest online library catalogue – was used. First, a list of books about presenting and public speaking was composed, using relevant search terms connected to these topics. After that, the search results were filtered. Books

---

1   This article is an adaptation of a Dutch-language paper that will appear in the proceedings of the 13th VIOT-conference which took place in Leuven (Belgium) in December 2014; this is a triennial conference for Dutch and Flemish communication scientists, rhetoricians and argumentation theorists.

without a reprint and results that seemed less relevant (books did not or only partially covered public speaking) were removed. To the remaining results a distribution criterion was applied: for each year within the period 1980–2009 the book available in most libraries was selected (according to WorldCat, reference point: January 2012).

Using this method 60 books were selected (30 for both languages). 10 English-language and 10 Dutch-language textbooks were added to this collection by way of repairing possible side-effects of the selection method. As the criterion of availability for the English-language part of the corpus was based on American libraries, some books with a more British or European perspective were added, such as Atkinson's *Lend Me Your Ears*. (Atkinson, Max: *Lend Me Your Ears. All You Need to Know about Making Speeches and Presentations*. Vermillion: London 2004) The same goes for the Dutch-language corpus: the list was compared to a corpus body of public speaking textbooks Andeweg and De Jong composed in 2004 based on experts' opinions, after which some extra books were taken into account. (Andeweg, Bas / Jong, Jaap de: *De eerste minuten. Attentum, benevolum en docilem parare in de inleiding van toespraken*. [The first minutes: attentum, benevolum and docilem parare in speech introductions]. PhD thesis Nijmegen University. Sdu Publishers: The Hague 2004) All this resulted in a final corpus of 40 English-language and 40 Dutch-language public speaking textbooks form the period 1980–2009.

The material was carefully inspected regarding passages connected to retention. The publications were read from cover to cover and passages in which an explicit link is made with retention were selected (based on key words such as 'memory', 'retention', 'remember' and 'stick'). After that, these key words were also used as search terms to check for any retention advice that may have been overlooked. Of each passage it was determined whether it contained advice on retention and, if so, which specific rhetorical technique was related to it. Furthermore, we took stock of advice that was explicitly linked to a specific part of the presentation, such as the introduction or conclusion.

About 5% of the entire body of work comprises passages in which a connection with retention is made (683 out of 12.707 pages). Remarkably, none of the textbooks contained a distinct part or chapter about retention or making a message memorable.

2.2 Retention techniques most frequently mentioned

A total of 87 techniques connected to retention by textbook authors were distinguished. Fig. 6.1 provides an overview of the ten most frequently mentioned techniques in the corpus.

Fig. 5.1: Overview of the most frequently mentioned advised retention techniques in the public speaking textbooks from the period 1980-2009, broken down into the English-language and Dutch-language textbooks. The frequency of the technique is expressed in the number of books in which it is mentioned, compared to the total number of books in that sub corpus (= 40).

English-language corpus (N = 40)		Dutch-language corpus (N = 40)	
Rhetorical technique	Frequency (% total number of books)	Rhetorical technique	Frequency (% total number of books)
Summary	52,5	Repetition	47,5
Anecdote	50	Summary	32,5
Repetition	47,5	Slides, flip-chart, blackboard	32,5
Imagery / vivid language	40	Using visual text	32,5
Chunking (clustering information into main points)	37,5	Partitio (overview of speech's main points in introduction)	22,5
Using an object / prop	35	Electronic presentation (PowerPoint)	22,5
Connecting to the audience	32,5	Systematic structure/ logical order	22,5
Metaphor	32,5	Circle technique (wrapping up by referring to introduction)	17,5
Slides, flip-chart, blackboard	32,5	Using images	15,0
Content-related humor	30	Clear main message	12,5

Although the corpus shows a wide variety in retention advice, three main conclusions can be drawn about retention in public speaking textbooks. First of all, techniques that enhance a clear *structure* and *organization* of the speech are often advised. Secondly, techniques used to *visualize* information are very frequently connected to retention. Both 'real-time' visualization (images, diagrams or graphs on a screen) and mental visualization (metaphors, concrete examples) are promoted. Finally, the conclusion or wrap-up of a presentation – and even more specifically, the summary or recapitulation – is the part of a speech that is most preferred by the textbook authors for improving retention.

Some advice shown in figure 6.1 corresponds to encoding principles that influence the storage and retrieval of information in the (long-term) memory (see introduction). For instance, some frequently advised retention techniques such as 'partitio', 'summary' and 'systematic structure' require a speaker to structure and organize the information in a presentation systematically. In English-language textbooks, when it comes to influencing the audience's memory, speakers are often encouraged to break down the body part of their talk into manageable chunks of information ('chunking'). This approach considers chunking to be a conscious process, which concurs with the subtype of *goal-oriented chunking* mentioned in cognitive sciences. (Gobet, Fernand et al.: "Chunking Mechanisms in Human Learning". *TRENDS in Cognitive Sciences*, 5 (6), 2001, pp. 236–243)

While figure 5.1 gives an overview of the most frequent retention advice, it is limited and superficial. Public speaking advisors use different definitions and labels for rhetorical phenomena and do not always explain their interpretation of a technique they sometimes introduce themselves. Moreover, some techniques mentioned are described ambiguously. For example, 'repetition' can take up any form and shape from literally repeating a core message to stylistically repetitive figures in sentence structure (such as an anaphor). On top of that, the table does not provide any insight into the comprehensibility or feasibility of the advice. Some authors lose themselves in elaborate examples, whereas others summarize their advice in a single concise phrase. Lastly, the effect of the advised techniques cannot be assessed: most authors do not back up their advice with research or theory.

3. Rhetorical analysis of research presentations and political speeches

Section 2 has made clear which techniques public speaking advisors advise to influence information retention. A follow-up question is whether this advice has found its way to speech-making practice, and if so, in what way. To find out, presentations of Dutch scholars in communication science (rhetoric and argumentation) and speeches given by Dutch politicians in parliament were analyzed[3]. The above overview of advised retention techniques serves as a starting point for the method of analysis. The analysis focuses on the use of structural retention techniques by speaking professionals (in this case: scholars), whose presentation behavior is seldom scrutinized. The ways scholars use retention techniques can be identified more precisely by contrasting the results to an analysis of political speeches, which usually differ in purpose and target audience. This section details the composition of both corpora (research presentations and political speeches) (3.1), followed by an explanation of the method used (3.2).

3.1 Composition of presentations and political speeches

The first corpus consists of 16 research presentations held at the triennial 'VIOT conference' for Dutch and Flemish communication scientists, rhetoricians and argumentation theorists. The presentations fit in a fixed format of about twenty minutes, followed by a short discussion. Only the twenty minutes the researchers had prepared were taken into account in this analysis. The composition of this group of texts has also been described by Hertz. (Hertz, Brigitte: *Spotlight on the Presenter. A Study into Presentations of Conference Papers with PowerPoint*. PhD thesis, Wageningen University 2015)

The second corpus comprises speeches given by the leaders of four large Dutch political parties during the annual governmental policy debates between 2010 and 2013. These debates evolve around the policy the government has proposed for the year to come. Political parties have the opportunity to criticize the policy, hand in amendments and debate each other's points of view. The speech that each party leader gives during these debates is considered to be one of the most important speeches of the year. In the corpus used for this study's analysis, the speeches of the following four parties that played an important role between 2010 and 2013 were selected: the Liberals of prime minister Mark Rutte (all years part of government), the Party for Freedom of Geert Wilders (both government support and opposition in the selected period), the Labour Party/ Social Democrats (first opposition, later part of government) and the Liberal Democrats (four years in opposition).

In both analyses, only the speech or presentation text was used. Since the analysis was aimed at structural retention techniques, which encompass a significant part of the retention advice in public speaking textbooks, delivery aspects (gestures, voice, and expression) were not taken into account. Therefore, video recordings were not used. Figure 6.2 gives an overview of the two corpora.

Fig. 5.2: Overview of the most important characteristics of the analyzed speech/ presentation corpora.

presentations (RP)	political speeches (PS)
N = 16	N = 16
Main purpose: to inform	Main purpose: to persuade
Total length: 48,535 words	Total length: 40,880 words
Average length: 3033 words, sd: 402	Average length: 2555 words, sd: 1548
Text transcribed based on video recording	Text used as recorded in the Proceedings of the Dutch Parliament
Slides / visual support used by speaker	No slides / visual support used by speaker

Figure 5.2 shows similarities as well as some differences. First of all, the main purposes differ. Research presentations are mainly aimed at informing about recent research and to a lesser extent at convincing fellow researchers, whereas political speeches focus chiefly on persuading fellow MPs present and their own

electorate outside of parliament. (cf. Leeuwen, Maarten van: *Stijl en politiek. Een taalkundig-stilistische benadering van Nederlandse parlementaire toespraken.* [Style and politics. A linguistic-stylistic approach to Dutch parliamentary speeches]. PhD thesis Leiden University. LOT: Utrecht 2015, p. 93) In spite of the difference in main purposes, it is plausible that retention is a (secondary) purpose for speakers. Both to inform and to persuade an audience, a certain extent of knowledge transfer and retention of information seems indispensable.

Furthermore, the research presentations are longer and do not vary much in length. The standard deviation of speech length is higher in the political speech texts, due to the fact that the amount of time allotted to each party leader depends on the number of parliament seats a party holds. In addition, for the research presentations a transcription of video recordings was used. The texts from the political speeches were taken from the Proceedings of the Dutch Parliament (exclusive of interruptions by other speakers); in which parliamentary clerks register transcripts of the debates. As a final difference, the scholars used (PowerPoint) slides, while the politicians did not use any support of electronic visuals. Because of this difference, the slides used by the scholars have not been analyzed. This finding means some retention techniques might not have been observed.

Despite the differences, we believe the texts are suitable for the analysis described in this study, since the focus is on structural retention techniques on the hierarchical level of the overall speech structure (not on word or sentence level). It has been noted that some retention techniques that are involved in other aspects of a presentation (such as the visual aids or delivery by a speaker) are not part of this analysis.

3.2 Selected retention techniques and method for analysis

Analysis of the public speaking textbooks has shown 87 techniques that are said to enhance the audience's information retention. For an effective and meaningful rhetorical analysis of the research presentations and political speeches, the number of techniques needs to be narrowed down. Therefore, we have focused on a limited number of structural or organizational rhetorical retention techniques that a speaker can use to shape a presentation on a higher hierarchical level (e.g., focusing more on overall speech structure than sentence structure). The selected techniques are first of all the frequently advised *circle technique, partitio* and *(explicit) summary*, and furthermore *announcing the conclusion, explicit transition* and *question figures* (see figure 5.3 for a short explanation and description).

The choice for these structure-focused techniques is based on two main considerations. To start with, textbook authors deem 'structuring' and 'organizing information' important strategies to make a speech or presentation memorable, which is in line with the fact that 'organization' is an encoding principle to store information in the long term memory, according to memory research. Next to those theoretical observations, these structural techniques can be made operational in a rhetorical analysis based on recognizable text features and characteristics such as transition phrases and structure markers. This seems to make an analysis based on these techniques suitable to be carried out by multiple raters. The analysis is aimed at taking stock of the way these retention techniques are used; no estimation of the possible effect of a technique or the rhetorical effect of a specific speaker is made.

Fig. 5.3: The definitions of the rhetorical retention techniques focused on structure/organization of the speech used in the analysis (research presentations and political speeches).

Technique	Brief description
Circle technique	In the conclusion, a speaker refers to an example or phrase already used in the introduction. Can cause the audience to experience a higher 'sense of closure'. (Andeweg et al. 2008)
Partitio	At the end of the speech's introduction, the speaker gives an overview of the speech or presentation structure (main points to be addressed). (Andeweg, Bas / Jong, Jaap de: "All's Well that Ends Well. The Problem of Peroratio in Ministerial Speeches". In: Strunk, Jeanne / Dam, Lotte / Holmgreen, Lise-Lotte (eds.): *Rhetorical Aspects of Discourses in Present-Day Society*. Cambridge Scholars Publishing: Newcastle 2008, pp. 31–50.)
Announcing the conclusion	The speaker announces the final part of the presentation, using an explicit signal phrase such as 'to wrap up'. Seems to influence the retention of information mentioned in the conclusion. (Andeweg et al. 2008)
Explicit summary	The speaker recaps the main points made in the core of the speech (Andeweg/ De Jong 2008) and explicitly marks this using signal phrases such as 'to summarize' and 'to conclude'.
Explicit transition sentence	The speaker explicitly marks the transition to a new part or topic of the speech/presentation, for example using a transition sentence ("First I will discuss the method of research. For this method… etc."). (Andeweg/ De Haan 2009)
Question figures	The speaker uses a direct question to the audience, a rhetorical question (answer is captured in the question's formulation), a *subiectio* (speaker poses a question and immediately answers it himself) or a *quaestio* (speaker asks multiple questions in a row). (Braet, Antoine: *Retorische kritiek. Overtuigingskracht van Cicero tot Balkenende*. [Rhetorical criticism: persuasion from Cicero to Balkenende]. Sdu: Den Haag 2007) A question figure can be used to structure a talk, for example when a *subiectio* is used as a transition sentence ("What method did we use? Well…"). It can also have an effect on the elaboration of information by making the audience think of the answer or tapping into existing knowledge. (Hoeken, Hans/ Anderiesse, R.: "Het effect van de positie van retorische vragen op de overtuigingskracht van een persuasieve tekst". [The effect of the position of rhetorical questions on the persuasive force of a persuasive text]. *Tijdschrift voor Taalbeheersing* 14, 1992, pp. 257–269) These functions are not mutually exclusive.

Two remarks should be made regarding figure 6.3 with respect to the quantitative analysis of the speech corpora:

- The first four techniques can only occur once per presentation or speech as a result of the definition used and they are dependent of the boundaries of a speech part (introduction or conclusion).
- The final two techniques, explicit transition and question figures, can repetitively occur throughout the entire text.

Furthermore, it is important to note that figure 5.3 shows the retention techniques as they are defined by the researchers in order to make a reliable and comparable analysis. These definitions can differ somewhat from various descriptions found in public speaking textbooks. For example, it was decided to only code those summaries that are explicitly marked as such by the speaker. The analysts have not made a content analysis to determine whether the speaker gave a complete and sufficient overview of the speech or presentation content in the summary. The explicit signal the speaker might or might not give the audience that he or she is about to summarize, was considered more important. This approach can be formalized better in a coding instruction and it is in keeping with the stronger effect of explicit conclusions compared to implicit conclusions in (persuasive) texts. (cf. O'Keefe, Daniel J.: *Persuasion: Theory and Research*. Vol. 2. Sage: Thousand Oaks, CA 2002, p. 216)

The speech and presentation texts from both sets of research were systematically coded in the data analysis software Atlas.ti, using a strict coding instruction in which the textual features and characteristics of each technique have been recorded (more specific than figure 6.3). It was possible to label a passage with more than one technique (e.g., a passage labeled as 'explicit transition' can also contain a question figure). The first step in the process of analysis was to determine the boundaries of the introduction and conclusion, since the labeling of some techniques (e.g., summary) depends on the part of the speech in which they occur.

First, two researchers independently coded 8 speeches from both sets of research (a total of 16, half of the total amount of speeches analyzed), using the coding instruction. This analysis showed a substantial inter-rater reliability between the raters: $\kappa = .69$ ($p < .001$). The explicit transition and question figures caused most rating disagreement; the agreement on the other techniques, which could only occur once every text, was good ($\kappa = .91$ ($p < .001$). After this, the remaining speeches were analyzed by one researcher. Based on this coding process the results have been obtained that are discussed in section 4.

4. The use of structural retention techniques in research presentations and political speeches

Can a typical use of structural retention techniques in research presentations and political speeches be pinpointed? To find out, the frequency of the different structural retention techniques taken into account in the analysis is shown (4.1). Thereafter, several similarities and differences between the speech and presentation texts are highlighted (4.2–4.4).

4.1 Frequency of structural retention techniques

Figure 5.4 shows the frequency of the techniques involved in the analysis, itemized per corpus and for both of the corpora together.

Fig. 5.4: Overview of the use of structural retention the techniques per data set and overall. The frequency of the upper four techniques is expressed in the percentage of the total amount of speeches in the corpus (they can only occur once every text); the frequency of the explicit transition and question figures is expressed in occurrences per speech and per 1000 words of the (sub)corpus.

	Scholars (N=16)	**Politicians** (N=16)	**Total** (N=32)
Circle technique	13%	44%	28%
Partitio	50%	6%	28%
Announcing the conclusion	63%	31%	47%
Explicit summary	56%	0%	28%
Explicit transition	5 per speech/ 1,5 per 1000 w	2 per speech/ 0,7 per 1000 w	3 per speech/ 1,1 per 1000 w
Question figures	9 per speech/ 2,9 per 1000 w	8 per speech/ 3,2 per 1000 w	8 per speech/ 3 per 1000 w

From figure 5.4 it can be concluded that the scholars use more partitios, explicit transitions, announcements of the conclusion and explicit summaries than the politicians. However, the circle technique is deployed more often by the politicians. Differences concerning question figures are negligible. These quantities show some general trends; next, the differences in use of structural retention techniques will be explained in more detail using examples from the analyzed corpora. All examples have been translated from Dutch to English by the authors.

4.2 "Tell them, tell them, tell them"

The scholars in this study use more partitios, explicit transitions, announcements of the conclusion and summaries than the politicians. In doing so, they stick to the often advised maxim *tell them what you are going to tell them – tell them – tell them what you have told them*. In five out of eight cases an overview of the presentation's structure (partitio) in a research presentation is followed by an explicitly marked summary in the conclusion. Zooming in on the partitio and the summary, the difference in use between scholars and politicians is considerable: the politicians only once announce what they are about to tell and they do not explicitly summarize at all.

Although the summary is employed in just over half of the analyzed research presentations, the form and shape of the recaps diverge quite a bit. In some cases the summary is short and concise, as in RP (research presentation) #14:

> I will summarize what we have found: a significant difference appears to exist between perception of understanding and real understanding, and clear relations exist between perception of understanding, appreciation, tendency to discussion of and attitude towards safe sex.

However, not all recapitulations in the corpus of research presentations are as concise as the example above from RP #14; the longest summary is 250 words (a little over 7% of the total presentation's length). Sometimes the main points of the presentations are almost literally repeated; sometimes a variation in formulation is used. Now and then, summaries are combined with a perspective on future research, which can be typical for scholarly presentations. An interesting question following from these observations is whether the form and presentation of the summary could influence its possible retention effect.

4.3 Politicians close the circle more often

The frequencies of the circle technique show the opposite trend: politicians use it more often than scholars. The circle technique refers less overtly to the presentation's structure; it is a more implicit structure marker. From that perspective, it might not fit that easily in the 'tell them' structure scholars prefer – which might also be a reason why politicians use it more often. An example of the circle technique can be found in PS (political speech) #13 given by Geert Wilders, party leader of the right-wing Party for Freedom (PVV). First, part of the introduction is shown; after that, the part of the conclusion that contains a reference to the introduction is presented:

> We are on the threshold of historical events. I belong to the generation that grew up in the shadow of the Berlin wall. No one could imagine that one day, this socialist wall would fall. But it fell!
>
> (…)
>
> I will wrap up. (…). We will continue to demolish our Berlin walls and make The Netherlands a better place for, as we call them, Henk and Ingrid
>
> [Wilders' equivalent for the Average Joe and Jane, MW].

Wilders stages the Berlin wall once more in the conclusion, implying that he has closed the circle. An experiment by Andeweg et al. (2008) has shown that such a circle technique increases the 'sense of closure' an audience has, but the audience's information retention only seemed to be affected positively when it was combined with an announcement of the conclusion. The combination of these two techniques (announcing the conclusion and a circle technique) only occurs twice in the corpus of political speeches; in both cases, Geert Wilders is the speaker.

4.4 Varied use of transition sentences and question figures

The scholars we analyzed use more explicit transitions than the politicians, but the frequency of question figures is nearly equal when both sets of research are compared. The way these question figures are used, does however differ. Scholars seem to prefer the *subiectio*: raising a question and directly answering it themselves. The *subiectio* is often used to emphasize structure or a transition to a new topic. This structural use of the *subiectio* by scholars is supported by the fact that the combination of an explicit transition and a question figure occurs 27 times in the corpus of research presentations (0, 6 per 1000 words). The following example is taken from RP #6, in which the speaker uses a *subiectio* to introduce a new topic in the speech – the discussion of the 'procedure' used:

> What was the procedure? We both instructed the participants to think out loud, and asked them to take notes in the program *Infocus* – I will elaborate on that later.

In the corpus of political speeches, the combination of explicit transition and question figure occurs only twice. Politicians seem to apply question figures rather differently, for example in a *quaestio* – a series of questions. In PS #8 Diederik Samsom, party leader of the Dutch Labour Party (or Social Democrats), uses such a series of questions in which he refers to a girl he introduced in an anecdote earlier in his speech:

> What country will she live in? How will we make our money? What kind of companies will we work in? How will we care for the sick and elderly? How do we actually educate

our children? What will our energy supply look like? In short: what do we all want to achieve these next few years?

The questions used in the example above do not seem to be deployed to structure and organize the speech, but rather to give the listener food for thought. This way of using question figures seems more related to the elaboration principle of encoding information, which entails the audience actively using information to process it (e.g., by trying to give an answer to the question) and connecting it to existing knowledge. (cf. Hoeken/ Anderiesse, 1992)

5. Conclusion

The purpose of this article is twofold: (1) to provide an overview of the rhetorical techniques public speaking advisors have connected to information retention over the last three decades and (2) to give insight into which and how structural retention techniques are used in presentations and speeches, and how they tend to be used in those of scholars (speaking professionals) and politicians (professional speakers).

Public speaking textbooks show a wide variety of techniques linked to retention. Many frequently advised retention techniques are connected to structure and organization (such as the summary) and visualization (literal: PowerPoint slides, or mental: metaphor). The conclusion (peroration) is a preferred part of the presentation to apply retention techniques, according to the textbook writers.

An explorative rhetorical analysis of research presentations and political speeches has been carried out, aimed at tracing two types of structural retention techniques: the techniques that occur only once in a presentation and often indicate a higher organizational level (circle technique, partitio, announcement of conclusion, summary) and the techniques that manifest themselves at a lower, more local organizational level (explicit transition sentences and question figures). This analysis showed that scholars more often than politicians use retention techniques that have an impact on a higher hierarchical level of the presentation, such as the partitio (content overview), the announcement of the conclusion and the summary. In other words: it seems to be typical for scholars to use retention techniques that explicitly, almost didactically, emphasize the overall structure of a presentation. Given that, it is remarkable that almost half of the research presentations do not contain a partition and a summary. This means some researchers in these presentations with an informative purpose might overlook an opportunity to influence retention. We assume that in some cases sheer time pressure may have caused these 'omissions': the speakers had problems to end their presentations within the time allotted.

The politicians, on the other hand, use the circle technique more frequently than the scholars. This technique not so much emphasizes the overall speech structure, but it has a more implicit structure effect providing a 'sense of closure'. Furthermore, the politicians use question figures mostly in an elaborative way, appealing to existing knowledge, for example by using a quaestio (series of questions). The scholars tend to use question figures to structure and organize, which is illustrated by their use of the *subiectio*. The specific rhetorical retention techniques politicians choose to employ might depend on another important purpose speakers have: to guard and shape their image (ethos). The use of partitios, transition sentences and summaries could have a retention effect, but at the same time it could be considered boring and too straightforward. This possible negative side effect, which might obstruct the politicians' persuasive purpose, could be a reason for them to avoid retention techniques that explicitly emphasize the speech structure and opt for other retention techniques not involved in this study's analysis, such as metaphors, anecdotes or repetition figures.

All in all, based on the analysis described in this research, scholars (speaking professionals) seem to prefer a more explicit structuring strategy to influence the audience's information retention than politicians (professional speakers) do. However, this analysis has only been explorative, which makes it difficult to pinpoint 'strategies'. Based on the rhetorical analysis performed we can interpret typical use of the techniques involved by these groups of speakers, but we can only make an 'educated guess' about their intentions and motivations. Also, this study focused on specific speakers (researchers at a conference on rhetoric and communication science, politicians during an important debate); therefore, results cannot be generalized as typical for all scholars and politicians. A focus on other advised retention techniques, such as visualization techniques (the scholars used PowerPoint slides, for example), and on other presentation genres, such as the usually well-prepared TED talks, would result in a more complete picture.

The analyses of the public speaking textbooks and the speeches have shown some promising research perspectives into retention effects of rhetorical techniques. We now know more about the typical uses of explicit structuring by scholars and the more implicit mode preferred by politicians. These insights offer valuable starting points for further research into the effects of structural retention techniques. The summary, for example, is often connected to retention in textbooks. The analyzed speech practice has shown it can take up many forms and shapes. So, does the summary indeed bring about a retention effect, and do variables such as its length and specificity matter in that respect? To gain more insight into question, an experiment into the effect of different types of summaries has already been conducted, its setup in line with that of Andeweg et al. (2008). This will be reported on in due time.

Knowledge of the advice, use and effect of rhetorical retention techniques is highly relevant in today's knowledge society. Presentations are popular events to transfer knowledge and make it widely accessible; to make their message memorable is therefore one of the key purposes speakers have. This study represents one important step in gathering more knowledge about the ways speakers use rhetorical retention techniques and the possible effects those techniques have. Speakers who master these precious techniques may even be remembered 2500 years from now – just as we still know Aristotle's words and ideas.

Acknowledgments

Many thanks to Bert Besterveld and Shari Helderman for the corpus analysis of the public speaking textbooks. Many thanks to Brigitte Hertz for sharing the corpus of research presentations and to Sebastiaan van Loosbroek and Carli van Winsen for their contribution to the analyses of the research presentations and political speeches.

References

Alley, Michael et al.: "How the Design of Headlines in Presentation Slides Affects Audience Retention". *Technical Communication* 53 (2) 2006, pp. 225–234.

Anderson, Ronald E.: "Implications of the Information and Knowledge Society for Education". In: Voogt, Joke/ Knezek, Gerald (eds.): *International Handbook of Information Technology in Primary and Secondary Education*. Springer 2008, pp. 5–22.

Andeweg, Bas/ De Haan, Corrie: "Overgangszinnen in een Powerpointpresentatie". [Transition sentences in a PowerPoint presentation]. In Spooren Wilbert / Onrust, Margreet / Sanders, José (eds.) *Studies in taalbeheersing 3*. Van Gorcum: Assen 2009, pp. 17–29.

Andeweg, Bas/ Jong, Jaap de: *De eerste minuten. Attentum, benevolum en docilem parare in de inleiding van toespraken*. [The first minutes: attentum, benevolum and docilem parare in speech introductions]. PhD thesis Nijmegen University. Sdu Publishers: The Hague 2004.

Andeweg, Bas/ Jong, Jaap de: "All's Well that Ends Well. The Problem of Peroratio in Ministerial Speeches". In: Strunk, Jeanne/ Dam, Lotte/ Holmgreen, Lise-Lotte (eds.): *Rhetorical Aspects of Discourses in Present-Day Society*. Newcastle: Cambridge Scholars Publishing 2008, pp. 31–50.

Andeweg, Bas/ Jong, Jaap de/ Wackers, Martijn: "'The End is Near'. Effects of Announcing the Closure of a Speech". In: *Proceedings of the Professional Communication Conference IPCC*. IEEE International Montreal 2008, retrieved 28.9.2015 from DOI 10.1109/IPCC.2008.4610194.

Atkinson, Max: *Lend Me Your Ears. All You Need to Know about Making Speeches and Presentations*. Vermillion: London 2004.

Atkinson, R.C./ Shiffrin, R.M: "Human Memory: A Proposed System and Its Control Processes". In: Spence, Kenneth W./ Spence, Janet T. (eds.): *The Psychology of Learning and Motivation: Advances in Research and Theory*. Vol. 2. Academic Press: New York 1968.

Baddeley, Alan/ Eysenck, Michael W./ Anderson, Michael C: *Memory*. Psychology Press: Hove 2009.

Braet, Antoine: *Retorische kritiek. Overtuigingskracht van Cicero tot Balkenende*. [Rhetorical criticism: persuasion from Cicero to Balkenende]. Sdu: Den Haag 2007.

Gobet, Fernand et al.: "Chunking Mechanisms in Human Learning". *TRENDS in Cognitive Sciences*, 5 (6), 2001, pp. 236–243.

Hertz, Brigitte: *Spotlight on the Presenter. A Study into Presentations of Conference Papers with PowerPoint*. PhD thesis Wageningen University 2015.

Hoeken, Hans/ Anderiesse, R.: "Het effect van de positie van retorische vragen op de overtuigingskracht van een persuasieve tekst". [The effect of the position of rhetorical questions on the persuasive force of a persuasive text]. *Tijdschrift voor Taalbeheersing* 14, 1992, pp. 257–269.

Kaplan, Robert M./ Pascoe, Gregory C.: "Humorous Lectures and Humorous Examples: Some Effects upon Comprehension and Retention". *Journal of Educational Psychology*, 69 (1), 1977, pp. 61–65.

Knoblauch, Hubert: *PowerPoint, Communication and the Knowledge Society*. Cambridge University Press: Cambridge 2013.

Leeuwen, Maarten van: *Stijl en politiek. Een taalkundig-stilistische benadering van Nederlandse parlementaire toespraken*. [Style and politics. A linguistic-stylistic approach to Dutch parliamentary speeches]. PhD thesis Leiden University. Utrecht: LOT 2015.

Lytras, Miltiades C./ Sicilia, Miguel Angel: "The Knowledge Society: A Manifesto for Knowledge and Learning". *International Journal Knowledge and Learning* 1 (1/2) 2005, pp. 1–11.

O'Keefe, Daniel J.: *Persuasion: Theory and Research*. Vol. 2. Sage: Thousand Oaks, CA 2002.

Wagenaar, Willem: *Het houden van een presentatie*. [Giving a presentation]. (Studeren). NRC Handelsblad: Rotterdam 1996.

Louise Schou Therkildsen

Uppsala University

Becoming a citizen: Knowledge and identity in European textbooks for citizenship tests

1. Introduction

In many Western countries[1] immigrants need to pass a citizenship test in order to obtain citizenship. Such tests are often intensely debated in the media, where they are typically criticised on a factual level for being either too easy or too difficult for even natural-born citizens to pass, and on an ideological level for equating national citizenship with trivial knowledge about kings, queens and geographical characteristics.[2] The central question in these debates has to do with the meaning of being a citizen in a national community: Is this meaning manifested in factual knowledge? In democratic practice? Or in an emotional bond?

This continuous criticism has not led, in practice, to many political changes. Once they are implemented, citizenship tests are not easily abolished, which leads one to believe that political parties across ideological orientations are in favour of such tests. It does happen that a test is abolished only to reappear with a new name, time frame, thematic focus and questions.[3] Also the textbooks some countries have chosen to publish in order for applicants to be able to prepare for these tests are subject to change. Among these countries are Denmark and Austria whose textbooks are analysed in this chapter.

In such official learning materials, the aforementioned trivial facts about kings and queens are interwoven into larger national narratives and thus exhibit institutionalized knowledge about the respective countries: their history, culture, norms and values. These narratives are presented as factual knowledge, but are

---

1 Among others the USA, Canada, Australia, France, Spain, the Netherlands, Latvia, Germany, the UK, Austria and Denmark.
2 See among others: Süddeutsche.de: "Da wird keiner überfordert," *Süddeutsche Zeitung*, München, 1. Juli 2010; Nielsen, Peter / Kassebeer, Søren: "Indvandrere memorerer indfødsretsprøve," *Berlingske*, København, 13.08.2007; Klingsey, Mette: "Bred kritik af ny indfødsretsprøve," *Information*, København, 28.02.2007; Kurier.at: "Einbürgerungen sanken rapide", *Kurier*, Wien, 13.01.2015.
3 As was the example in Denmark in 2013, when the law on the current test was passed.

at the same time selected and recreated within the texts. In this way, these testing and learning materials are interesting elements in the context of the knowledge society, where knowledge is conceptualised as a concrete resource, often equated with commodity; a knowledge worker offers and gets paid for her knowledge. The ontology of knowledge has been debated since antiquity, but what we know today is that knowledge is most often the result of a continuing process of deliberation and destabilization, including narratives about our countries' past, present and peoples. The question still relevant today is: What are the rhetorical consequences, when processual knowledge is presented as stable knowledge? And at a higher level, what are the roles of uncertainty and process in a knowledge society?

This chapter will not provide exhaustive answers to these questions, but contributes examples pertaining to the first one. The Danish and Austrian textbooks are not only central to the question of how applicants receive citizenship, but also to the reader's positions within the textual universe and potentially also within society: How do applicants for citizenship fit into these national narratives?

Rhetoric understood as "the use of symbols to influence thought and action" (Foss, Sonja K.: *Rhetorical Criticism: Exploration and Practice*. Waveland Press: Long Grove 1989, p. 4) is the foundation of this rhetorical criticism through which I seek to uncover the more subtle meanings of such textbooks. The notions of discursive essentialism (Shome, Raka: "Postcolonial Interventions in the Rhetorical Canon. An 'Other' View". *Communication Theory* 6 (1), 1996, pp. 40–59) and constitutive rhetoric (Charland, Maurice: "Constitutive Rhetoric: The Case of the Peuple Québécois". *Quarterly Journal of Speech* 73 (2), 1987, pp. 133–150) form the basis of my rhetorical close reading (Leff, Michael C. /transl. Villadsen, Lisa S.: "Fortolkende retorisk kritik". *Rhetorica Scandinavica* (26), 2003, pp. 6–19; Jasinski, James: "The Status of Theory and Method in Rhetorical Criticism". *Western Journal of Communication* 65 (3), 2001, pp. 249–270) in which I argue that both the Danish and the Austrian textbooks exhibit essentialist constitutive mechanisms, but in different degrees and with different significance. Whereas the national narrative of the Danish textbook is primarily connected to the past, highlighting homogeneity and continuity and thus potentially leaving little space for the applicant for citizenship, the narrative of the Austrian textbook highlights diversity and change and thus to a greater extent positions the applicant for citizenship within the national narrative.

At first glance, the examples I highlight here will not seem unusual: A learning material about Danish/Austrian society naturally contains stories of Denmark/Austria and their respective populations. Likewise, the ministries that have commissioned and published the two textbooks are not necessarily aware of the texts' symbolic functions. And that is precisely why these texts are interesting: their symbolic functions do not necessarily leap to the eye – neither the readers' nor the publishers' – which gives them a status of generally accepted assumptions, thus even more important to be subjected to rhetorical analysis. As part of the intellectual and linguistic common property of the respective countries, they are – in an unobtrusive way – significant to the way in which these countries, their citizens and applicants for citizenship are presented and positioned.

1.1 Danish and Austrian tests and textbooks

The Danish and Austrian tests are both multiple choice tests, but they vary in terms of the time frame and the number of questions. The first Danish citizenship test was implemented in June 2006. The Danish textbook (Ministeriet for Flygtninge, Indvandrere og Integration: *Danmark før og nu - læremateriale om historie, kultur og samfundsforhold til indfødsretsprøven*, København, April 2007, henceforth *Denmark Then and Now*) was published in April 2007 and in force until June 2014[4]. It formed the basis of 35 of the 40 questions in the test. Applicants were given 45 minutes to complete the test. In order to pass the test, 32 of the questions had to be correctly answered.

The 165-page-long book consists of four chapters: *Danish History* (54 pages), *Danish Democracy* (34 pages), *Danish Welfare Society* (16) and *Denmark and the Outside World* (19 pages). Following the historical chapter, there are 25 thematic spreads (42 pages in total) about topics such as Danish geography, language, the royal family, Christianity, literature, music and architecture.

The Austrian citizenship test was implemented in 2006. The textbook *My Austria* (Bundesministerium für Europa, Integration und Äußeres: *Mein Österreich*, 2nd printing, Wien, November 2014) was first published in April 2013 and forms the basis of two out of three test categories: Austrian history and Austrian institutions. The third category consists of questions about the specific federal state the applicant lives in. The test contains a total of 18 questions, 6 questions in each category. To successfully pass the test, applicants must correctly answer at least either half of the questions in each category (9) or two thirds of all questions, regardless of which categories (12).

My Austria is a 75-page-long textbook with a main part consisting of a chapter on Austrian history (20 pages) and a chapter on the fundamental values and

---

4   The test in Denmark was changed in 2014 and I have not yet had the opportunity to study the current version. Today, the test consists of 30 questions of which 22 must be answered correctly.

institutions of democracy (35 pages). They are followed by a practice section (8 pages), where example questions appearing throughout the book are collected and answered. The textbook is prefaced by the Minister of Internal Affairs (1 page) and the Minister of Europe, Integration and Foreign Affairs (1 page), who greet the applicants and wish them good luck with the test. These brief forewords are followed by an introduction (2 pages) by the chairman of the independent integration committee, specifying its central role in the creation of the textbook and outlining the structure and content of the book. Finally, the introduction is followed by a didactical section (8 pages) explaining how the test is structured, what the different signs and boxes in the textbook stand for, and giving instructions on different ways to prepare for the test.

In the following section, I will present the notion of discursive essentialism from the perspective of constitutive rhetoric before taking a closer look at the national narrative of Denmark and Austria.

2. Discursive essentialism and constitutive rhetoric

The Danish and Austrian textbooks are addressed to a group of readers who are applying for a new nationality and thus in a very concrete manner are applying for admission in a nationally constituted community. Until September 1st, 2015, applicants for Danish citizenship legally had to give up their prior citizenship in order to receive the Danish citizenship, and at the time of writing, applicants for Austrian citizenship are still not allowed to have double citizenship. The two textbooks openly concern themselves with national identity and the role of the individual in the larger community, and they do so not only by giving the reader specific knowledge about the community, but also by positioning the individual within a larger frame of concrete practices, norms and values.

Crucial to my close reading of these two textbooks is therefore the issue of identity and how such a phenomenon comes into being in texts and discourse. This is also a central question to Maurice Charland (1987), who is interested in displaying how certain texts interpellate and constitute identities at the same time. The consequences of such rhetoric, however, are not purely theoretical or textual; they potentially have normative and argumentative consequences that reach beyond the textual universe, for instance to the way we perceive ourselves and our position in society as well as how we legitimise new laws and policies.

Along with postmodern thinkers such as Louis Althusser, whom Charland also invokes in his adaptation of the concept *interpellation*, Charland believes that subject positions are not static; we are constituted within several communities, identity formations and discourses at one and the same time. (1987, p. 142)

One ideological effect of constitutive rhetoric, however, is the creation of a transhistoric subject: constitutive rhetoric offers consubstantiality between a past and contemporary collective community, often based on assumptions of a certain commonality uniting the interpellated subjects. (Charland 1987, p. 140) In other words, a central and very interesting mechanism in constitutive rhetoric is that it offers a narrative universe where temporal, spatial and ideological differences are toned down, if not completely absent.

The notion of essentialism is borrowed from the scholarly fields of critical and postcolonial theory. (cf. among others: Said, Edward W.: *Orientalism*. Pantheon: New York 1978; Spivak, Gayatri C.: *The Postcolonial Critic: Interviews, Strategies, Dialogues*. Routledge: New York 1990) It was brought into the field of rhetoric primarily by Shome with the purpose of directing more attention to essentialist perspectives in rhetorical studies. (1996, p. 41) It is by now a well-established concept within rhetorical scholarship, which is the case with constitutive rhetoric as well. However, with the continuous political attention given to migrants, refugees and foreigners in general, these thoughts on identity and how identities come into being seem just as relevant today as they did when they were first introduced in the late 1970's and 1980's.

By bringing essentialism into my theoretical framework, I wish to highlight the reciprocal relationship between different subject positions within a given text: How are subjects – implicitly[5] or explicitly – positioned? And in this context, how do the essential characteristics attributed to the Dane/the Austrian influence the applicant for citizenship and her position within the national narrative? Since Charland's objective in his classic article (1987) is first and foremost to describe the mechanisms of constitutive rhetoric and how it functions, and less how such rhetoric influences the different subject positions within the text, I find it useful in this study to combine the notions of essentialism and constitutive rhetoric.

In the following, I analyze some mechanisms of essentialist constitutive rhetoric through a rhetorical close reading of the Danish textbook *Denmark Then and Now* and the Austrian textbook *My Austria*. More specifically, I examine their use of national metaphors, strategies of generalization and linguistic internalization of norms.

---

5   For instance through negation. See Philip Wander's notion of *the third persona*. Wander, Philip: "The Third Persona: An Ideological Turn in Rhetorical Theory". *Central States Speech Journal* 35, 1984, pp. 197–216.

3. The national narrative of Denmark

The analysis of the national narrative of Denmark falls into three sections focusing in turn on organic metaphors, democracy and homogeneity.

3.1 Organic metaphors

The discourse analysts Marianne Winther Jørgensen and Louise Philips (Jørgensen, Marianne Winther / Philips, Louise: *Diskursanalyse som teori og metode*, Roskilde Universitetsforlag 1999) have studied national metaphors and their rhetorical significance. According to them, it is characteristic of this type of metaphors that they structure the nation as an organic, coherent entity – as opposed to a political or institutional entity – to which people are connected through soil or upbringing. (1999, p. 178–180) When portraying the history and origin of the country, the national narrative of Denmark in the textbook is structured first of all by a root-metaphor[6]:

> 1[7]. The Danish society has <u>roots</u> that reach several thousand years back in time. Denmark's history is important to know, if you wish to understand the Danish society as it looks today. The welfare society, the political system, its culture and everyday life are results of a long historical development. (*Denmark Then and Now*, p. 10)
> 2. In Denmark, there is a strong tradition for local democracy and self-governance. Local self-governance has <u>deep roots</u> in Danish history. (*Denmark Then and Now*, p. 106)
> 3. Local self-governance is a <u>cornerstone</u> in Danish democracy. It is a <u>deeply rooted</u> practice back in time that local communities solve many of society's common tasks. (*Denmark Then and Now*, p. 121–123)

With its deep, old roots metaphor, this texbook anchors Denmark several thousand years back in time in the shape of a natural, organic entity, as, for instance, a tree. In the third anecdote[8] it is complemented by a house-metaphor comparing local self-governance to a cornerstone in a house, thus indicating its primary function in democracy. Another organic metaphor is exemplified in the following anecdote, where etymological explanation of the name "Denmark" leads to the metaphor of Denmark as an individual:

---

6 All translations and underlinings are mine unless otherwise indicated.
7 All anecdotes are given a number, which I will refer to in the following discussion.
8 I use the term "anecdote" to signify a small story which supports a larger narrative, as described and used by William Lewis (Lewis, William F.: "Telling America's Story: Narrative Form and the Reagan Presidency". *Quarterly Journal of Speech* 73 (4), 1987, pp. 280–302).

4. The word "Denmark" is first noted at the end of the 800s. "Dan" originates from "Dane" and signifies the people living in the Danish area. "Mark" means "border area". [...] The first time we see the name Denmark used within the country's borders is on a rune stone from around 955. [...] On the stone it is written that King Harald won the whole of Denmark and Norway and made the Danes Christians. Harald Bluetooth's rune stone in Jellinge is therefore called the birth certificate of Denmark. (*Denmark Then and Now*, p. 13)

The metaphors portraying Denmark as a tree with deep roots in anecdote 1, 2 and 3 and as a person with a birth certificate in anecdote 4 suggest that, as a nation, Denmark is a delimited and organic entity, which blurs internal differences. As a result, Denmark is implied to be an entity with essential characteristics that have not changed substantially over hundreds of years. Denmark, in other words, becomes a synecdoche for the Danish population, despite their qualitative and quantitative differences, very much in line with Michael McGee's thoughts on 'the people' as a linguistic, ideological abstraction (McGee, Michael C.: "In Search of 'The People': A Rhetorical Alternative". *Quarterly Journal of Speech* 61 (3), 1975, pp. 235–249); a myth that allows us to deduce from individual to collective without further argumentation. (McGee 1975, p. 238–239)

This reasoning is a necessary move in the direstion of constitutive rhetoric, since such discourse seeks to transcend individual or class specific interests in order to create a collective identity. (Charland 1987, p. 138) Therefore it is paramount to pay attention to what is being said and deduced on behalf of this collective identity. (Charland 1987, p. 139) Furthermore, anecdotes 1–4 suggest a diachronic similarity between past and present Denmark, anchoring contemporary institutions, such as the nation and democracy, back in time in a substantial, historical community: The nation and democracy seem to be – for lack of a better metaphor – deeply rooted in one another.

3.2 Democracy

Another characteristic of the Danish narrative is its focus on democracy. The root/house metaphors in 1–4 above are not only important to the understanding of Denmark, but also of democracy. They indicate that democracy and local self-governance play important roles in the understanding of Denmark and the way democracy is practiced in the country.

This close linkage between nation and system of government is also highlighted through repetition: more than 50 times concepts such as 'democracy' and 'popular rule' are linked to words such as "Denmark," "national," "Danish," "Danes," as in this introductory anecdote:

5. Danish popular rule has a lot in common with democracy in other countries, but it has also found its own distinctive form. In this chapter, some of the most important characteristics about the way democracy functions in today's Denmark are described. Danish democracy is founded on a written constitution, The Constitution of the Kingdom of Denmark. The Constitution focuses on national democracy, as it takes place in parliament. (*Denmark Then and Now*, p. 106)

This national anchoring suggests that democracy has a distinctive Danish manifestation, which the text also states explicitly, though it is not elaborated wherein this distinctiveness consists. In the following anecdote, however, democracy is portrayed as a deeply rooted practice in Danish culture, described as something the Danes are raised into as children:

6. The general high voter turnout in Denmark can have several explanations. One of them is that Danes are raised into democracy as children and adolescents. They get to know democratic values early on in primary school and in high school. Another explanation is the strong tradition of being part of different associations, which strengthens the democratic values of the citizens. (*Denmark Then and Now*, p. 130)

This anecdote internalizes Danish democracy as an intrinsic quality within the individual. Thus, democracy is first of all connected to a time before questions of citizenship were even relevant to the applicant: in the childhood.

3.3 Homogeneity

The portrayal of internal consistency described in the section on organic metaphors is accompanied by the third characteristic of the Danish narrative, namely its anecdotes of homogeneity, displayed in the following anecdote about Denmark's previous position as the large kingdom of the North:

7. Geographically Denmark is the gate to the Baltic Sea. Several European powers have in the past been interested in having free access to this sea. They have therefore wanted to weaken Denmark, though without destroying the state that guarded the entrance to the Baltic Sea. Denmark, which once was part of a great North Atlantic empire with many different groups of people, has therefore gradually been reduced to a small nation state with a relatively homogenous population. (*Denmark Then and Now*, p. 10)

This is a depiction of Denmark as a previous great power, which has gradually decreased due to its exposed geographical position, and which, as a result, lost its demographic diversity, which has led to a "relatively homogenous population." A similar portrayal is seen in an anecdote about Denmark after the war against Prussia in 1864:

8. Denmark now consisted of the kingdom, Greenland, the Faroe Islands and Iceland as well as – until 1917 – the three small West Indian islands [the US Virgin Islands]. Thus, the population in Denmark after 1864 became more homogeneous than ever before. The citizens of the kingdom spoke the same language, had the same constitution and were culturally quite similar, even when there was still great difference between rich and poor. Facing the hardships after the defeat in 1864, the Danish national identity grew strong. Language and culture came to mean a lot. (*Denmark Then and Now*, p. 37)

Again, the greater the external threat, the greater the internal (cultural and linguistic) build-up, seems to be the premise. And in the contemporary times:

9. The Danish population is relatively homogenous. This means that most people share the same language, culture and history. (*Denmark Then and Now*, p. 68)

Along with the previous anecdotes (1–6), these anecdotes of homogeneity point towards the past when portraying the Danish population, and they do so by creating a story where Denmark fights against the hardships and threats brought upon it by the outside world, again highlighting internal coherence. Whereas the metaphors portraying Denmark as a tree and a person establish a diachronic similarity between past and contemporary Denmark, the anecdotes about homogeneity among the Danes establish a diachronic as well as a synchronic similarity between Danes of the past and of the present.

When looking at the text from a factual perspective, the knowledge it conveys is not false: Denmark *is* a relatively homogenous country in comparison to Germany or France, for instance. And it *is* an old country with uninterrupted democracy since 1849 (at least for some parts of the society), which distinguishes it from many European countries, among them Spain and Poland. The rhetorical significance of the Danish textbook lies somewhere else: In the overall emphasis on knowledge that highlights homogeneity, coherence and continuity rather than other relevant perspectives, such as for instance the diversity within the population, which was created, among many other factors, by geographical expansion in Sweden, Norway, Prussia, Iceland and Greenland and the guest worker arrangement of the 1960's.

In summary, by articulating Denmark and Danish democracy as a tree with deep roots, or as a person with a birth certificate, and Danish democracy as a cornerstone in society (anecdote 1–4), Denmark becomes a delimited, organic entity. An interrelation between the Denmark of the past and contemporary Denmark is suggested. Adding the anecdotes (7–9) about the homogeneity resulting from previous threats from the outside, and about democracy (1–6) as a nationally anchored and highly developed skill that is passed onto Danes as children, coherence and continuity are emphasized.

4. The national narrative of Austria

The analysis of the national narrative of Austria falls into four sections: Anecdotes on Austrian identity, change and diversity, the use of possessive pronouns and anecdotes on democratic engagement.

4.1 Austrian identity

In *My Austria*, essentialist constitutive mechanisms come to light, not surprisingly, first and foremost in the expressions of Austrian identity, as shown here in an anecdote about multiculturalism in Austria, and in two anecdotes about the economic and industrial recovery in the post-war period in the 1950's and 1960's:

1. People with different origin and history live together peacefully in Austria. This positive coexistence has evolved over centuries, it is part of our identity and it is secured by our laws. (*My Austria*, p. 7, foreword by Sebastian Kurz, Minister of Europe, Integration and Foreign Affairs)
2. The economy grew, and the currency remained stable. The victorious powers of the Second World War - in particular the United States - helped rebuild the country. More and more people were now proud to be Austrian. (*My Austria*, p. 34)
3. Since people were recovering economically, many began believing in the future of Austria. This contributed to an emerging Austrian identity, which today is self-evident. (*My Austria*, p. 35)

Whereas Austrian identity in anecdote 1 is connected to norms of diversity and positive coexistence[9], in anecdote 2 and 3 it is founded upon a belief in the future of Austria concretized in a collective participation in the economic success of the country. This is first of all an expression of the prevailing hopelessness in Austria after WWII, but underneath this expression appears an essentializing understanding of identity similar to the one we saw in the Danish textbook with a synecdochic relationship between nation state and population: The constitution of an Austrian identity is rooted in the constitution of Austria as a nation.

---

9   In itself a disputed notion, which, however, is beyond the scope of this chapter. For further reading, see among others Phillips, Kendall R.: "The Spaces of Public Dissension: Reconsidering the Public Sphere". *Communication Monographs* (63), 1996, pp. 231–248; Ivie, Robert: "Rhetorical Deliberation and Democratic Politics in the Here and Now". *Rhetoric & Public Affairs* 5 (2), 2002, pp. 277–285 and Berg, Kristine M.: *Intercultural Dialogue as Rhetorical Form: a Pyrrhic Victory*. (doctoral thesis), Copenhagen University, 2011.

4.2 Change and diversity

Similar to the Danish textbook the Austrian textbook also highlights age, though not connected to homogeneity and coherence, but to change and diversity, such as in the following anecdotes:

4. An Austrian state as such did not exist until the "Empire of Austria" was founded in 1804. (*My Austria*, p. 22)
5. Many different peoples lived in Austria. In the 19th century, eleven languages were officially recognised. This state was also called a "multi-ethnic state." The inhabitants had very different religions. There were catholic, protestant and orthodox Christians. Judaism and Islam were also recognised religions within the monarchy. (*My Austria*, p. 26)

And today:

6. Currently, 8.5 million people live in Austria. 1.4 million of them were born in a different country. This means that every sixth inhabitant of Austria is an immigrant. This is also a clear sign that Austria has become more modern and international. (*My Austria*, p. 39)

What these anecdotes have in common is their focus on ethnic diversity and the dynamic that this diversity conveys. It is not primarily portrayed in evaluative terms of its being either good or bad, but as a founding premise of the country. In the last anecdote, diversity in population is connected to the "modern" and the "international," thus articulating immigration as a step towards the future; the comparative determiner "more" suggests that the present situation is only a step towards even more modernity and internationality.

4.3 Possessive pronouns

Another characteristic in the Austrian textbook is its use of the possessive pronouns "mein" (my) and "unser" (our). The title itself, *My Austria*, opens the textbook with the assumption that the applicant considers Austria to be her country. In the same way, seven sections in the chapter on democratic institutions are all concluded by short paragraphs headlined with the following seven sentences:

7. What does human dignity mean to our daily coexistence? (*My Austria*, p. 42)
8. What does the liberal state mean to our daily coexistence? (*My Austria*, p. 46)
9. What does the constitutional state mean to our daily coexistence? (*My Austria*, p. 49)
10. What does democracy mean to our daily coexistence? (*My Austria*, p. 57)
11. What does "Republic" mean to our daily coexistence? (*My Austria*, p. 60)
12. What does the federal state mean to our daily coexistence? (*My Austria*, p. 64)
13. What does the separation of powers mean to our daily coexistence? (*My Austria*, p. 69)

In these sentences, explanations of seven fairly abstract concepts are anchored in the repetitive "our daily coexistence." The text turns to the reader and explains what these complex ideas mean on a daily basis, thus quite concretely positioning the reader already as a member of the Austrian society.

In the following anecdotes, however, the positioning is more ambiguous:

14 (and 1). People with different origin and history live together peacefully in Austria. This positive coexistence has evolved over centuries, it is part of <u>our</u> identity and it is secured by <u>our</u> laws. (*My Austria*, p. 7, foreword by Sebastian Kurz, Minister of Europe, Integration and Foreign Affairs)

15. The idea of human dignity has spread since the 18th century. Today this idea forms a very important foundation of <u>our</u> society. (*My Austria*, p. 40)

16. As voters <u>we</u> communicate how satisfied or dissatisfied <u>we</u> are with the policy and the conditions in <u>our</u> country. (*My Austria*, p. 57)

Grammatically, the possessive pronouns in these three anecdotes can be interpreted as inclusive ("us" as natural-born and new citizens) as well as exclusive ("us" natural-born citizens as opposed to "you" new citizens). The orientation towards the past in anecdote 14 and 15 also contribute to further ambiguity: By anchoring Austrian multiculturalism and the idea of human dignity in the past, "our identity," "our laws" and "our society" are connected to previous times; times when the applicant and her relatives were not necessarily a part of Austrian society. But at the same time these concepts are connected to the present: "People with different origin and history live together peacefully in Austria."

What makes these pronouns interesting is the way they normalise diversity, if understood as inclusive: By simply articulating "our daily coexistence," "our society," and "our country" as something quite ordinary, the dynamics and diversity represented by the applicants for citizenship are potentially positioned within the Austrian narrative in a very unspectacular way, thus emphasizing its normality, provided, we might argue, that they adopt the same norms and practices as described in anecdotes 14–16.

The question is how this textual ambiguity is interpreted by the reader. Due to the positioning initiated by the title of the book and the seven sections about "our daily coexistence," other more ambiguous uses will most likely be read in this context as well. But, as we know, even though the more ambiguous anecdotes are few, they are potentially significant, depending on what we notice and how we attribute meaning.

4.4 Democracy

The fourth and last aspect of the Austrian textbook is the way it portrays democratic engagement:

17. At elections we have the opportunity to actively shape policy. Elections are also a response to the politicians. As voters we communicate, how satisfied or dissatisfied we are with the policy and the conditions in our country. (*My Austria*, p. 57)
18. Active political participation as a candidate is easier for citizens of a federal state. The number of votes that one needs to get into a local council or individual state parliament [Landtag] is lower. This makes it easier to engage politically in your own community or state. For the National Council candidates need more votes to be elected. Moreover, it is often easier to mobilise the citizens in your close surroundings. (*My Austria*, p. 65)

In these two anecdotes, democratic engagement is displayed not as a specific quality of the Austrian society or citizen, but as concrete practices of citizenship. Furthermore, they are portrayed as practices you can learn: In the Danish textbook, democratic engagement is deeply rooted in Danish society and connected to the individual citizen as an internalized practice you are raised into. In the Austrian textbook, simply described democratic practices and their functions are to be understood as something recurring and universal that one can be a part of in the present and the future; not as something one needs to learn as a child.

In summary, essentialist constitutive mechanisms occur in the Austrian textbook in anecdotes connected to Austrian identity, wherein Austrian citizens appear to be generic parts of the generalized notion of Austria. At the same time, *My Austria* highlights diversity and change within the Austrian population by simply articulating diversity as something that has always existed and which is an important contribution to future development. Furthermore, by using possessive pronouns (i.e., "our") in a primarily inclusive manner and by articulating democratic engagement as a universal and recurring practice of citizenship, applicants for citizenship are often positioned in the text within the national narrative, as an already existing and important part of Austrian society; again, provided they adopt the same norms and practices.

5. Identity in a globalized world

What is the broader rhetorical significance of national narratives in textbooks of this kind? Above I have given analytical examples from two European textbooks for applicants for citizenship. These texts are significant, first of all because they exhibit institutionalized knowledge about the history, culture, norms and values of Denmark and Austria and indicate how these countries and their citizens are portrayed to potential new citizens.

The national narrative of the Danish textbook is founded on the view of the nation as something organic and homogenous: a stable, fundamental institution that reaches several hundreds of years back in time. As two sides of the same coin, the Danish citizens smoothly form the society in Denmark, based on the prevalence of similarity, which transcends the contradictions, differences and inequalities Danish society also contains. Cultural similarities between the nation and its citizens are to be expected and are not necessarily wrong. But the focus on homogeneity and coherence in the Danish textbook leaves very little space for people who for one reason or another do not form part of society as smoothly as depicted or who form a contrast to this supposedly homogeneous population. By presenting what has been selected and created within the text as factual, stable knowledge, the textbook fails to acknowledge that society is an intellectual, cultural and linguistic construct, susceptible to change just like every other construct. It presupposes a trans-historic, consubstantial community, thus, in small but noticeable measures, essentializing what it means to be Danish.

By contrast, the Austrian textbook in many ways illustrates in alternative way to write textbooks of this kind: By articulating a country in change, a past and present community characterised by multiculturalism, it interpellates a national identity that is not fixed, but open to change and influence from other identities and cultures. As Shome and Charland note, in today's globalized world we are, in different degrees, cultural hybrids, constituted within several communities, identity formations and discourses at the same time. (Shome 1996, p. 52; Charland 1987, p. 142) Although many anecdotes in the Austrian textbook express a similar thought by highlighting diversity, at the same time, it does maintain a homogenous notion of identity that is closely related to the nation of Austria. As a result, this text also, albeit in smaller and less noticeable measures essentializes what it means to be Austrian.

Secondly, these texts are significant because they do more than simply present knowledge; they position the reader in relation to the society they depict. With anecdotes about Denmark and Danish citizens as a static unchanging backdrop, the applicant for citizenship is positioned as an outsider, who must adapt to and integrate into an already well-established community. Applicants who, by being who they are, embody the opposite characteristics (e.g., dynamics and diversity), are positioned in this relationship as the only subjects of change.

In the Austrian textbook, we see a different relationship: With a history of changeability and multiculturalism displayed in the national narrative, several points of identification are offered, which will most likely make it easier for the applicant to identify with the country in which she applies for citizenship and to see herself as a part of it in the future as well.

The close reading of the two textbooks, *Denmark Then and Now* and *My Austria*, provides examples of how the well-known notions of discursive essentialism and constitutive rhetoric prove relevant in contemporary rhetorical contexts. With complex challenges, such as increasing globalization and increased mobility, the national narratives of Denmark and Austria also expose a more general challenge in contemporary European societies: How do we meet and manage these phenomena if we simultaneously maintain understandings of identity as something coherent and unchanging? This is a question that seems even more important to address in light of the current refugee situation, which does not seem to be lilely to end any time soon.

References

Berg, Kristine M.: *Intercultural Dialogue as Rhetorical Form: a Pyrrhic Victory*. PhD thesis Copenhagen University 2011.

Bundesministerium für Europa, Integration und Äußeres: *Mein Österreich*, 2nd printing, Wien November 2014.

Charland, Maurice: "Constitutive Rhetoric: The Case of the Peuple Québécois". *Quarterly Journal of Speech* 73 (2), 1987, pp. 133–150.

Foss, Sonja K.: *Rhetorical Criticism: Exploration & Practice*. Waveland Press: Long Grove 1989.

Ivie, Robert: "Rhetorical Deliberation and Democratic Politics in the Here and Now". *Rhetoric & Public Affairs* 5 (2), 2002, pp. 277–285.

Jasinski, James: "The Status of Theory and Method in Rhetorical Criticism". *Western Journal of Communication* 65 (3), 2001, pp. 249–270.

Jørgensen, Marianne Winther /Louise Philips: *Diskursanalyse som teori og metode*, Roskilde Universitetsforlag 1999.

Klingsey, Mette: "Bred kritik af ny indfødsretsprøve". *Information*, København, 28.02.2007. http://www.information.dk/136856, retrieved 30.09.2015.

Kurier.at: "Einbürgerungen sanken rapide". *Kurier*, Wien, 13.01.2015. http://kurier.at/chronik/burgenland/einbuergerungen-sanken-rapide/107.874.182, retrieved 30.09.2015.

Leff, Michael C. Trans. Villadsen, Lisa S.: "Fortolkende retorisk kritik". *Rhetorica Scandinavica* (26), 2003, pp. 6–19.

Lewis, William F.: "Telling America's Story: Narrative Form and the Reagan Presidency". *Quarterly Journal of Speech* 73 (4), 1987, pp. 280–302.

McGee, Michael C.: "In Search of 'The People': A Rhetorical Alternative". *Quarterly Journal of Speech* 61 (3), 1975, pp. 235–249.

Ministeriet for Flygtninge, Indvandrere og Integration: *Danmark før og nu - læremateriale om historie, kultur og samfundsforhold til indfødsretsprøven*, København, April 2007.

Nielsen, Peter/ Kassebeer, Søren: "Indvandrere memorerer indfødsretsprøve". *Berlingske*, København, 13.08.2007. http://www.b.dk/danmark/indvandrere-memorerer-indfoedsretsproeve, retrieved 30.09.2015.

Phillips, Kendall R.: "The Spaces of Public Dissension: Reconsidering the Public Sphere". *Communication Monographs* (63) 1996, pp. 231–248.

Said, Edward W.: *Orientalism*. Pantheon: New York 1978.

Shome, Raka: "Postcolonial Interventions in the Rhetorical Canon. An 'Other' View". *Communication Theory* 6 (1), 1996, pp. 40–59.

Spivak, Gayatri C.: *The Postcolonial Critic: Interviews, Strategies, Dialogues*. Edited by Sarah Harasym. Routledge: New York, 1990.

Süddeutsche.de: "Da wird keiner überfordert". *Süddeutsche Zeitung*, München, 1. Juli 2010. http://www.sueddeutsche.de/politik/schaeuble-zum-einbuergerungstest-da-wird-keiner-ueberfordert-1.211710, retrieved 30.09.2015.

Therkildsen, Louise T. S.: "Du fødes som dansker – Essentialistiske fortællinger i læremterialet til den danske indfødsretsprøve". *Journal of Media, Cognition and Communication* 1 (1), 2013, pp. 149–165.

Wander, Philip: "The Third Persona: An Ideological Turn in Rhetorical Theory". *Central States Speech Journal* 35, 1984, pp. 197–216.

David Isaksen

University College of Southeast Norway

From calutrons to Congress: The democratic challenge of specialized knowledge

> *When only a few individuals have access to all the technical data needed to decide a given point, how can collective [...] wisdom play its part, and how can it be effectively expressed when the natural spokesmen for the profession become confidential advisers to government?*
>
> Alice Kimball Smith

1. Introduction

I take my working definition of rhetoric from Kenneth Burke who claimed that it is the use of symbols to induce cooperation. (Burke, Kenneth: *A Rhetoric of Motives*. University of California Press: Berkeley et al. 1969, p. 38) Rather than a separate genre of text or speech, rhetoric is a perspective or lens one can use to study how the use of symbols, such as letters, phonemes, or images, can induce actions or thoughts in the audience. (Burke, Kenneth: *Essays Toward a Symbolic of Motives: 1950–1955*. Rueckert, William (ed.) Parlor Press: West Lafayette, IN 2007, p. 41) A rhetorical analysis thus defined is the study of attempts made, by a rhetor or rhetors, at inducing cooperation by use of symbols. The critic should study to what extent the attempt is successful, and also try to find good reasons for the failure or success of the attempt or attempts.

Rhetoric is an essential function of language in all societies, since they can exist as societies only by using symbols to coordinate thoughts and actions. Following the stasis system from classical rhetoric, we may say that we use rhetoric to determine socially what the facts are, what they should be called, their relative importance, and what should be done about them. In the example of science, an individual researcher may discover something about nature which one could call empirical fact, or knowledge; however, this does not become *public* knowledge until it has been authorized or accredited by a public. (Bitzer, Lloyd: "Rhetoric and Public Knowledge". In: Burks, Don M. (ed.) *Rhetoric, Philosophy, and Literature. An Exploration*. Purdue University Press: West Lafayette, IN 1978, p. 68) The first public that must be induced to accredit the discovery will be a scientific community, which members are seen as the sole possessors of ability to evaluate the legitimacy of the discovery. (Kuhn, Thomas: *The Structure of Scientific Revolutions*, 4th ed. University of Chicago Press: Chicago et al. 2012, p. 167) If they give their approval then that often concludes the rhetorical work the discoverer must conduct. However, sometimes the discovery has implications for a greater public or seems to call for actions that the scientific community by itself does not have the means or rights to authorize. The scientific community claims competency to judge in matters of fact and, at times, definition, but no competency to judge in matters of quality (relative importance) or procedure (what should be done).[1] Yet, in order to make judgments of quality one first has to establish questions of fact and definition. In such instances, the scientist or scientists must take the arguments developed for a scientific audience and make them persuasive to a greater public that does not share the competence, values, and common assumptions of the scientific community. This transition is fraught with difficulty, but it is crucial work that must be done in order to enable the general public to make public policy decisions based on scientific knowledge. Citizens do not have to be experts, but they need clear explanations of the problem and open public debate "in order to sort through the available options and the trade-offs involved." (Hauser, Gerard A.: *Introduction to Rhetorical Theory*, 2nd ed. Waveland Press: Prospect Heights, IL 2002, p. 85) Only an enlightened general public can be a "knowledge society"; otherwise we will rather have to talk of "societies" of specialized knowledge that is not widely shared among the non-specialists.

My main object of study here will be how scientific knowledge is accredited or authorized as public knowledge, and what roles scientists take on in that process, arguing questions of quality rather than fact and trying not merely to inform but to persuade. I will look primarily at texts and illustrations that are remnants of a historical attempt at making the public accept a specific instance of scientific knowledge as truth: the 1945–46 debate about the control of atomic energy.

Most of the scientists who had participated in the development of the atomic bomb were horrified after the war with how the Truman administration and the military sought to gain solitary control of atomic policy and curb debate about

---

[1] The logical positivists labeled questions of quality and procedure as meaningless and metaphysical. (Carnap, Rudolf: "The Elimination of Metaphysics through Logical Analysis of Language". In: Ayer, Alfred. J. (ed.): *Logical Positivism*. The Free Press: New York et al. 1959, p. 76; Schlick, Moritz: "The Turning Point in Philosophy". In: Ayer, Alfred. J. (ed.): *Logical Positivism*. The Free Press: New York et al. 1959, p. 56) Edward Teller claims that the scientist has done his job when he has increased man's control over nature and has no business deciding about how that power will be used. (Teller, Edward/ Brown, Allen: *The Legacy of Hiroshima*. Doubleday: Garden City, NY 1962, pp. 56–57)

the issue. They walked out from their labs and into the public sphere to voice their protest against what they saw as precursors to atomic war and tried desperately to wake and alert the public about this new technology and its implications. (Smith, Alice K.: *A Peril and a Hope. The Scientists' Movement in America 1945–47*. MIT Press: London et al. 1971, p. 16) This time has been described as the dawn of Big Science, with powerful and advanced machinery like calutrons taking center stage in nuclear research and pushing the sciences towards increased specialization. (Peierls, Rudolf: *Bird of Passage. Recollections of a Physicist*. Princeton University Press: Princeton et al. 1985, pp. 225–226; Frisch, Otto R.: *What Little I Remember*. Cambridge University Press: Cambridge et al. 1980, p. 178) Some senior scientists believed the public would not be able to grasp the importance and meaning of such advanced subjects, so they rather trusted that, through their influence, the government would make the right decisions on behalf of the public. Most of the atomic scientists disagreed, and they believed the public needed to have a say in this decision and tried to enable them to do so. This required different tools and different premises than those that were native to their scientific discipline, such as what Chaim Perelman and Lucie Olbrechts-Tyteca (Perelman, Chaim/ Olbrechts-Tyteca, Lucie/ Trans. Wilkinson, John/ Weaver, Purcell: *The New Rhetoric. A Treatise on Argumentation*. University of Notre Dame Press: Notre Dame 1969) have labeled the argument of authority, appeals to emotions, and argument by example, illustration, and analogy. I will try to highlight the challenges of this transition and the successes and failures of the scientists in relation to them.

Many of the scientists working on the bomb realized what they saw as inevitable political implications of their project. After Hiroshima and Nagasaki, the scientists were appalled to see that this understanding was not widely shared, and most of them began to argue for openness and civilian control of nuclear weapons. (Smith 1971, p. 140) Their initial attempts at persuading the public failed due to what may be called "disciplinary blindness."[2] In order to make their specialized knowledge

---

[2] This blindness has been commented on by many historians and philosophers of science. Thomas Kuhn writes that "A paradigm can […] insulate a community from those socially important problems that are not reducible to the puzzle form, because they cannot be stated in terms of the conceptual and instrumental tools the paradigm supplies." (Kuhn 2012, p. 37) Michael Polanyi writes that "It is by the assimilation of the framework of science that the scientist makes sense of his experience" (Polanyi, Michael: *Personal Knowledge. Towards a Post-Critical Philosophy*. University of Chicago Press: Chicago 1962, p. 60), but this may also make the scientist disregard evidence which "conflicts with the current teachings of science" or set aside facts that have no place in the "established framework of science" (p. 138).

understandable and persuasive to the public and the U.S. Congress, these scientists had to reinvent themselves rhetorically. In this, they both succeeded and failed: The rhetoric of these scientists led to the passage of the McMahon Act (1946), yet it failed to achieve the international openness that might have prevented the nuclear arms race. I argue that this historical example shows how scientists have to rely on and nurture a broader culture of rationality than what fits within the narrow scope of positivistic science in order to make the case for the significance of scientific knowledge on public policy.

2. Background

During WWII, scientists from all over the world came to the United States to participate in the development of the atomic bomb. The purpose for and meaning of this work was articulated primarily by three influential texts. In each instance, they convey a mixture of scientific facts and a less scientific interpretation of those facts.[3] The basic initial premise of the scientists' participation in the project can be found in the Frisch-Peierls memorandum of 1940, which basically states that since the design of an atomic bomb is relatively simple, Nazi Germany may successfully develop such a weapon. In other words, because there is a certain potentiality, this potentiality will inevitably be unleashed for destructive purposes. If so, then the Allies should have their own weapon for the sake of parity and deterrence, although "the bomb could probably not be used without killing large numbers of civilians, and this may make it unsuitable for a weapon for use by this country." (Frisch/ Peierls 1992, p. 81) Even pacifists, such as Robert R. Wilson, were drawn in by these arguments and started working on the bomb. (Wilson, Robert R.: *From Pacifist to Warrior*. TS. Robert R. Wilson Papers. Carl A. Kroch Library. Cornell University, Ithaca, NY 1990, p. 9)

Once the scientists arrived at Los Alamos, they either attended or read a series of lectures by Robert Serber, which later became known as the *Los Alamos Primer*. The document describes itself as an "indoctrination course," and starts with this purpose statement: "The object of the project is to create a practical military

---

3 Smith claims that every scientist sets the line between fact and interpretation at a different place. Polanyi sees interpretation and judgment as a feature inherent in every empirical observation (p. 19). Kuhn claims that the paradigm of a researcher determines from the outset which observations are seen as valid and which ones are discarded as anomalies (p. 82). Yet there is a general agreement that, of the two, fact is the one where the researcher stands on the most solid empirical ground.

weapon in the form of a bomb." (Serber, Robert: *The Los Alamos Primer. The First Lectures on How To Build an Atomic Bomb.* Rhodes, Richard (ed.) University of California Press: Berkeley et al. 1992, p. 2) The details of nuclear bomb assembly are described with the ultimate goal being to maximize damage and "efficiency." As Serber states, "Since the one factor that determines the damage is the energy release, our aim is simply to get as much energy from the explosion as we can." (1992, p. 12) The whole development process is here described as a scientific problem, or, more broadly viewed, a great experiment. This pattern of thought is mirrored in J. Robert Oppenheimer's statement that "when you see something that is technically sweet, you go ahead and do it and you argue about what to do about it only after you have had your technical success." (United States Atomic Energy Commission. *In the Matter of J. Robert Oppenheimer. Transcript of Hearing before Personnel Security Board.* United States Government Printing Office: Washington, DC 1954, p. 81) The incessant work towards creating the atomic bomb allowed little time for reflection and reevaluation of the purpose of their work, even after it became known in 1944 that Germany's nuclear program had failed.

Niels Bohr, the father of quantum physics, joined the project in 1944, and he quickly became the ideological leader of the Los Alamos scientists. Oppenheimer later stated that "he made the enterprise, which often looked so macabre, seem hopeful." (Smith 1971, p. 6) Bohr's vision was similar to that of H. G. Wells in *The World Set Free* where he hypothesizes that the release of nuclear energy will cause "an epidemic of sanity" to break out among the nations and leaders of the world. (Wells, Herbert G.: *The World Set Free. A Story of Mankind.* Macmillian: London 1914, p. 2; Bohr, Niels: "A Challenge to Civilization". *Science.* (102) 12.10.1945, pp. 363–364) The basic argument is relatively simple: War is the nation state asserting its superiority and sovereignty over other nation states. Weapons are used to conquer land and property. However, this new weapon makes such conquest impossible, since it can be easily developed by both sides in a conflict and allows no options for a defense. Therefore, only international control through a superstate or World Federation which supersedes the sovereignty of nation states can save us all from extinction. With such a system, war on a large scale becomes impossible. This sentiment was echoed by Oppenheimer in the speech he gave at Los Alamos October 16th, 1945:

> The people of this world must unite, or they will perish. This war, that has ravaged so much of the earth, has written these words. The atomic bomb has spelled them out for all men to understand. Other men have spoken them, in other times, of other wars, of other weapons. They have not prevailed. There are some, misled by a false sense of human history, who hold they will not prevail today. It is not for us to believe that. By our words we are committed, committed to a world united, before this common peril. (Oppenheimer,

Robert: "Speech to Los Alamos Scientists, October 18th, 1945". Robert R. Wilson Papers. Carl A Kroch Library, Cornell University, Ithaca, NY)

As Alice Kimball Smith would later write, "Mankind now faced a common destiny of destruction as represented once before by the universal story of the flood." (Smith 1971, p. viii) We here see displayed three of the dominant concepts of the atomic bomb: (1) the atomic bomb as a defensive measure in order to establish a balance of powers based on deterrence, (2) the atomic bomb as a scientific experiment and measure of progress, and (3) the atomic bomb as the invention which will end all war and make victory in war impossible.

Of these three concepts of the atomic bomb, most of the scientists chose the third as their ideological commitment. The first concept of deterrence held greater sway among the administration and political establishment, the second concept of the bombs as experiments and progress was echoed by Edward Teller and other scientists who pushed relentlessly for development of the hydrogen bomb and a greater range of nuclear weapons to be added to the weapons arsenal (Teller/Brown 1962, p. 42), but the third was the only one that provided any solace for the scientists who were ethically troubled by what they had brought forth. For many of the scientists, the political reality of the bomb hit them at the Trinity test explosion. This is well exemplified in the account from Robert R. Wilson's unpublished memoir *Pacifist to Warrior*: "Sensations and emotions press in. A momentary ecstasy of creation is replaced by remorse and fear as the realization of the immensity of what we have done is pounded in by the rolling of the thunder from the mountains, mountains that are now dwarfed by the scale of the fireball – and the question grows: what have we done? – what have we made?" (1990, p. 1–2)

3. First attempts at informing the public and the public response

Already before the atomic bombs had been released over Japan, the scientists were organizing to educate the public about this terrible new reality. Organizations started popping up all over the Manhattan Project, to the great dismay of their bosses (Robert Oppenheimer, Arthur Compton, and the military): The Association of Los Alamos Scientists (with the fitting acronym ALAS), the Association of the Manhattan Scientists, and many other political organizations were established during this period (Smith 1971, p. vii). Oppenheimer was sympathetic to the movement goals, but believed that these issues should be entrusted to government committees rather than the people. The ALAS scientists went out to speak about atomic weapons with anyone who would listen to them. The message was pretty unanimous and closely followed the argument developed by Bohr. As Jane Wilson writes:

More than forty years later the message is still the same. It was indelibly engraved on my brain: (1) The atomic bomb is an entirely new kind of weapon, (2) The atomic bomb is a deadly weapon which can devastate cities at a single blow, (3) There is no defense against an atomic bomb, and (4) The 'secret' of the atomic bomb is that it is possible to make it. Since that secret is now revealed, many nations – unless there is some control – can soon have the bomb. (Wilson, Jane: *Jane Wilson Memoir*. TS. Hans Bethe Papers. Carl A. Kroch Library, Cornell University, Ithaca, NY)

Whether one could say that these points are all objectively true and therefore true knowledge, it is nevertheless the case that they were accepted *as true* by the atomic scientists, and therefore were accredited as "scientific knowledge." There was little disagreement about this among the two camps; they mainly differed as to the methods that should be used to obtain the policies that these facts demanded.

If we look at these four points from the perspective of stasis theory, we can see that they primarily fit in the stases of definition and quality. (Crowley, Sharon/ Hawhee, Debra: *Ancient Rhetorics for Contemporary Students*, 5th ed. Pearson: Boston et al. 2012, p. 64) The atomic bomb is already a fact, but it is unclear exactly what kind of a fact it is and what implications it may have for the future of the world. A scientist is at home in arguments of fact, but arguments of definition and especially quality are further away from their area of expertise. This is because arguments of quality "always depend on the values maintained in the community" (Crowley/ Hawhee 2012, p. 77) and values have been deemed by positivism as "devoid of scientific value" since questions of value elude the methods of the mathematical and natural sciences." (Perelman/ Olbrechts-Tyteca 1969, p. 512)[4] Arguments of quality naturally call for tools such as description, concretization, narrative, comparisons, and appeals to emotion as well as logic, since "in the absence of an objective standard, things are measured only by the value people attach to them." (Perelman, Chaim. Trans. Kluback, William: *The Realm of Rhetoric*. University of Notre Dame Press: South Bend 1982, p. 77) Yet, the scientists initially treated all four points as arguments of fact, and self-evident fact at that. This approach is evident in the documents released by ALAS and Robert Wilson between

---

4   Carnap writes that "Logical analysis […] pronounces the verdict of meaninglessness on any alleged knowledge that pretends to reach above or behind experience" and "the same judgment must be passed on all philosophy of norms, or philosophy of value, on any ethics or esthetics as a normative discipline. For the objective validity of a value or norm is neither empirically verifiable nor deducible from empirical statements; hence it cannot be asserted (in a meaningful statement) at all." (Carnap 1959, pp. 76–77) Viewed from these criteria, all but the second claim made by Jane Wilson could be viewed as meaningless or metaphysical.

October 1945 and January 1946, such as "Open Letter to President of the United States," "Summary of Arguments Press Release," "Atomic Spectre," "Manifesto of the Association of Los Alamos Scientists," and quotes given to Senator Glen Taylor for his address "Creation of a World Republic."

Perhaps predictably, the first attempts were not favorably received. In the midst of the exultation of victory in WWII and triumphant nationalism, the messages from the scientists sounded like sour grapes. One instance may be a good illustration of this: Despite security restrictions, Robert Wilson sent out a letter to the editor of nearly every major newspaper and magazine in the United States. It starts out with, "A spectre is haunting this country – the spectre of nuclear energy. As a scientist who worked on the atomic bomb I am appalled that the public is so apathetic and so uninformed about the dangerous social consequences of our development" (Wilson, Robert R.: "Atomic Specter". *Time Magazine* (17) 10.22.1945, p. 1). The statement then basically recounts the four main points mentioned by Jane Wilson and states that, "It is my sincere conviction that a satisfactory solution will be forthcoming, but only as a result of an enlightened and strong public opinion." He ends with the somewhat feeble statement that "It was our hope in developing the bomb that it would be a great force for world cooperation and peace..."

The tone here is a bit arrogant and condescending, and seems to shift responsibility and blame from the scientists to the American people. The thesis claims there is a danger, and moreover he identifies himself as someone who created that danger. Then he goes on to castigate a war-weary American public for being apathetic and uninformed about the dangers of nuclear energy. In other words, the public is ignorant of the specialized knowledge the scientists have and they are scolded for being ignorant. The form of the argument is that of a declaration or manifesto without the normal reasoning expected of a preamble. He states his arguments as if they were matters of fact, with no explanation of why there can be no effective defense, why it is impossible to keep the method of creating it a secret, or why the United States is inevitably doomed unless international control of atomic weapons is established. There is no point of reference here for the general public, no connection to the reality they know or anything tangible they can relate to. Wilson here speaks as an expert that expects to be believed, even though the audience have not worked with these materials for two years or personally witnessed an atomic explosion like he has. The same tendencies can be found in their "Open Letter to the President of the United States" where the ALAS claim "Such old concepts as armed might, and spheres of influence, lost their meaning with the obliteration of Hiroshima" (Association of Los Alamos Scientists: "Open Letter to the President of the United States". TS. Robert R. Wilson Papers. Carl A Kroch Library, Cornell

University, Ithaca, NY, p. 3). They do not give any evidence to support this view, but rather treat this as a self-evident fact.

"Atomic Specter" received many negative responses. One reader wrote back to Wilson in person, and it must have made an impact since he kept the letter with his collection of papers that was donated to Cornell University:

> Was it not a wonderful tale you put at the end of your article. 'It was our hope in developing the bomb that it would be a great force for world cooperation and peace.' Oh my God, I say with earnestness, How could it ever come about by killing innocent women and children in the most horrible way yet devised by a degenerate mankind? It is fanatic to believe such. (Beck, J. K.: "Letter to Robert R. Wilson, 6.11.1945". TS. Robert R. Wilson Papers. Carl A Kroch Library, Cornell University, Ithaca, NY, p. 1–2)

Yet, for all its faults, it is one of the first large-scale attempts to inform the public and let them have a say in the future of nuclear weapons and atomic energy. Wilson trusts the public where Oppenheimer, Fermi, and Compton have chosen to trust the closed halls of government in committees and private discussions. This creates a rift between the two approaches to this question, which come to a head in the debate over the May-Johnson bill in October the same year. The text of the bill establishes and determines the composition of an Atomic Energy Commission that would regulate all affairs relating to atomic energy, giving the commission widespread powers even to impose fines or prison sentences on scientists who speak of matters the commission deems to be restricted. The focus of the bill is on secrecy, and the committee would be mainly under the control of the military and the president, without congressional oversight. The president could also replace members of the committee at any time without any explanation. (Smith 1971, pp. 129–131) Representative May, who introduced the bill, pushed it through committee after only 5 hours of debate, and claimed to have the support of the military, administration, and the scientists for this approach. (Smith 1971, pp. 134–135)

Compton, who was a close advisor to the government, defended this bill to his colleagues even though he conceded that the committee would not be democratic "It is indeed true that democracy can last only as long as our leading citizens are inspired by the desire to work for the benefit of the public rather than of themselves. If this spirit prevails, however broad the commission's power may be, we are in no danger. If it is absent, democracy is already gone." (quoted in Smith 1971, p. 179) In essence, if we can trust our leaders then we are safe, if we cannot then we have no recourse to action. Such is the concept of democracy that sprung out of the experience of WWII for Arthur Compton. This met with massive opposition from the younger and more idealistic scientists who were already disillusioned by the Nagasaki bombing. They openly challenged the authority of

Fermi, Oppenheimer, and Compton, and pushed for an extension of debate on the May-Johnson bill, contacted legislators, and organized the Federation of Atomic Scientists (FAS) as an official lobbying group in D.C. (Smith, 1971, p. 180–192) Faced with this barrage of criticism, the Senate extended the debate for the bill until the beginning of 1946. The scientists had won a brief interlude, but they had made little progress on gaining acceptance of their main four theses.

4. New approach

One can see in the following months how the scientists developed their methods in order to be more persuasive. In addition to publishing the best-selling book *One World or None*, the Federation of American Scientists started publishing a non-technical journal called *Bulletin of the Atomic Scientists*, and encouraged popular opinion pieces by scientists in venues such as *LIFE, Collier's* and *The New Republic*. Their work was augmented by the August 1946 publication of *Hiroshima* by John Hersey in *The New Yorker*, which soon became "the talk of the town" and played a significant role in educating the public about the dangers of nuclear weapons. What we see is a rhetorical approach that to a greater extent takes the audience into consideration. We see less bombast and "manifesto language," more humility, greater focus on emotional appeals, metaphors, images, descriptions, even pictures that look a bit like propaganda posters, and a broad involvement in the political process through new and old channels.

For example, in "A Plea for Atomic Freedom," published on 25th of March, 1946, Aaron Novick introduces himself in this way: "I am not a world-famed scientist, nor am I experienced in speaking of political affairs. I am a young man who worked on the atomic-bomb projects at the University of Chicago and Los Alamos" (Novick, Aaron: "A Plea for Atomic Freedom". *The New Republic*. (12) 25.3.1946, p. 399). This is clearly a different approach, with a more humble and pleading tone. He addresses the audience personally and asks rhetorical questions to engage them in the issue at hand:

> Have you ever feared for every political expression you ever made? Working under Army security rules was much like living in the kind of totalitarian society which existed in Germany and Italy. We often saw men discharged after several years of service because suddenly their 'loyalty was questioned.' What had they done [...] given aid to the enemy, divulged secrets to foreign spies? They received no hearing. Their colleagues were given no explanation. We became frightened, insecure, under constant vague threat. During the war we had to accept it. In peacetime we cannot. (Novick, 1946, p. 400)

In the context of WWII one can imagine the emotional impact a comparison with Germany would have. Rather than simply stating that "this is unacceptable," Novick shares his concerns through narrative and descriptions, describing sensations and emotions such as "frightened" and "insecure." Novick draws the audience in by his narrative and urges everyone to press for civilian control of nuclear weapons with the warning, "Do otherwise, and America begins a nuclear armament race which will destroy us all." (1946, p. 400)

Although Novick theoretically has the credentials to call himself an expert, he willingly relinquishes that mantle in order to speak simply as a concerned citizen. Rather than appealing to logic and scientific facts, Novick appeals to a sense of justice and the legal right to due process and freedom from persecution. The comparison with Italy and Germany and the opposition of acceptable conditions in wartime and peacetime act together with what Richard Weaver named devil-terms and god-terms throughout the text to highlight the importance of the choice between civilian and military control of atomic energy. (Weaver, Richard: *The Ethics of Rhetoric*. Hermagoras Press: Davis, CA 1985) On the one hand, we have "civilian control, American tradition, world peace, peacetime, progress, basic rights" and on the other hand we find "military control, revulsion, suppression, secrecy, stops the progress of science, intolerable, totalitarian, threat, fear, wartime, censorship, sterile, destroy us all" (Novick 1946, pp. 399–400). The rhetorical effect of such comparison is "less to inform than to impress" (Perelman 1982, p. 77) and is often listed as one of the primary strategies to create pathos or emotional appeal. (Hatch, Gary L.: "Rhetorical Proofs: Ethos, Pathos, and Logos". In: McInelly, Brett C./ Jackson, Brian (eds.): *Writing and Rhetoric*. Hayden-McNeil: Plymouth, MI 2011, p. 67)

The use of all these emotional appeals begs the question as to whether Novick is speaking as a citizen or a scientist. He relinquishes the mantle or ethos of an expert in order to relate to his audience, but he still makes a number of claims about fact that a positivist would have to label as metaphysical or pseudo-scientific. He claims that the nature of science and military control are incompatible, that science and secrecy cannot dwell in the same house, that "military control stops the progress of science" (Novick 1946, p. 400), and that total annihilation is the inevitable result of a nuclear arms race. Most atomic scientists regarded these as fact, but they belong in the realm of interpretation. A positivist would even label them metaphysical or meaningless.

Another example of effective rhetorical appeals is "Beyond Imagination" by Phillip Morrison, a Los Alamos scientist who had personally visited Hiroshima after the bombing. In this popular article published on 11th of February 1946, Morrison gives detailed descriptions of the horrors at Hiroshima and describes exactly why the atomic bomb is different to all other weapons. At this time, his point had been made before, but it was not yet fully accepted by the public. He makes the difference vivid by comparing the heat from the bomb to that of a small sun, carefully describing the different stages of the blast with its effects, such as "instantly all organic material was burned up. For some distance it burned up the flesh". (Morrison, Philip: "Beyond Imagination". *The New Republic* (26) 11.02.1946, p. 178) Where the scientists before had simply claimed that the atomic bomb was a new kind of weapon, Morrison is one of the first to make a lay person understand exactly why. He describes the minimal effort required to destroy and other ways in which the atomic bomb is totally different:

> The atomic bomb is a weapon of saturation. It destroys so quickly and so completely such a large area that defense is hopeless. Leadership and organization are gone. Key personnel are killed. With the fire stations wrecked and the firemen burned, how control a thousand fires? With the doctors dead and the hospitals smashed, how treat a quarter of a million injured? (Morrison 1946, p. 178)

With painful precision he details the deaths of the citizens of Hiroshima: the people in the street are burned in a flash, the people inside are crushed by the blast wave knocking their roofs and walls over their heads or the heat starting fires that burns them alive as they are trapped under rubble. Some crawl virtually unharmed from the rubble of their homes, but "they died anyway" from radiation poisoning where "the blood does not coagulate, but oozes in many spots through the unbroken skin, and internally seeps into the cavities of the body" (Morrison 1946, p. 180) and the patient dies within two to three weeks. The implications of the narrative are obvious: there is no escape from an atomic bomb.

Unlike Novick, Morrison clearly speaks with the mantle of a scientist, referring several times to his title and expertise, as well as the limits of his knowledge and the limit of his expertise. For example, he says of radiation that "I am not a medical man, but like most physicists I have studied this disease a little" (1946, p. 180) and clarifies when he has been able to confirm rumors by empirical evidence and when he has not been able to do so. The narrative is detached, but not objective. For example, his focus is clearly on those who died and not on those who survived, making it seem like all who did not die from the heat or the blast wave finally succumbed to radiation poisoning, leaving no hope of deliverance, although there were some survivors closer to the blast. His information is factual, but his selection of information is deliberate and is intended to make the main four points mentioned by Jane Wilson in a more forceful and effective way, to create presence. (Perelman 1982, p. 34) This clashed with the official narrative of the military and administration, which downplayed the effects of the bomb and particularly radiation. General Groves, who led the Manhattan Project and had claimed in Congress that radiation death was "very pleasant" (Jungk, Robert. Trans. Cleugh, James: *Brighter than a Thousand Suns. A Personal History of the Atomic Scientists*. Harcourt: New York et al. 1970, p. 228), later labeled the rhetorical efforts of the atomic scientists as "propaganda." (Smith 1971, p. 250) Although that is a common way of denigrating the rhetoric of an opponent, at least some aspects of the scientists' rhetoric bear some resemblance to propaganda.

Perhaps the best example of this is a pamphlet developed by Science and Philosophy Group of the California Labor School. Although not an official publication of the FAS, Giacomo Patri, the artist who illustrated the pamphlet, had a connection to many of the atomic scientists, and the CIO served as an organizational link between the FAS and the Labor School. The pamphlet could be mistaken for WWII propaganda. It starts with "The Horror" and shows a multitude of people incinerated and helpless against the nuclear bomb in their midst.

Fig. 7.1: Front page of pamphlet issued by Science and Philosophy Group of the California Labor School. Illustrations by Giancomo Patri

The text of the pamphlet echoes the same four points Jane Wilson mentions in her unpublished memoir, but the impact through visual aids is undeniably greater. The arguments are succinct and sharpened, claiming that the May-Johnson bill would "gag the scientist and close the mouths and stop the ears of the people" and "create a dictatorial power over not only this nation but the world." (Patri, Giancomo: "Pamphlet on the May-Johnson Bill". TS. Robert R. Wilson Papers. Carl A. Kroch Library, Cornell University, Ithaca, NY 1946, p. 2) The text is accompanied by a face that shows simultaneously fear, hatred, and suspicion. Contrasted with this we see two smiling men talking to each other openly over the heading "International Unity" and a quote from H. G. Wells that says "This can wipe out everything bad or good in this world. It is up to the people to decide." (Patri 1946, p. 3) The final page is a call to action and shows a family facing a line of bomber airplanes and facing away from a bounteous harvest of fruit, highlighting the future consequences of this decision.

Both these rhetorical efforts of Morrison and Patri serve to make the threat of atomic weapons concrete and therefore relatable to the general public. However, as the rhetoric becomes sharper and the difference between the alternatives is made to seem greater, we also see a tendency towards demonization, fear appeals, and other aspects of argument that clearly go beyond the "objective reasoning" that formerly was the mark of the scientist in public perception. Otto R. Frisch, for example, claims that the unique training scientists have to think "objectively and dispassionately" enables them to make better decisions (1980, p. 176), yet Harold Urey writes in January 1946, "I write this to frighten you. I am a frightened man, myself. All the scientists I know are frightened – frightened for their lives – and frightened for *your* life." (Urey, Harold C.: "I'm A Frightened Man". *Collier's Weekly* (18) 05.01.1946, p. 18) Whether or not this statement can be called objective it is hardly an example of dispassionate thinking.

5. Results and lessons

The immediate result of the strenuous efforts of the atomic scientists, led by the FAS, was the rejection of the May-Johnson bill and the signing of the McMahon Act or Atomic Energy Act on August 1st, 1946, but it also led to a temporary reduction in the prestige of the scientists. Even though they had been almost unanimous in their opposition to the May-Johnson bill, this unanimity soon started to show cracks. When they were not successful in promoting a World Federation or in averting a nuclear arms race, the scientists were unable to agree upon what should be the next step. Teller argued in 1947 that the only answer now was to secure nuclear superiority for the United States, others argued the main effort had to be educating the public, and the community in general saw no way of getting a clear and unanimous answer to which way to go forward. Hans Bethe, Nobel laureate in physics, argued that without a clear case to be made, scientists would lose their present prestige in politics. He chose not to involve himself further to preserve his credibility until a time came when scientists could speak with one voice again. (Smith 1971, pp. 350–351)

Bohr's vision and the hope that came with it was largely abandoned, leaving the scientists with the "fragile hope" that deterrence would prevent the end of humanity. Oppenheimer writes later to Bohr that "Even in our gloomy moments we did not succeed quite in thinking how difficult it would get to be." (Oppenheimer 1946, p. 1) As scientists either abstained from war work or signed confidentiality agreements in top secret laboratories and government posts, the advocates for restraint fell out of the loop on nuclear weapons. Wilson made a moral choice to abstain from war work and making bombs, but later laments that "since I was no longer connected with it, I was an amateur – almost lost any expertise that I had previously. I lost it all, so I had no effect on what was happening." (Palevsky, Mary: *Atomic Fragments. A Daughter's Questions*. University of California Press: Berkeley et al. 2000, p. 131)

What are some lessons we can learn from this historical case study? I think the first lesson is that scientists must learn to adapt their arguments to their audience if they want to empower the public to make informed decisions on technical matters. John Dewey claims that improving the conditions of debate is of utmost importance. (Dewey, John: *The Public and Its Problems*. Ohio University Press: Athens, OH 1954, p. 208) The experts must make it possible for the public to understand and develop their own opinions concerning an issue so that they can participate in democratic decision-making. The public will be more enabled to do so if scientists use Morrison's rhetoric rather than that of Wilson's "Atomic Specter," showing them the reasons behind their claims and conclusions.

A second lesson is that maybe the scientific community needs to accept a reduction in prestige to create more openness about the debates among scientists. Smith writes: "Because scientists have claimed to provide the medium for revelation of truth about the physical world, one answer to any given question is expected of them [...] and when they disagree publicly, the authority of science is undermined to a greater degree than is that of other disciplines." (1971, p. 367) It was the realization of this loss of prestige that made Hans Bethe withdraw from active politics. Yet, as Smith mentions, other disciplines do not experience loss of prestige in the same degree, showing that it is possible to retain prestige without unanimity. If the public is supposed to have an active role in shaping public policies, they have to become educated about the basis for the expert advice that they receive.

Despite their focus on participation, the FAS by themselves functioned more or less as expert elites that led the public somewhat like sheep. They knew that the May-Johnson bill was a bad idea, and they used all their expertise and knowledge to convince others that they were right.

It was perhaps the public clash of opinions among scientists that gave the greatest educational benefit to the public, since it forced the FAS to reveal the basis for their claims and make more comprehensive arguments, and allowed the public to see the extent and limits of agreement among scientists on the issue at hand. This helped the public to question the different judgments scientists made on what was fact and what was interpretation, since every scientist privately defines the line between the two a little bit differently. (Smith 1971, p. 368) For example, there was great agreement among scientists that there could be no defense against an atomic bomb and that there was no essential secret as to how to make one, but there was less agreement about what kind of "international organization" could be set up to be entrusted with managing all the world's atomic energy. This created a real opportunity for citizens to become educated enough to judge between competing claims.

Specialized knowledge may be an even greater challenge to democracy today, as scientific knowledge is being produced at an accelerating rate and is becoming increasingly specialized. To a greater extent than before WWII, scientists now operate as advisors to governments or even as government officials themselves. Dewey claimed already in 1927 that "no government by experts in which the masses do not have the chance to inform the experts as to their needs can be anything but an oligarchy managed in the interests of the few" (1954, p. 206), but the technocratic tendencies of modern political debate tend to create ever greater barriers to citizen participation and mask ideological commitments as scientific truth.[5]

Greater openness and exposure to debates among scientists would educate the public and perhaps make them more able to participate in the process of

---

5   One example could be how some economists have made a case for austerity in Europe based on "economic facts" that are in fact controversial and to a certain extent ideological interpretations. Paul Krugman claims this was the case with Alberto Alesina's research on "expansionary austerity." (Krugman, Paul: "The Austerity Delusion". *The Guardian*. 29.04.2015) Similarly, Katherine Magraw claims that Edward Teller misrepresented the likelihood of developing "clean thermonuclear bombs" and disguised opinions and hopes as facts in order to foil the Comprehensive Test Ban Treaty. (Magraw, Katherine: "Edward Teller and the 'Clean Bomb' Episode". *Bulletin of the Atomic Scientists* (44)4, 1988, p. 36)

questioning and spreading knowledge in the knowledge society. If the public were to become more rhetorically savvy as to how scientific debates arise and are resolved then science may not necessarily suffer a loss of prestige whenever disagreement occurs, since the public will understand that this is a natural part of the process in the scientific elimination of error.

One feature of this rhetorical savviness would be to know what questions to ask of science and the kind of answers one can expect. As Teller writes, politicians are disoriented when they ask scientists for their conclusions and are faced with contradictory responses, but "If the question had been: 'What are the facts? What are your arguments?' then the answers would have been more consistent." (Teller/Brown 1962, pp. 153–154) Exact scientific answers can most clearly be found in questions of fact, but scientists speaking on matters of quality or procedure (such as public policy) are often required to go well beyond what they can give clear factual evidence for.

Another feature would be greater familiarity with the kinds of arguments that are decisive in a scientific context. The most common argument cited for climate change in public policy debates is that the majority of climate scientists believe in anthropomorphic climate change, and yet, except for in questions of definition (such as "is Pluto a planet or a dwarf planet?"), the *argument from authority* is not a decisive scientific argument.[6] Richard Feynman famously claimed that, "Science is the belief in the ignorance of experts" (Feynman, Richard: "What is Science". *The Physics Teacher.* 7 (6), 1969, pp. 313–320), and Perelman states that science has historically attacked this form of argumentation violently and *it* is of interest "only in the absence of demonstrable proof." (1982, pp. 94–95) Climate policy advocates have used this argument because they perceive the current public to be too ignorant of climate science to refer them to the relevant scientific facts and theories (demonstrable proof), and yet this argument still requires a basic level understanding of scientific controversy. As Perelman writes, "Except for the case of an absolute authority, the conflict of authorities requires a criterion by which a settlement is brought about" (1982, p. 95), and climate scientists have

---

6   As A.J. Ayer writes, "One reason why we trust 'the scientists of our era' is that we believe that they give an accurate account of their observations. But this means that we shall be involved in a circle if we say that the reason why we accept certain evidence is merely that it comes from the scientists of our era." (1959, pp. 233–234) In other words, the authority of scientists rests on empirical observation and not on any inherent quality that makes them oracles of nature and truth. To say we believe scientists because they are credible is a circular argument.

had difficulties in convincing the public about what criteria should decide who is an authority on climate science.[7]

Exposure to scientific controversies can bring out and display the basic assumptions of the scientific community and the foundations for agreement and disagreement. Though this may not be an immediate solution to the climate change controversy, I believe it would still have an educational effect on the public. As John Dewey writes, "No matter the differences in native intelligence, the actuality of mind is dependent upon the education which social conditions effect," and "A more intelligent state of social affairs, one more informed with knowledge, more directed by intelligence, would not improve original endowment one whit, but it would raise the level upon which the intelligence of all operates." (1954, p. 208) In either case, it is the only way democracy can be less than a blind belief in the judgments of experts.

References

Ayer, Alfred. J.: "Verification and Experience". In: Ayer, Alfred J. (ed.): *Logical Positivism*. The Free Press: New York et al. 1959, pp. 228–243.

Association of Los Alamos Scientists: "Open Letter to the President of the United States". TS. Robert R. Wilson Papers. Carl A Kroch Library, Cornell University, Ithaca, NY.

Beck, J. K.: "Letter to Robert R. Wilson, 6.11.1945". TS. Robert R. Wilson Papers. Carl A Kroch Library, Cornell University, Ithaca, NY.

Bitzer, Lloyd: "Rhetoric and Public Knowledge". In: Burks, Don M. (ed.) *Rhetoric, Philosophy, and Literature. An Exploration*. Purdue University Press: West Lafayette, IN 1978.

Bohr, Niels: "A Challenge to Civilization". *Science* (102) 12.10.1945, pp. 363–364.

Bohr, Niels: "Niels Bohr's Memorandum to President Roosevelt, July 1944". In: Jungk, Robert/ Trans. Cleugh, James: *Brighter than a Thousand Suns. A Personal History of the Atomic Scientists*. Harcourt: New York et al. 1970, pp. 344–347.

---

[7] The question of competence is hard for the public to judge without understanding of scientific controversy. Why believe the climate scientists who agree when over 9000 scientists disagree with their conclusions? (Oregon Institute of Science and Medicine. *Global Warming Petition Project*, retrieved 23.11.2015, from http://www.petitionproject.org/index.php) Why believe James Hansen when the likes of Edward Teller, Freeman Dyson, Philip Abelson, and Fredrick Seitz oppose or question his findings? The criteria set by climate scientists are that only those who specialize in climate science and have published recently in climate science journals have competence to judge in these matters, but these criteria and the reasoning for them are not well grounded among the public.

Burke, Kenneth: *Essays Toward a Symbolic of Motives: 1950–1955*. Rueckert, William (ed.) Parlor Press: West Lafayette, IN 2007.

Burke, Kenneth: *A Rhetoric of Motives*. University of California Press: Berkeley et al. 1969.

Carnap, Rudolf: "The Elimination of Metaphysics through Logical Analysis of Language". In: Ayer, Alfred. J. (ed.): *Logical Positivism*. The Free Press: New York et al. 1959, pp. 60–81.

Crowley, Sharon/ Hawhee, Debra: *Ancient Rhetorics for Contemporary Students*, 5th ed. Pearson: Boston et al. 2012.

Dewey, John: *The Public and Its Problems*. Ohio University Press: Athens, OH 1954.

Feynman, Richard: "What is Science". *The Physics Teacher*. 7 (6), 1969, pp. 313–320.

Frisch, Otto R.: *What Little I Remember*. Cambridge University Press: Cambridge et al. 1980.

Frisch, Otto R./ Peierls, Rudolf: "The Frisch-Peierls Memorandum". In: Rhodes, Richard (ed.): *The Los Alamos Primer. The First Lectures on How to Build an Atomic Bomb*. University of California Press: Berkeley et al. 1992, pp. 79–88.

Hatch, Gary L.: "Rhetorical Proofs: Ethos, Pathos, and Logos". In: McInelly, Brett C./ Jackson, Brian (eds.): *Writing and Rhetoric*. Hayden-McNeil: Plymouth, MI 2011, pp. 55–81.

Hauser, Gerard A.: *Introduction to Rhetorical Theory*, 2nd ed. Waveland Press: Prospect Heights, IL 2002.

Jungk, Robert/ Trans. Cleugh, James: *Brighter than a Thousand Suns. A Personal History of the Atomic Scientists*. Harcourt: New York et al. 1970.

Krugman, Paul: "The Austerity Delusion". *The Guardian*. 29.04.2015.

Kuhn, Thomas: *The Structure of Scientific Revolutions*, 4th ed. University of Chicago Press: Chicago et al. 2012.

Magraw, Katherine: "Edward Teller and the 'Clean Bomb' Episode". *Bulletin of the Atomic Scientists* (44)4, 1988, pp. 32–37.

Morrison, Philip: "Beyond Imagination". *The New Republic* (26) 11.02.1946, pp. 177–180.

Novick, Aaron: "A Plea for Atomic Freedom". *The New Republic* (12) 25.3.1946, pp. 399–400.

Oppenheimer, Robert: "Letter to Niels Bohr, 30 March, 1946". Niels Bohr Papers. Niels Bohr Archive, Copenhagen University, Copenhagen.

Oppenheimer, Robert: "Speech to Los Alamos Scientists, October 18th, 1945". Robert R. Wilson Papers. Carl A Kroch Library, Cornell University, Ithaca, NY.

Oregon Institute of Science and Medicine. *Global Warming Petition Project*, retrieved 23.11.2015, from http://www.petitionproject.org/index.php.

Palevsky, Mary: *Atomic Fragments. A Daughter's Questions*. University of California Press: Berkeley et al. 2000.

Patri, Giancomo: "Pamphlet on the May-Johnson Bill". TS. Robert R. Wilson Papers. Carl A. Kroch Library, Cornell University, Ithaca, NY 1946.

Peierls, Rudolf: *Bird of Passage. Recollections of a Physicist*. Princeton University Press: Princeton et al. 1985.

Perelman, Chaim/ Trans. Kluback, William: *The Realm of Rhetoric*. University of Notre Dame Press: South Bend 1982.

Perelman, Chaim/ Olbrechts-Tyteca, Lucie/ Trans. Wilkinson, John/ Weaver, Purcell: *The New Rhetoric. A Treatise on Argumentation*. University of Notre Dame Press: Notre Dame 1969.

Polanyi, Michael: *Personal Knowledge. Towards a Post-Critical Philosophy*. University of Chicago Press: Chicago 1962.

Schlick, Moritz: "The Turning Point in Philosophy". In: Ayer, Alfred. J. (ed.): *Logical Positivism*. The Free Press: New York et al. 1959, pp. 53–59.

Serber, Robert: *The Los Alamos Primer. The First Lectures on How to Build an Atomic Bomb*. Rhodes, Richard (ed.) University of California Press: Berkeley et al. 1992, pp. 79–88.

Smith, Alice K.: *A Peril and a Hope. The Scientists' Movement in America 1945–47*. MIT Press: London et al. 1971.

Teller, Edward/ Brown, Allen: *The Legacy of Hiroshima*. Doubleday: Garden City, NY 1962.

United States Atomic Energy Commission. *In the Matter of J. Robert Oppenheimer. Transcript of Hearing before Personnel Security Board*. United States Government Printing Office: Washington, DC 1954.

Urey, Harold C.: "I'm a Frightened Man". *Collier's Weekly* (18) 05.01.1946. pp. 18–19, 50–51.

Weaver, Richard: *The Ethics of Rhetoric*. Hermagoras Press: Davis, CA 1985.

Wells, Herbert G.: *The World Set Free. A Story of Mankind*. Macmillian: London 1914.

Wilson, Jane: *Jane Wilson Memoir*. TS. Hans Bethe Papers. Carl A. Kroch Library, Cornell University, Ithaca, NY.

Wilson, Robert R. *From Pacifist to Warrior*. TS. Robert R. Wilson Papers. Carl A. Kroch Library. Cornell University, Ithaca, NY.

Wilson, Robert R.: "Atomic Specter". *Time Magazine* (17) 10.22.1945.

Part Three:
National varieties of rhetorical action

Gabriela Scripnic

"Dunărea de Jos" University of Galați

Emotion-invoking strategies in the presentation of Roşia Montană Project in the Romanian public sphere

1. Introduction

Roşia Montană Project was a gold and silver mining project developed by Roşia Montană Gold Corporation, owned by a Canadian resource company (about 80%), which in 2013 divided the Romanian society into two parties. The project generated largely mediated debates and public manifestations in which each party attempted to impose their standpoint and to gain people's commitment through votes given via Internet sites.

This chapter reports on the analysis of a series of pro-Roşia Montană presentation texts, in terms of pointing out the rhetorical strategies used to create emotions and, subsequently, to persuade the audience of a particular standpoint. The study draws on the concept of cultural public sphere (McGuigan, Jim: "The Cultural Public Sphere" 2011, Web) perceived as realm of affective and cognitive engagement as opposed to Habermas's concept of public sphere, (Habermas, Jürgen/ Trans. Burger, T. /Lawrence, F.: *The Structural Transformation of the Public Sphere: An Inquiry into a Category of Bourgeois Society*. Polity Press: Cambridge 1989) envisaged as an arena of rational deliberation. From the wide range of verbal products related to Roşia Montană, we have chosen the official presentation of the project available online and two advertisements broadcast on the Romanian television, with the view to identifying the emotion invoking strategies through which the authors of the products intended to reach the Romanian public. We assume that pathos is accomplished not only through the traditionally acknowledged strategies such as rhetorical figures or topoi, but also through objective information, namely statistical data. We argue that providing this type of knowledge functions as an audience-oriented strategy aiming at inducing the "feeling good" state of being in the population and in the nation itself if the project were implemented.

2. The Roşia Montană project within the Romanian public space

The name of *Roşia Montană*[1] became notorious in 1999 when the Romanian-Canadian company called Roşia Montană Gold Corporation (RMGC) got the concession license which allowed it to extract the gold and silver assumed to exist on an area of 12 square km. The mining project was scheduled to spread over 17 years during which hundreds of tons of gold and silver were meant to be extracted by cyanidation. The project consists of opening the largest surface gold exploitation in Europe which encompasses, in the valley of the Red River, four open pits and a gold and silver processing plant which uses cyanide and, farther in the area, a pond for chemical decantation of a surface of approx. 400 ha.

One of the biggest fears related to the project is an ecological accident which may occur in case the dam of the decantation pond breaks. A series of experts, among which the ones from the Norwegian Geotechnical Institute, were called to testify on dam safety and environmental specialists were asked to speak out in relation to the risk of water pollution. Moreover, in the project it is stipulated that, once the exploitation is over, three of the open pits will be filled with earth, the fourth one will be transformed into a recreational lake, while the entire area will be closely monitored for the next 50 years.

The project raised a lot of issues within the public sphere and many NGOs claimed that the European parliament forbids the use of extraction technologies based on cyanide. However, the commissary for environment of the European Commission (Janez Potocnik) stated in 2010 that "after an in depth analysis of the issue, the Commission considers that a general ban of cyanide in mining activities is not justified from environmental and health point of views."[2] The area affected by the development of the project covers about 25% of Roşia Montană. It involves drastic measures such as the relocation of households situated in the industrial part of the village, including churches and cemeteries. These propositions, partly put into practice, were severely condemned by the Romanian Academy in whose

---

1 Roşia Montană is a village situated in the Apuseni Mountains, Department of Alba, Transylvania. The village is crossed by a river Roşia (*The Red River*), rich in minerals, iron in particular, which give it a reddish colour. This feature explains the name of the village itself – *The Red Mountain*. For 2000 years the region has undergone excessive mining in order to extract the iron cores existing in the area.
2 Answer given by Janez Potočnik on behalf of the European Commission on June 23rd, 2010, retrieved 10.4.2015, from http://www.europarl.europa.eu/sides/getAllAnswers.do?reference=P-2010-3589&language=EN.

declaration[3] the members stand against the destruction of a 2000-year old community by actions totally unacceptable for a civilised society.

We aim to highlight the reactions in Romanian public sphere that were triggered by the implementation of the project. In 1962, the German cultural theorist Jürgen Habermas put forward the model of the public sphere whose ideal form was identified as the "bourgeois public sphere" of the 18th century (Habermas 1989, pp. 5–32) in the attempt to answer a fundamental philosophical question: "what are the conditions under which rational, critical, and genuinely open discussion of public issues becomes possible?" (Melton, James van Horn: *The Rise of the Public Enlightenment Europe*. Cambridge University Press: Cambridge 2001, p. 4) In Habermas's perspective, the public sphere was envisaged as

> a realm of communication marked by new arenas of debate, more open and accessible forms of urban public space and sociability, and an explosion of print culture in the form of newspapers, political journalism, novels, and criticism. (Melton 2001, p. 4)

It refers to "a theatre in modern societies in which political participation is enacted through the medium of talk", "an institutionalized arena of discursive interaction." (Fraser, Nancy: "Rethinking the Public Sphere: A Contribution to the Critique of Actually Existing Democracy". *Social Text* 25/26, 1990, p. 57)

Distinct from the state and its apparatuses or from the economy and its trade markets, the public sphere provides citizens with a space in which to "deliberate about common affairs" (Fraser 1990, p. 57) and, hence, to generate public opinion through participation and debate. (Popa, Diana: "Dimensiunile afective și cognitive ale spațiului public cultural" [Affective and cognitive dimensions in the cultural public sphere]. In: Gâță, Anca/ Popa, Diana (eds.): *Discurs și interacțiune în spațiul public românesc* [Discourse and interaction in the Romanian public sphere]. Galati University Press: Galati 2008, p. 109) It relies on three claims: (1) a reason lies at the basis of any discourse and debate and therefore participants should be able to provide ideas disseminated through the various form of print culture, which is detrimental for speaker's identity or status; (2) any topic developed in the public sphere may theoretically undergo severe criticism as well as individuals and institutions that may be subject to a careful examination by the public opinion; (3) the public sphere rejects secrecy and, in this regard, publicity, seen as the act of making something public, played an important part. (Melton 2001, p. 7) Moreover, the democratic public sphere, in its ideal form, involves the joint deliberation of socially equal interlocutors, stemming from or forming a

---

3   The complete form of the declaration can be found at http://www.acad.ro/forumuri/doc2013/d0619-ProiectulRosiaMontana-AnalizaAR.pdf.

"single, comprehensive public sphere" rather than "a nexus of multiple publics." (Fraser 1990, pp. 62–63) These deliberations should concern issues of "common good" (political, social) whereas the intrusion of private matters (family, marriage) is to be avoided.

Although Habermas (1989) dwelt in his presentation of the traditional public sphere on the three sides of the deliberation process (i.e. speaker's status, rational discourse and public opinion's critical response), in this chapter, Habermas' public sphere is taken as a starting point of the presentation of the contemporary public sphere, namely the cultural public sphere, in order to point out a distinction relevant for our analysis: reason based public discourse vs. emotion based public discourse.

In modern societies, as a consequence of the excessive trivialisation of issues under focus within the public sphere, which is invaded with values and topics that used to be the prerogative of the private space and as a result of the manipulative role assumed by the media, the traditional public sphere undergoes a series of changes. These changes are seen from a double, quite opposite perspective: on the one hand, the changes equal an irreversible alteration of the public sphere which is perceived as lacking substance; (cf. Becker, Carol: "The Artist as Public Intellectual". In: Giroux H.A./ Shannon P. (eds.): *Education and Cultural Studies: Towards a Performative Practice*. Routledge: New York and London 1997, p. 13) on the other hand, the modifications are envisaged as a normal process of moving from an initial state to other, more complex, states. (cf. Popa 2008, p. 110) In this perspective, the traditional public space has moved forward, to a network of new hybrid and mobile forms, (Popa 2008, p. 110) among which the cultural public sphere. Perceived as an updated form of the Habermas's literate public sphere, the cultural public sphere includes "the whole range of media and popular culture" and points to "the articulation of politics, public and personal, as a contested terrain through affective (aesthetic and emotional) modes of communication." (McGuigan 2011) We are dealing with a new conception of the public sphere that "accounts for affectivity as well as cognition" since "aesthetic and emotional engagement with lifeworld issues might be felt passionately and experienced as especially meaningful." (McGuigan 2011)

If the dictates of reason dominate Habermas' public sphere, with the cultural one, the emphasis is placed on emotion and feeling as a stimulating tool in encouraging debate (cf. Popa 2008, p. 110). With this study, we argue that emotion and pathos are not just discussion generating devices, but they orient the thinking and the public opinion towards the persuasive goal assumed by the instance which brought the topic to the fore. Moreover, we argue that emotion can be related to public issues (the development and implementation of a mining project in Romania): emotion displayed in private matters is put to good use in order to trigger debate in a public aspect and is granted with persuasive objective. Therefore, private and public, emotion and reason intermingle in a public arena which fostered a wide range of manifestations: talk shows, reunions, festivals, to name but a few.

Since 2005, when the Canadian government declared its support for the implementation of Roşia Montană Project, the public reaction has been overwhelming and it stemmed from state authorities, cultural and religious institutions, public personalities, locals living in the area and, last, but not least, from ordinary people who felt like it is their duty to support either of the two sides on the issue. Thus, in 2009, the Romanian Minister of Economy stated they wanted to include in the governmental programme the swift start of Roşia Montană Project as the gold market was prone to such projects[4].

The public sphere has hosted so far a war of statements for and against the project and we will mention at this point a few examples: in order to show their support for Roşia Montană Project, the inhabitants of the area formed NGOs meant to encourage its implementation as a measure of sustainable development; on the other hand, the Romanian Academy first made known its position in 2003 and later renewed it in 2009 and 2011 through a declaration addressed to the Romanian authorities. By means of an elaborate argumentation (more than 20 pages) backed by examples and legal provisions, the academy aims at preventing the Romanian government from making an error with negative effects on the community, the environment and on the archaeological landmarks and at drawing attention on the risky consequences that the project may have for the Romanian state. Moreover, famous Romanian actors got involved into advertising campaigns, namely *Save Roşia Montană*: People are worth much more than the gold they wear. A country is worth much more than the gold it has. Find the truth about Roşia Montană, not about its gold[5].

---

4   The statement is available in Romanian at http://www.kmkz.ro/investigatii-2/rosia-verde/%E2%80%9Ecianura%E2%80%9C-sparge-guvernarea-romaniei/.
5   It is the English translation of the statements made by famous Romanian actors in a series of public advertising campaigns against the implementation of Roşia Montană Project. These commercials (available at https://www.youtube.com/watch?v=OdYPoYk9dXQ; https://www.youtube.com/watch?v=22O9J8PRK-Y) were broadcast on the Romanian television in 2013 as a reaction to the pro Roşia Montană Project commercials that will be discussed further in this chapter.

3. Emotion-invoking strategies in pro Roşia Montană discourse

In this study, we dwell upon two media products issued by RMGP with the view to convincing / persuading the public of the well-being that the project brings about once implemented: the Internet site of the project and the series of advertisements that were broadcast on the national and private televisions in 2013, till they were banned by the National Audiovisual Council. The reason was, as the members of the council claimed, that the advertisements proved to be misleading, advertising a political campaign rather than a commercial one. We argue that these products are pathos-oriented since aesthetic engagement is sought, more often than not through an allegedly objective presentation of facts.

3.1 Pro Roşia Montană internet site

We shall start with a brief presentation of the site available at http://en.rmgc.ro/rosia-montana-project/community.html. At the top of the page, in black and white, there is a series of questions that animated the public and to which answers are provided, based on various analyses (geological, environmental, and social): *What is the truth about the technology used in the mining project? How will the environment be protected? What is the size of Romania's benefit? How safe will the dam in Roşia Montană be? Can mining save the area?* All the questions are closely followed by the motto of the campaign: *Find the truth about the Roşia Montană project*. This motto was overtly attacked by the opponents of the project, who, in their advertisements stated: *Find the truth about Roşia Montană, not about its gold*. Furthermore, what strikes the eye are the four captions (*economy, environment, patrimony* and *community*) highlighted not only by using the yellow background, but also by the association with images with great emotional impact, such as images of a large number of gold bars. We will tackle each part in order to point out how the appeal to emotion is accomplished in terms of linguistic structures and rhetorical strategies.

In Aristotelian rhetoric, the orator's act of knowing the audience's passions is considered as indispensable as it strongly contributes to conviction. (cf. Amossy, Ruth: *Argumentation dans le discours*. 2nd edition. Cursus: Paris 2009, p. 179) The inseparable functioning of logos and pathos together is expressed by Plantin (Plantin, Christian: *L'argumentation*. Seuil: Paris 1996, p. 4) under the form of a complete persuasion which should necessarily include three operations: a discourse is bound to teach, please and touch the audience as the intellectual, rational way is not enough to trigger action.

Specialized literature has so far led to two main directions as far as the construction within the discourse of the emotional effect: the case when emotion is explicitly brought to the fore due to the use of terms pertaining to the lexical field of emotion and passion; the case represented by the situation in which emotion is generated without making use of any terms lexically designating emotions. In this category we can include acknowledged topoi or commonplaces, syntactical phenomena – word order, interjections, exclamatory sentences, stylistic devices – repetitions, emphases. (cf. Amossy 2009)

In the study, we attempt to highlight the strategies of pathos used in the Roşia Montană discourse, placing a special emphasis on the strategies that are dissimulated under the effects of objectivity. (Sukiennik, Claire: "Pratiques discursives et enjeux du pathos dans la présentation de l'Intifada al-Aqsa par la presse écrite en France". *Argumentation et analyse du discours* [on line], 1, 2008, Web) We mainly deal with a discourse which a priori bears no trace of linguistically expressed emotion, with an intended objectivity rendered by scientific data. Therefore, the inquiry is directed towards identifying how pathos is produced and, secondly, how an objective and allegedly pathos-free discourse can stir emotion by putting to good use exactly those "notorious objectivity effects" (Sukiennik 2008): (1) numerical indications, (2) descriptions, and (3) quotations.

(1) When reading the information provided in each section of the RMGP website, we are struck by the agglomeration of numerical data whose role is to render the arguments as less subject to criticism as possible, since these numbers are presented as statistics issued from an expert authority in the field of economy, environment, chemistry, etc. These numbers generally point to:

- amounts of money (in US dollars[6]) that the Romanian state will benefit from: *Roşia Montană Project represents a direct investment of more than two billion dollars in the Romanian economy. The project will bring an estimated $5.3 billion into the Romanian economy: 2.3 billion - the direct benefit of the Romanian state*;
- amounts of money (in US dollars) that will be invested in the country in order to improve its main sectors: *Out of 5.3 billion, 2.3 billion USD will go directly to the State budget. The remaining 3.0 billion USD will be spent in Romania for human resources, construction, electricity, materials, transportation, reagents, spare parts and others. The investment necessary to develop the mining project in Roşia Montană is around 2.7 billion dollars including capital spent to date*

---

6 The inconsistency in the notation of the currency ($, USD, dollars) is present in the website.

(550 million, construction activities 1.4 billion, sustaining capital 570 million and closure activities 150 million);
- the price of gold and silver: *These economic benefits are estimated taking into account an average price of 1,200 dollars / ounce for gold and 20 dollars / ounce for silver.* It is repeatedly pointed out the increase in the state budget that the project is claimed to bring: *During its life cycle, with its multiplier effect, the Roşia Montana Project offers Romania a potential GDP expansion of 19 billion USD;*
- the investments made in order to promote Roşia Montană as a historical and archaeological site: *RMGC invests 70 million USD to bring the history to light.*
- the numerous jobs that the project is meant to create. These numbers are further explained for the public to react better: *The mining project will create over 2,300 direct jobs during the mine construction phase, 880 direct jobs during mining operations and 3,600 jobs in total during operation.*
- the households that chose to be dislocated from Roşia Montană and moved to a village nearby, in a newly created neighborhood: *To date, 125 families have chosen to become citizens of Alba Iulia, opting for one of the types of houses built by RMGC in Recea.*

The numerical indications are endowed with a double rhetorical function due to their association with realities vital for the functioning of each and every society: money and jobs. They are audience-oriented because they address different groups of the public: the ones interested in their personal well-being (jobs), the ones concerned with the country's economic situation (state budget), and the ones aware that an increased gross domestic product (GDP) means a high life standard for all citizens. Therefore, the numerical indications act in the direction of building a positive ethos for the company which describes itself as caring about both the people and the state. Secondly, the figures are meant to generate emotion as they promise the fulfilment of the norms that should ideally be respected in a modern society. As in the Romanian society these norms are not always accomplished, the promise of their accomplishment (the future tense used reinforces this idea) inevitably triggers emotion and induces the feeling of well-being among the population. The topoi of having a job and living in a society whose economy is speeding up generate emotion in all communities, but for the Romanian audience who used to be accustomed to the austerity of the communist regime and who, after the fall of communism, has always heard about economic drawbacks and low state budget, these topoi are even stronger in generating emotion and enthusiasm towards the prospects brought to the fore.

(2) Descriptions are normally envisaged as objectivity devices as the effect sought for is truthfulness, namely to make the audience believe in the accurate

reproduction of reality (Sukiennik 2008) In our case, description is used to draw a parallel between the dark present reality of Roşia Montană in terms of environment and community and the bright future in store for the region after the implementation of the project.

- environment: *Because of these acid waters, the flora and fauna are almost inexistent downstream of the Roşia and Abrud rivers. In the water streams from Roşia Montană, the chemicals concentrations exceed several times the legal limits, as follows: 1.3 times for cadmium, 5.2 times for arsenic, 73.6 x for iron and 96.3 x for zinc* vs. *The acidic waters which are currently flowing freely into the hydrographical system will be collected behind the Cetate acid water catchment dam, and from there, they will be pumped towards the Processing Plant, where they will be treated in an acidic water treatment station.*
- community: *As a result of the acute lack of jobs, people - especially the young ones – are leaving the area for developed urban areas in the country or abroad. Consequently, the area is going through a continuous depopulation and demographic ageing process* vs. *the revenues to be earned by the employees will be twice as high as the average salary earnings at the level of the national economy.*

The description of the current situation (a seemingly tragic one since chemical waters flow freely in an area abandoned by local people) helps putting in a favorable light the future situation which is presented as the only escape from a potential environmental and demographic disaster. The description becomes therefore a means to create emotions, combining the enthusiasm towards the implementation of the project with the relief of having survived such outrageously difficult times.

(3) The quotations provided stem from credible sources, or presented as such, that act as experts in the field, therefore their words cannot be cast doubt on. In our case, the quotations are largely used in relation to two aspects that were massively tackled by the public opinion: the economic benefits for the state and the safety of the technology employed. The quotations function as arguments of authority and are meant to strengthen the standpoint brought to the fore:

- Alan Roe, Director and Principal Economist, Microeconomics and Financial Economics, Oxford Policy Management *"During its life cycle, with its multiplier effect, the Roşia Montană Project offers Romania a potential GDP expansion of 19 billion USD".*
- James Otto, World renowned expert on mining taxation *"The Romanian government gains a fair share from the Roşia Montană Project – 44% to 48% of the cash flow".*

- Terry I. Mudder, an attributed technical statement regarding the use of cyanide in mining: *There are nearly endless rumors and unsubstantiated reports published in newspapers and on the Internet regarding the dangers associated with cyanide. This fear of cyanide arises from several historical sources. This fear is sometimes exploited to generate negative public reaction against mining".* Terry Mudder, an American chemist with over 30 years of experience in cyanide use, has been involved in over 200 mining and industrial projects on 6 continents. He is considered the number 1 expert in the world in this field.

The reinforcement of the authoritative status of the people called for to testify is accomplished by the function they have (*director*), by the internationally acknowledged expertise (*world renowned expert, number 1 expert*), by the fruitful scientific activity performed and the experience accumulated so far (*an American chemist with over 30 years of experience in cyanide use*), by the place where they work (*Oxford*), relying on the doxastic knowledge shared by the Romanian community according to which the representatives of western and northern companies are trustworthy, serious and committed to values and norms. Much concern is given to the choice of these authorities in terms of avoiding any accusations of inconsistency between the standpoint defended and the nature of expertise they are supposed to have.

Theoretically, the use of quotations proves to be cognitively relevant since the authorities have deeper knowledge of the topic than the ordinary public who becomes aware of certain issues due to these interventions. These quotations which disclose statistics and percentages resulting from specialized analyses are not a direct appeal to the audience's emotions, but an exploitation of the main interests shared by all members of community who are more likely to be persuaded when self-advantage is at stake. Through objective data, the authorities reinforce the feeling of well-being induced by the presentation of the project.

Another type of argument of authority is exploited when referring to the world-wide use mining techniques: *90% of the gold extracted today in the world is obtained using cyanide technology. Mines from the USA, New Zealand, Canada, Italy, Finland, Spain and Sweden use this technology safely.* The enumeration of the countries, which cognitively explains the 90% already mentioned, touches the audience who is bound to respond better when examples of richer countries are brought into the discussion. Here is activated the association with prosperity by the parallel with those countries.

The discourse is also centered on persuasion from ethos as it places a special focus on depicting the company as worthy of respect. Ethos is mainly enhanced by putting forward the company's:

- commitment to norms successfully approved and implemented in other (benchmark) countries and full compliance with international standards; at this point, the presence of temporal circumstances highlights the long term commitment to safe practices (all emphases mine): *From the very first year of its operations, the project proposed by Roşia Montană Gold Corporation provides for measures to put an end to this historical pollution and improve water quality in the Roşia Montană area. After more than 100 years of cyanide use in the mining industry, the methods to use and neutralize cyanide are very well known, so that the risks to the people and environment are minimized. Our practices in the field of sustainability are based on ISO 26000 standards.*
- concern with the people living in the area: the list of benefits (jobs, business opportunities, compensations, newly built infrastructure) is reinforced by the enumeration of all the facilities that Roşia Montană will have in its future resettlement site: *The Central Area of the site will include public buildings, the mayoralty, the police, the post-office, a bank, the church, the school, the kindergarten, a multifunctional center, a museum, a dispensary, a pharmacy, commercial spaces, entertainment areas or amenities for tourism development in the area, a hostel, a hotel, an area to organize fairs, sports activities, a gym, a skating rink, a football field, a park, playgrounds for children.*

The creators of the site address all levels of the public in order to touch all sensitive issues of life (job, health, entertainment, authority) and to prove the company's comprehensive perspective on the project as they do not leave aside any of what is important for a community. Persuasion is targeted due to the ideal perspective on life they offer in the direction of which the audience naturally bend.

Another pathos-oriented strategy is the highly modalized discourse. The certitude of the positive impact of the project is rendered by:

- the indicative mood of the verbs (present and future) which places the actions in the sphere of the achievable, actions are already validated or are about to be validated in the real world;
- lexical items that bear the sense of certitude (all emphases mine): *environmental rehabilitation is guaranteed; we will ensure that employees fulfill their obligations in a manner sufficient to safeguard labor protection and security. The results are clear: apart from gold and silver, there are no other exploitable rare metals in Roşia Montană.*
- modal verbs: *This account can only be accessed by the competent governmental authorities and with the purpose of environmental rehabilitation.*

Linguistic traces of subjectivity are to be identified in an apparently objective discourse: qualifying adjectives (often pre-modified by adverbs of intensity or used at superlative): *the project will have a <u>significant</u> economic impact; Another <u>important</u> benefit of the project; the benefit for the local and county community is <u>extremely important</u>. The dam in Roşia Montană will be <u>the safest</u> mining dam in the world, designed so far.*

3.2 Pro Roşia Montană advertisements

Other forms used by the project owners in order to persuade people to consent to its implementation are the series of advertisements broadcast on national and private televisions. These advertisements address the average people who might not understand the scientific and economic data presented on the project site, but who often take a stance when daily and ordinary problems are highlighted. The advertisements can be divided into two categories according to the commonplaces exploited to trigger emotion: on the one hand, there are the advertisements which bring to the fore miners themselves or their representatives; on the other hand, there are the ones where ordinary people from Roşia Montană appeal to the population to join them in the attempt to raise engagement in the project. Below, we will dwell upon a sample of each category with the view to highlighting the rhetorical strategies used to generate emotion and to persuade the audience to accept the standpoint adopted by the speaker. The transcript and the translation of the advertisements from Romanian into English belong to the author of the study.

In the first 35-second-long advertisement, the miners' union leader has taken the floor to speak out about the injustice that miners have to cope with. He is surrounded by other miners who silently consent to his words. While he is speaking, images are presented of usual mining activities. Below, there is the transcript of this advertisement.

I'm Cristian Albu, I work in Roşia Montană and I am a union leader. Here, for 2000 years, people have known how to perform only one activity: mining. When the mines closed down, people here became desperate, they could no longer provide for their families. We do not want to beg, we just want to work, to do what we have been taught to do for generations.

In Romania, there is a shortage of jobs and mining can provide thousands and thousands of jobs. I am calling for Romanians' solidarity: stick with us, vote for mining, vote for jobs at Roşia Montană.

Voice off: *Go to DaRosiaMontana.ro and sign for jobs at Roşia Montană (an initiative of the Union "The future of mining").*

Generally, the advertisement focuses on arousing the feeling of unfairness towards the miners' present situation. The advertisement aims at making the audience vote for Roşia Montană project in order for the justice to be made, for the miners to enjoy the benefits of a fair world in which the right to work is not denied to its members. In this respect, the pathos-oriented devices are:

- universally acknowledged topoi: the responsible adult who is in charge with providing for his family, the sharing of best practices from one generation to the other, the right to work in a field where one has acquired knowledge and experience. When these social norms are not fulfilled, a new and reversed picture is created and the feeling of pity and indignation is triggered among the audience. Persuasion is reached due to the fact that the public sympathizes with the miners who are forced to live in an unfair world;
- stylistic devices: opposition between the demeaning behavior they are forced to adopt (begging) and the proper behavior for a democratic society (work to earn a living); opposition between the gloomy atmosphere in Romania in terms of available jobs and the bright prospective view announced, where thousands and thousands of jobs will be created to meet the needs of the community. The repetition of the numerals emphasizes the idyllic perspective meant to sway the audience's mind and work on their emotions.

In the second advertisement (1 minute and 41 seconds long), a female resident of the area is describing her life in poverty because of the lack of jobs in Roşia Montană. Images of a modest household are meant to back up the speaker's words:

I've never thought that at 42 years old, I would live out of my mother's pension. With no job, everybody knows that one cannot provide for their children, in terms of basic needs and education. My son is 12 years old; he is in the sixth grade at the Roman Catholic College in Alba Iulia. My daughter is studying at "Avram Iancu" College in Câmpeni. They both have very good results at school; they are my pride and my very soul. I am at a loss of words.

I've given up a lot of things, going on holidays, for instance. We spend our holidays here, on these mountains. It is very hard. It is very cold; we need a lot of wood for the fire. I knitted socks, I knitted sweaters, I sewed bed sheets, whatever was asked from me. I even baked cakes. But enough is enough. A pair of socks is 5 lei. How many pairs are required for somebody to lead a normal life and to ensure their children's education? It is very hard. That is why I ask everybody who comes to Roşia Montană or the ones who only heard of Roşia Montană to support us, to give us the chance to raise our children, because it is very hard to have children and not to have a job, not to have anything to offer them or to offer them only the very basic necessities. It is painful for a parent, for a mother to realise that she cannot raise her kids as she should. That is why I ask everybody: give us a chance, help us. It is a call, it is a cry, it is a form of despair.

Voice off: *People in Roşia Montană have no other wish but to work. Find out their life stories at scrisoarecatreRomania.ro*

The advertisement is both ethos- and pathos-centered. The speaker is presented as a responsible parent who is mainly concerned with her children's education, who did not hesitate to give up her joys (holidays) in order to provide for them, who was ready to accept even lower activities (bake cookies, knit socks) provided they ensured even the smallest revenue, who cannot accept to lead her life out of her mother's pension. This positive discursive ethos enhances the impact of her appeal to the population to sustain the project.

The discourse is persuasive through the appeal to emotion: pity and anger are again the main emotions exploited in order to make the audience act on it and sign to show the support. These emotions are triggered by:

- the appeal to doxastic knowledge (*With no job, everybody knows that one cannot provide for their children, it is very hard to have children and not to have a job, not to have anything to offer them or to offer them only the very basic necessities. It is painful for a parent, for a mother to realise that she cannot raise her kids as she should.*)
- the description of her children's school performances together with the indications of the name of the institutions: especially the mention of the Roman-Catholic School is very important as the Romanian society has a very high confidence in religious institutions and representatives; the description of the hard life they have to cope with: the image of children living in freezing houses during winter has a strong emotional impact on the audience.
- the repetition of adjectives pertaining to the evaluation of the life they lead and to the situation they face on a regular basis: *it is hard, it is painful.*
- the enumeration of the activities that she was forced to do in order to have a revenue. The rhetorical question *How many pairs are required for somebody to lead a normal life and to ensure their children's education?* makes the audience bend in the direction of the numerous, yet vain, efforts made by the woman.
- the self-evaluation of the testimony presented under the form of a gradual enumeration: at the end of her intervention, she assesses her speech and the evaluation is presented gradually, from a relatively neutral assessment (*it is a call for help*) to more dramatic characterizations which point to the attitude felt by the speaker: *it is a cry, it is a form of despair.* She counts on conveying the

same feeling to the audience so that they should be dominated by the despair directly suggested or indirectly depicted in the advertisement.
- the direct implication of the audience: the perlocutionary act she performs with the intention of making people sign in favor of the project is rendered explicit by the verb "ask". The interlocutor is addressed to by different formulas that are also gradually put forward: first there are envisaged the interlocutors who have had a direct contact with the region (*everybody who comes to Roșia Montană*), then the referential sphere is enlarged by including those who have had a direct contact with Roșia Montană, by hearsay (*everybody who has heard about Roșia Montană*) and, at the end, the addressees overarch every single person who has seen the advertisement (*I ask everybody to give us a chance*). By means of a powerful emotional impact, the audience is urged to adopt a position regarding the issue and to act in the direction desired by the speaker.

4. Conclusion

After a brief presentation of Roșia Montană mining project, we described the Romanian public sphere as an arena of debate in order for the citizens to deliberate about an issue of common interest: whether or not the Roșia Montană project should be implemented. This public sphere has deviated from the traditional concept introduced by Habermas (1989) as a consequence of the transgression of private into the public, by the blending of reason and emotions. Currently we are faced with a cultural public sphere where the engagement of the citizens is therefore the result of a combination of cognitive / rational and emotional approaches to deliberation. The study dealt with some representative examples of how manifestations related to Roșia Montană played on both reason and emotion, on public and private.

Through the analysis performed, we highlighted that emotion can be related to public issues and, sometimes, is dissimulated under the effects of objectivity the discourse is displaying. For example, the information provided on the RMGC site is presented as obtained from analyses or from experts in order to make it as less likely to be subjected to attacks or criticism. The numerical indications are audience-oriented because they address different groups of public and are meant to generate emotion as they promise the fulfilment of the norms that should ideally be respected in a modern society. Moreover, the description also becomes a means to create emotions, combining the enthusiasm towards the implementation of the project with the relief of no longer living in that polluted and depopulated area. Last, but not least, the quotations become an exploitation of the main interests shared by all members of the community who are more likely to be persuaded when self-advantage is at stake. On the other hand, the advertisements focus on arousing the feeling of unfairness towards the miners' present situation and the feeling of pity regarding, for example, a mother who cannot raise her kids. The intrusion of the private in the public sphere generates heated debates and, through the feelings of pity and indignation arisen, it contributes to obtaining or enhancing the audience's commitment to the thesis brought forth.

As a general conclusion, we may state that emotion-invoking strategies such as topoi, stylistic devices and the emotional responses dissimulated under the effects of objectivity prove that a thorough analysis of the target audience was performed by the creators of the site and of the advertisements in order, firstly, to get to know and understand them and, secondly, to deliberately use those rhetorical devices that the Romanian audience is, mainly because of economic and social reasons, particularly sensitive to.

References

Amossy, Ruth: *Argumentation dans le discours*. 2nd edition. Cursus: Paris 2009.

Becker, Carol: "The Artist as Public Intellectual". In: Giroux H.A./ Shannon P. (eds.): *Education and Cultural Studies: Towards a Performative Practice*. Routledge: New York and London 1997, pp. 13–24.

Fraser, Nancy: "Rethinking the Public Sphere: A Contribution to the Critique of Actually Existing Democracy". *Social Text* 25/26, 1990, pp. 56–80.

Habermas, Jürgen/ Trans Burger, T./ Lawrence, F.: *The Structural Transformation of the Public Sphere: An Inquiry into a Category of Bourgeois Society*. Polity Press: Cambridge 1989.

McGuigan, Jim: "The Cultural Public Sphere" 2011, retrieved 23.4.2015 from http://openinstitutions.net/2011/03/the-cultural-public-sphere/.

Melton, James van Horn: *The Rise of the Public Enlightenment Europe*. Cambridge University Press: Cambridge 2001.

Plantin, Christian: *L'argumentation*. Seuil: Paris 1996.

Popa, Diana: "Dimensiunile afective și cognitive ale spațiului public cultural" [Affective and cognitive dimensions in the cultural public sphere]. In: Gâță, Anca/ Popa, Diana (eds.): *Discurs și interacțiune în spațiul public românesc* [Discourse and interaction in the Romanian public sphere]. Galati University Press: Galati 2008, pp. 103–107.

Sukiennik, Claire: "Pratiques discursives et enjeux du pathos dans la présentation de l'Intifada al-Aqsa par la presse écrite en France". *Argumentation et analyse du discours* [on line], 1, 2008, retrieved 20.4.2014 from http://aad.revues.org/338.

Websites

http://en.rmgc.ro/rosia-montana-project/community.html

http://www.rosiamontana.org/en/argumente/all-about-rosia-montana-mining-project

http://www.paginademedia.ro/2013/10/spoturile-pentru-rosia-montana-interzise-de-la-tv/

http://www.europarl.europa.eu/sides/getAllAnswers.do?reference=P-2010-3589&language=EN

http://www.acad.ro/forumuri/doc2013/d0619-ProiectulRosiaMontana-AnalizaAR.pdf

http://www.kmkz.ro/investigatii-2/rosia-verde/%E2%80%9Ecianura%E2%80%9C-sparge-guvernarea-romaniei/

Hilde van Belle

KU Leuven

Polemics and paradoxes in the media: The case of the Dutch TV-show *Pauw*

1. Introduction

In *Apologie de la polémique*, Ruth Amossy (Amossy, Ruth: *Apologie de la polémique*. Puf: Paris 2014) studies the place of polemical discourse in public space. This "argumentative modality" guarantees the possibility of non-violent coexistence of groups in political situations, in other words, situations of dissensus. In our pluralistic democratic society, where agreement often is not possible, polemics have a distinct social function, she claims, as they verbally manage conflicts that take place in the modus of dissent. They insure a way of coexistence in a complex society, and enable participants to share the same space and to communicate without reverting to physical violence. (Amossy 2014, pp. 12–13)

As a genre, polemics exist within a rich tradition throughout Western history: from Martin Luther to Karl Marx, from Robespierre to Noam Chomsky, from Desiderius Erasmus to Michael Moore. A polemic is a widely accepted and appreciated genre, and it certainly deserves a place in the study of rhetoric and argumentation. Scholars such as Arthur Schopenhauer or Marc Angenot (Angenot, Marc: *La parole pamphlétaire. Typologie des discours modernes.* Paris: Payot 1982) undertook elaborate efforts to classify every possible trick and move in polemical discourse. While in a democratic environment polemics exist in every domain of public life, their socio-political function is not all that widely acknowledged. In a context of increasing globalization, where people with the most diverse opinions and ways of life live together, it is important to expand our knowledge about conflict and polemics.

This chapter focuses on the phenomenon of polemics in the media. More particularly, I explore the complex role of journalists, who act alternately as reporters, moderators and even participants in polemical situations. As such, they often struggle with various expectations from the public: do they simply convey knowledge and information, do they moderate the discussion, or do they actively participate in the public debate? First, I introduce some aspects of Amossy's work on polemics, and secondly, I focus on a media case with an explicit polemical character. This analysis should deepen our insight in the function and possibilities of polemics in the media.

2. An apology of polemics

In her *Apology*, Amossy takes on the defense of polemics in the public debate. It is not as much a matter of accepting the phenomenon as it is a question of appreciation. This appreciation should result in a better insight in the function and necessity of polemics in a democratic setting. Amossy ascertains that dissensus is often defined in a political sense as the difference of opinions in public life. It functions as an antonym for political consensus resulting from the opinion of a majority. (Amossy 2014, p. 17) Our constant struggle for consensus has given rise to a dislike for dissensus and the polemics that accompany this. In most traditional and actual visions on public communication, disagreement and dissensus are rejected, or at least considered as a necessary step towards consensus and deliberation, a utopian idea based on an ideal of rationality and social harmony. (Amossy 2014, p. 29)

The rhetorical tradition does not really embrace polemical discourse, as rhetoric focuses on the art to negotiate the differences in order to reach an agreement. As such, dissensus functions as a generator of the democratic process that in itself mainly is based on "logos" and regulated by the process of "agon," which is not to be confounded with the classical concept of "eristic," the "pernicious" art of winning a debate at any price. (Amossy 2014, p. 20) To Perelman and Olbrechts-Tyteca, who also consider agreement as the aim and reasonableness as a way of escaping arbitrariness and violence, the distinction between a reasonable "discussion" and an eristic "debate" is extremely important, both on a social and philosophical level. Nevertheless, they do mention the difficulties of maintaining this distinction in the field. (Amossy 2014, p. 24)

The principle of reasonableness is also favored by the so-called Informal Logic scholars, as their work focuses on the resistance to fallacies and the overall education of citizens through the improvement of their critical skills. Yet, it was Douglas Walton, one of their founders, who classified "eristic dialogue" at the lowest position on the proposed scale. Likewise, the Amsterdam school of pragma-dialectics considers dissensus as the failure of a process that aims at the solution of a conflict on a reasonable basis. This focus on reasonableness and the general social appeal to goodwill for the sake of conflict resolution inevitably result in rather normative analysis methods. (Amossy 2014, p. 27) These views also connect to Habermas' ideas of the public sphere as a place where deliberation can take place in the interest of the public, based on the rational quest for an agreement. This explains Habermas' problems with mass communication that, due to its tendency to drama and spectacle, threatens to reduce the public sphere to a battlefield. (Amossy 2014, p. 28)

However, the dislike for dissensus and the estimation of consensus is not universal. Amossy points out two important questions: the implied link between reasonableness and consensus (in both directions), and the supposed necessity and function of consensus in democracy. For example, Robert Fogelin, who coined the idea of "deep disagreement", refers to an unsolvable variance caused by the incompatibility of the underlying principles of two parties. Also Marc Angenot (Angenot Marc: *Dialogues de sourds. Traité de rhétorique antilogique.* Mille et une nuits (Fayard): Paris 2008) speaks in terms of failure, when he challenges rhetoric's very definition as "the art of persuasion by discourse", whereas in reality, this "persuasion" is rather an exception than the rule. According to him, the more important question is why philosophers, politicians, friends or partners keep arguing, knowing that persuasion will never happen. As such, Angenot puts the notion of universal reason into question, and moves the center of rhetorical studies from persuasion to the polemical. (Angenot 2008, p. 32) However, as this move towards the polemical seems to be based on the philosophy of skepticism, Angenot does not seem to appreciate polemics all that much, Amossy concludes. (Amossy 2014, p. 33)

At this point, Amossy refers to other domains where the revalorization of dissensus is at stake, such as sociology or political sciences. Scholars such as Lewis A. Coser (1912) and later Georg Simmel stress how conflict is indispensable in social evolution and revolution, a claim that also is developed from a Marxist perspective. (Amossy 2014, p. 35) Amossy refers to the work of political scientist Chantal Mouffe, who rejects the concept of consensus as a key to democracy. Consensus is a misleading ideal, and the image of the rational citizen denies the role of power structures and socio-cultural frames, as well as the antagonistic dimension of politics. Mouffe claims that it is a key task of democratic politics to create the conditions that prohibit or play down those forms of antagonism. Politics should rather promote agonism, which involves a relation not between enemies, but between adversaries, or "friendly enemies". As they share a common symbolic space, they are friends, but as they want to organize this common symbolic space in a different way, they are enemies at the same time. Democracy's function is to allow and legitimize the conflicts that prove how society is marked not by homogeneity but by plurality. (Mouffe, Chantal: *The Democratic Paradox.* London/New York: Verso 2000, p. 105)

According to political scientist Pierre-André Taguieff, the function and value of dissensus is an important question for rhetoricians, who should move beyond the actual "angélisme dialogique" that forgets how conflict is fundamental to any political interaction. (Amossy 2014, p. 37) Amossy finally refers to the rhetorician Kendall Phillips who in his examination of the public sphere suggests "that the dominance of consensus has restricted our understanding of contemporary public argument and resistance" and explores the "possibility of de-centering consensus and the public sphere and reconsidering dissension." (Phillips, Kendall R.: "A Rhetoric of Controversy". *Communication Monographs* 63 (4), 1996, p. 231)

How could this "rhetoric of dissensus" come about? An important reference in the development of this topic is the famous pessimist philosopher Arthur Schopenhauer, who produced an overview of dishonest tricks in "The Art of Being Right" (cf. also http://coolhaus.de/art-of-controversy/). However, as Amossy notes, the motivation of his work comes down to developing the skill of self-defense, while any mentioning of the social function or heuristic value of polemics is missing. (Amossy 2014, p. 40) More recently, Marcelo Dascal did recognize a heuristic element in the confrontation and struggle between positions, but in his work on public polemic he focuses mainly on procedures that can de-dichotomize and unblock them. Amossy claims that even Christian Kock, who firmly defends dissensus as the normal expression of all practical rhetoric, aiming at action and not at truth, does not really celebrate polemics in public space. (Amossy 2014, p. 42)

3. A definition of polemics

Amossy tries to trace the rationality of polemics, its socio-discursive functions, and the difference between polemics and dialogue. She proposes some characteristic features: polemics are firmly based on conflict, tend to create dichotomy and polarization, and to disqualify the other. (Amossy 2014, p. 64) To put it more systematically:

1. The topic is presented or experienced as a matter of public interest and concerns (ephemeral) actuality.
2. There is an explicit argumentative move that presumes a counter-position ("un contre-discours"). This is a basic feature of polemical discourse, an ascertainment which leads Ruth Amossy even to wonder how the difference with ordinary argumentation should be understood. In order to map the relation between polemics and ordinary argumentation, Amossy introduces the concept of modality. In this concept, polemics is an argumentative modality

located at one pole of the continuum between the co-construction of answers and the "*choc des thèses antagonistes*" (the shock of antagonistic propositions).
3. Understood as the (verbal) management of conflict, polemics is characterized by a tendency to dichotomize and as such impede any solution.
4. Apart from this conceptual abstract function, polemics also have a social function: they organize and divide groups in different camps, defended by a variety of individual "actors" that all have their own reasons and take on the role of spokespeople ("*actant*") for the group. Both this variety and the problems of individuals in separating their function as actor and *actant* make this social polarization hard to estimate and overcome.
5. This polarization often implies rhetorical strategies of vilification of the other. Not only the words, but also the person of the opponent are discredited and targeted in different ways, up to the notorious strategies of dehumanization and demonization. Another strategy is to simply deduct the opponent towards silence and try to kill him symbolically by excluding him from the dispute altogether.

Those strategies do not prevent polemics from functioning as an argumentative modality within the domain of argument. The subjective, emotional and often passionate character of some polemics often functions as a target for critics who blame polemics mainly for their lack of rationality. Yet, it is important to notice that verbal violence and pathos do not seem to be fundamental characteristics of polemics. Polemics always develop in a balance between the violence of social polarization and confrontation with dichotomies on a burning topic on the one hand, and the social, cultural and institutional regulations that determine the public space on the other hand. Moreover, passion and emotion do not necessarily exclude rationality and reflection. Polemic speech should not be confounded with savage speech, as it is both authorized and constrained by the democratic space in which it develops. (Amossy 2014, p. 68)

4. Polemics and media

In a democratic environment, polemical discourse can be allowed and tempered at once. This reveals an important function for the media: they manage the tension between a heretic discourse marked by ruptures and verbal violence and the highly ritualized media frames within which the polemic discourse can develop. Polemics cannot function without a strong adherence to common norms and values. Both parties at least have to recognize one another and agree more or less about the urgency and the content of the topic, the rules of the game, etc. Blaming the media for their appetite for spectacle and drama is not always appropriate, since they often stage two quarreling parties that in the first place try to convince a third party: the audience. Giving the floor to public debate that is oriented towards an audience is exactly their function, and whereas the commercial incentives for drama and spectacle often are evident, they are not fundamental. (Amossy 2014, pp. 68–69)

It is clear that the media play an important role in the promotion and management of polemics. It is one of their basic responsibilities to report on them, but often media also initiate polemics, launching a topic and plainly taking sides as well. How do media regard their function in conflicts? The ideal of a democratic society that is guided by decisions on a rational basis finds its complement in the media concept of objectivity. Within the traditional objectivity paradigm, media primarily consider it their role to inform the public about existing conflicts, and to give the floor to both (or all) parties. Media should render factual knowledge to the citizens as the foundation for the rational decisions they have to make. Journalists that violate this code of factuality (e.g., the Jayson Blair affair in 2003) are mercilessly expelled from their professional group both by their peers and the public. The claim to factuality and truth functions as a basic paradigm. This is all the more remarkable since the belief in the possibility of objective representation has been largely abandoned in the academia. According to Marcel Broersma, this is a typical example of the anthropological concept of "Rücklauf," a process in which a notion already debunked by scholars is embraced by the general public. (Broersma, Marcel: "The Unbearable Limitations of Journalism. On Press Critique and Journalisms' Claim to Truth". *The International Gazette*, 72 (1), 2010, p. 27)

> The general idea behind the objectivity norm is that a true account of reality can be presented if journalists depersonalize and rationalize their working methods. [...] The objectivity norm prescribes neutrality and only the transmission of facts and not personal opinions. Reporters have to write in a detached tone and balance stories by presenting various points of view. The objectivity norm is an important way to distinguish journalism from propaganda and PR, claim autonomy as a profession and reinforce the profession by creating and controlling a group identity. It has become a central concept in journalism's collective discourse. (Broersma 2010, p. 28)

Although the power of the objectivity norm cannot be underestimated, it has never been absolute. Newspapers reserve separate sections for "opinion" (guaranteeing that the rest of the paper is opinion-free), and many media "take responsibility" in representing or defending social groups that have their particular sensitivities and ideas of justice. Clearly, the idea that political or social groups adhere to their own particular truths is generally acknowledged just as well. Many journalists take their role as critical and responsible citizens seriously and undertake actions to support minorities and help emancipate diverse social groups. (cf. Carpentier, Nico: "Identity, Contingency and Rigidity. The (Counter-)hegemonic Constructions of the Identity of the Media Professional". *Journalism* 6 (2), 2005, pp. 199–219) Also, the popularity of such phenomena as travelogue or literary journalism proves that telling a good (non-fiction) story is widely appreciated. Moreover, movements such as peace journalism even explicitly debunk the objectivity paradigm as a system of media habits that rather encourage conflict than appease it. (McGoldrick, Annabel: "War Journalism and 'Objectivity'". *Conflict and Communication online* 5 (2), 2006; Peleg, Samuel: "Peace Journalism through the Lens of Conflict Theory: Analysis and Practice". *Conflict and Communication online* 5 (2), 2006) In short, the role of the journalist as a neutral conveyor of facts/ knowledge/ information is challenged while other possible roles come to the fore, for example a moderator or maybe even a participant of the public debate.

5. The *Pauw* case

In his plea for greater attention to the notions of consensus and dissent, Kendall Phillips mentions different temptations to be avoided: "Finally, and most insidious, is the temptation to 'embrace' diversity and difference and continue business as usual." (Phillips 1996, p. 246) It is indeed the question how the concept of dissent "may expand the current struggles over the roles of communication in contemporary society", and how "struggles over the place of dissent in rhetoric, argumentation, and philosophy may unleash diverse theoretical, critical, and practical possibilities for communications in the contemporary age." (Phillips 1996, p. 246) In an attempt to deepen our understanding about the presentation and realization of dissensus in the media, I will analyze a fragment of a TV-show with an explicit polemic character.

Here the polemic confrontation between the moderator Jeroen Pauw on the one hand and Muslim fundamentalist Okay Pala on the other hand is staged in the Dutch talk show *Pauw*. I will argue that in this confrontation, the moderator shifts between various positions for different reasons. In the first place, he tries to help solve the conflict by inviting a fundamentalist representative and by assuming his expected role as moderator. Similarly, he explicitly chooses to side with the other guest who defends democracy in a general, almost stereotypical way. In this position, the journalist explicitly goes for a polemic style, in an attempt to discredit Pala as a non-democratic participant in a democratic debate. As such, Pauw symbolizes the struggle of journalists between their roles as neutral moderators, participators in the debate, and polemicists who recognize the insolubility of the fundamental problems they are tackling.

On September 4, 2014, the Dutch House of Representatives discussed jihadism and possible measures against radicalization of Muslims and support for IS violence. The debate was widely covered by the media, and they offered a variety of opinions and critique on (former) minister Ivo Opstelten's proposition to penalize "potentially dangerous ideas". The evening before, the Christian-democratic (CDA) leader Sybrand Buma had refused vehemently to debate with Okay Pala, the media representative of the radical Muslim organization Hizb ut-Tahrir ("Liberation Party," an international Sunni-Islamic political party), who was invited as well to the daily television talk show *Pauw*. Buma explained in detail why he refused to accept Pala at the discussion table, as his organization promotes the caliphate and attacks our Western rule of law system.

The next day, Okay Pala was invited again, and did sit at the table with other guests, such as the Christian Union MP Gert-Jan Segers, who was asked for a reaction to the presented video fragments about the political debate and as such got the chance to deliver a passionate defense of our rule of law system and our democracy, as well as his view on jihadism. Then the moderator turns to Okay Pala:

5.1 Description of material

Pauw (4 Sept 2014 – VARA) (translation HVB)

- J.P.: Okay Pala, your organization was mentioned today. Buma, the leader of the Christian Democrats asked the government again if this organization of yours can't be forbidden. The answer was "we have examined it already, it's not forbidden, but we will examine it again". Buma, who was here yesterday, refuses to debate with you: *[video fragment of Buma's arguments the day before]*
- J.P.: Your reaction to this?
- O.P.: He probably doesn't know us, because we're known in the Islamic world since 1953, when we were founded, as an intellectual political party …
- J.P.: In the Islamic world… In many countries, your movement is forbidden. Pakistan! Right?
- O.P.: Yes, forbidden, but that is because we fight corrupt regimes and want to change society. Our fight is a fight for hearts and minds […]
- J.P.: [quotes] "It is a duty to declare war to a government that is not governed according to Allah's laws"
- O.P.: Did I say that?
- J.P.: No, your organization did.
- O.P.: Where did you get this?
- J.P.: I got this from a piece from 1989 written by the American branch of your movement.
- O.P.: No, it's not like that.
- J.P.: Well, that's what it says, literally.

O.P.: We want to change society. We want to persuade people's minds and hearts [...] to create public opinion without violence, we defend Islam and Islamic state.
J.P.: No violence, you say.
O.P.: Absolutely.

J.P.: OK, I have a couple of questions for you and it would be nice that you would agree to answer in the first instance with "yes" or "no" in order to achieve some clarity, and after that we could together with Gert-Jan Segers have a look at the possible problems in our society for your organization, because why should it be forbidden, for instance? Are you for democracy?
O.P.: To start with ...
J.P.: Yes or no.
O.P.: No no no, I've come to discuss the proposed measures, not whether our organization should be forbidden or not. It's typical here in Holland: the focus is always shifted. I have to defend myself once more. [...]
J.P.: But this is surely the news. You might of course deplore this... It's not about..., it's about extremism. It's ...
O.P.: Can I, Paul? This is always the problem in the Netherlands, we broach a topic, and ...
J.P.: Who is "we"?
O.P.: We, as Hizb ut-Tahrir, we bring up a problem where all Muslims are targeted, and you push us into defense. I have to talk about why my organization should be forbidden, but I want to talk about the real problems. We ...
J.P.: You don't have to defend yourself, they're just questions.
O.P.: Can I please...
J.P.: You don't have to defend yourself...
O.P.: the focus is always shifted ... [...]

J.P.: Yes. Now, time for my questions: are you for democracy?
O.P.: I don't believe in democracy
J.P.: Do you promote the caliphate?
O.P.: Yes
J.P.: Do you want to turn to armed struggle for this?
O.P.: No
J.P.: Do you want to install the sharia?
O.P.: Yes
J.P.: Is there room for homosexuals in the caliphate?
O.P.: Homosexuality is forbidden in Islam.
J.P.: So: no!
O.P.: It's forbidden!
J.P.: What does it mean actually when you're a homosexual in the caliphate.
O.P.: I refuse to play this jingle!
J.P.: Jingle?
O.P.: Typical for Dutch anti-Islam policy [...] we want [...]

J.P.: This is what you want, and that's why the government wants to examine whether we can forbid it. This is exactly the extremist fundamentalism a whole lot of Muslims in the Netherlands don't fancy in the least!
O.P.: let me …
J.P.: I asked to answer a couple of questions
O.P.: This is the Islam discussion in the Netherlands. We want a lot more, we want […], we have […] …
J.P.: You want a caliphate…
O.P.: We want […]
J.P.: You don't answer the question. Why don't you? Because you think, "well, this doesn't work too well when they see …"
O.P.: It's been for years like this: the same topics […]
J.P.: Why, you've been thinking the same for years!
O.P.: For years, we want […]
J.P.: You want an organization, you want to organize a country without democracy, where women have less rights, where …
O.P.: [That's not true. Women's rights, what does that mean?]
J.P.: where there is no place for homosexuality, where capital punishment is performed when you want to convert to another religion than the religion you had at first: to be Muslim. It's all very well that you want this, you must get the chance to say this; the question is only: how dangerous is this and how many Muslims you think really would want this?
O.P.: Look, Paul, …
J.P.: And the government thinks it's dangerous.
O.P.: 13 centuries of Islam government would not have existed if they had been all too barbarian … […]

5.2 Analysis of rhetorical devices

The dispute still goes on for a while; this fragment shows the most polemic episode. We will mainly focus on the role(s) of the journalist: how does he position himself? When does he take on the standard role of the moderator, the "third party", the "representative of the public", when is he participating in the discussion, and how does he organize the polemical discourse?

The context of this discussion is quite familiar: it is a daily talk show with Jeroen Pauw as moderator. The style is confrontational, and the authority of the moderator is well-defined: he opens the debate, asks questions, interrupts and redirects, and closes the debate. He also determines the order in which the guests can speak. Pauw first gives the floor to everybody else: the politicians in the video fragments, the Christian-democrat (Gert-Jan Segers) in the studio, the refusing guest from the night before (Sybrand Buma) in a video fragment, and finally - as a kind of climax - he turns to Pala himself in the studio. Note that he does not properly introduce Pala or the organization he represents, and that he does not give him the chance to do so either.

Pauw is clearly assuming his role as media professional, referring to basic media values and procedures. For example, he reaffirms his questions by referring to the news value: "But this is surely the news!" Later on, he explicitly reaffirms his position as moderator: "Yes. Now, time for my questions." And when at some point Pala is protesting against the course of events, Pauw even tries to claim his position as a "neutral observer" by firmly declaring: "I only ask questions!"

However, it is not difficult to see that Pauw uses his professional authority in order to disqualify Pala. Moreover, he also takes part in the discussion itself, taking sides with Segers and challenging Pala. He delivers arguments against him, he asks suggestive questions, and as such he is clearly involved in the polemic discourse.

Let us take a closer look at the argumentation. To start with, there is no agreement about the topic. Pauw wants to have Pala confess that Hizb ut tahrir promotes violence which would allow the government to prohibit it, and when this is denied, he connects Pala's fundamentalism to the suppression of women, homosexuals, and atheists. Pala wants to shift the topic to what he allegedly has been invited for: the discussion of the measures that were proposed by minister Opstelten. To prove his point, Pauw confronts Pala with a loose sentence in an American text of 1989 that propagates violent struggle against non-Muslim governments. It is not a very strong argument, since the quote is old and far-fetched, but it is an argument about a vital point: provocation of violence.

The next argument that "In the Islamic world your organization is forbidden in some countries," suggests that the provocation of violence is the reason for this interdiction. If an Islamic organization is forbidden even in Islamic countries, it must be highly suspect, that is the suggestion. But no actual reason or explanation is given, which leaves us with a suggestive argument. Then, Pauw confronts Pala with yes/no questions that lay bare basic differences between Western democracy and Muslim fundamentalism. Pala simply has to follow and has to "admit" he is a fundamentalist. Time and again, he is prevented from giving information or arguments about his views. Pauw explicitly repeats the differences in summing up the features of the caliphate (on democracy, law, women's rights, homosexuality, atheism, death penalty) that serve as the familiar arguments against fundamentalism.

He asks for arguments why the organization could be dangerous and should be forbidden. Pauw brings down his basic questions finally to "how dangerous is this and how many Muslims you think really would want this?" The first one is directed towards the wrong person, because it will undoubtedly be answered negatively by a representative of Hizb ut-Tahrir: Pauw is shifting the burden of proof. The second question is quite irrelevant, keeping in mind the progress of ISIS and the fact that Hizb ut-Tahrir is active in 40 countries and counts two million members, according to Wikipedia. Pauw's intended message is clear: the organization is dangerous but it only represents a small minority. Finally, he uses the government as an authority argument that proves the danger, whereas the government has not decided yet: "And the government thinks it's dangerous."

Whereas Pauw did invite a Muslim fundamentalist to his show, it is clear that he does not aim in the least at an open and reasonable debate. Rather he takes sides in a very vaguely defined discussion, coming up with stereotypical, weak and suggestive arguments. Pala's arguments and his suggestion to discuss the proposed measures of minister Opstelten are dismissed altogether. This course of events is not unusual in the media: the ritual of asking questions in order to obtain information goes together with the ritual of critical enquiry, and it is the journalist who has the power to determine the course of the discussion. Yet, this discussion is particularly grim and confrontational.

The questionable quality of the argumentation aligns with Pauw's strategy to discredit Pala on the discourse level as well. For example, Pauw confronts Pala with a series of fundamental yes/no-questions, whereas Gert-Jan Segers was allowed to develop his argument freely, and so was Sybren Buma. He uses a strong you/we opposition throughout the discussion ("Problems in our society for your organization"), while he confronts Pala several times when he uses "we" ("Who is 'we'?"), suggesting the difference between the large group of moderate Muslims and the small minority of fundamentalist Muslims. Moreover, Pauw never even cares to mention the name of Pala's organization ("this organization of yours"), and he is particularly negligent when he is formulating the danger of Muslim caliphate in a very awkward way: "where capital punishment is performed when you want to convert to another religion than the religion you had at first: to be Muslim."

5.3 Discussion

It is clear that this debate is marked by a number of polemical features. If we follow the line of Amossy's suggestions, we can start with ascertaining that the confrontation definitely concerns a topic of public interest, and that it is based on the concrete (political) actuality. This is what the journalist mentions at the beginning. In his opening words, he simply states that "we will talk about extremism in the Netherlands, because today, there was the jihad debate," which then is evoked by the video fragments with different politicians explaining their views. When Pauw later on turns to Okay Pala, he states: "your organization was mentioned today" and he tells how Buma proposed the government to interdict it. (Note that the evening before, it was Buma who refused to speak to Okay Pala in the same television talk show, which reveals once more the imbrications between politics and media: a controversial guest in a TV-show becomes a political issue the next day.)

Furthermore, there is clearly an argumentative situation, albeit a very distorted one. If we accept Amossy's suggestion to consider a modular concept of argumentation that can be presented by a continuum that shifts from the co-construction of answers at one pole and the shock of antagonistic theses at the other, we can safely assume that in this case, the confrontation with the *choc des idées* prevails. Or rather, it is one of the parties that imposes this shock while the other party tries to move the discussion towards a more reasonable dialogue. Disagreement about the degree of dissensus, with discussants pushing towards different directions is no exception in polemical discourse. Amossy's concept of argumentative modality enables us to explicate this tension as well. We can make a distinction between the discussants that try to move towards complete dissensus, and the ones that move in the other direction.

In Pauw's accusations, the dichotomies abound: between democracy and the caliphate, between free speech and oppression, between the rights of women, homosexuals and atheists versus their suppression. According to Amossy, conflict is at the heart of the polemical, and dichotomies are the polemical expression or construction of this conflict, as they antithetically suggest the exclusion of a middle and the impossibility of any solution or alternative. These dichotomies are constructed very strikingly by Pauw's provocative yes-or-no questions about very complex and meaning-laden concepts such as democracy or the caliphate. They are used almost as a kind of shibboleth that can enable Pala to take part in the discussion, or not. Pauw carefully and elaborately sees to it that all possibilities of common ground are blocked.

Abstract dichotomies do not stand for concrete people. Within the polemical discourse, all kinds of people bring up all kinds of arguments, which reveals the social aspect of this phenomenon. People choose positions and form camps that strive for or against one of the poles of the dichotomy. Their choice and their arguments are often based on various motives, but the polarization between the groups is firmly based on the abstract dichotomous structure of the polemics, and according to Amossy this explains why polarization is so difficult to overcome.

The explicit attribution of the two actors' roles in this talk show is to Gert-Jan Segers, the defender of democracy and rule of law, and to Okay Pala, the defender of the caliphate. However, this argumentative situation is complicated by the ambiguous role of a third actor, the journalist who plays the role of moderator on the one hand but takes sides with Segers on the other hand, provoking a polemical confrontation. This ambiguity also holds for the exact definition of the argument (see also 4.2.). The link between Hizb ut-Tahrir and violence is suggested by Pauw and denied by Pala. The American quote serves to suggest that Pala is a liar. Pala in his turn tries to play down this fundamental discussion where his very right of speech is questioned and threatened, in favor of the question he assumedly was invited for: a reaction on Opsteltens measures. When this does not work, he calls Paul directly by his name, refuses to "play the jingle," and finally accuses him (and the media) for pushing him once more into the defense.

In our case, Pauw makes different moves where social groups are shifted. First, he creates a polarization between the Dutch House of Representatives, representing the Dutch in general, including himself, on the one hand, and Okay Pala and his misty organization that promotes violence and that is even forbidden in parts of the Islamic world on the other hand. Later on, he is struggling with his own definition of "we": sometimes this large group of the moderate Dutch Muslims seems to be implied, but sometimes they appear as a third group in the picture, somewhere between the "regular" non-Muslim Dutch and the Muslim fundamentalists. This struggle also reveals the appeal to the audience, and particularly its heterogeneous formation. As mentioned before, Pauw is quite severe about Pala's use of "we," interrupting him several times to make sure that Pala is not representing the moderate Dutch Muslims but only the very small and dangerous group of fundamentalists.

The strategies of identification with one group go together with the strategies that disqualify "the other" and vilification strategies that construct Pala as an enemy and as a symbol of evil. Not only are his words and arguments attacked and debunked, but also the person himself. For example Pauw accuses Pala of lying about violence, and tries to kill Pala symbolically by suggesting that he should not even be allowed to join the debate. A typical strategy of enemy construction here is Pauw's stress on the danger of the enemy on the one hand, but at the same time the assurance that he is not invincible on the other hand, which he tries to prove by suggesting the lack of support of Dutch "moderate" Muslims for Hizb ut Tahrir. (Jasinski, James: "Enemy Construction". In: Jasinski, J. (ed.): *Sourcebook on Rhetoric. Key Concepts in Contemporary Rhetorical Studies*. Sage Publications: Thousand Oaks, CA 2001, p. 203)

I have examined so far the basic aspects of polemics as defined by Ruth Amossy and as they appear in this case: there is the public interest, the conflict aspect, the dichotomization and polarization, and the desire to disqualify the other. This means that we have not turned to the questions of verbal violence and passions yet, which are actually the most noticeable terms by which polemics tend to be characterized. According to Amossy, these features are not inherently connected to polemics, in the same way that rationality is not excluded. Polemics take place in certain contexts, frames, rituals that determine their course and possibilities. They are not possible without some agreement about the rules of the game, the way the communication is organized, and, to Amossy, it is the tension between the rules and the verbal violence that create the dynamics of the phenomenon.

In the case of Pauw, we cannot really speak of verbal violence or passion, indeed, but it is particularly interesting to see how the journalist shifts positions throughout the debate. This way, it is Pauw who violates the rules of the game while Pala strictly conforms to them. This reveals a paradoxical situation: Pauw, as a representative of democracy and free speech uses his institutional power as a media professional, in order to "debunk" his guest, who does not stand for democracy and free speech, but strictly keeps to the rules. Eventually, Pala can play the role of the victim who is suppressed by Western media, thus finding refuge in the appeal of an *ad misericordiam*.

The strategy of ambiguity enables Pauw to invite a representative of a fundamentalist Muslim organization for a discussion that allegedly is impossible for the lack of common ground, which he makes very clear. Pauw stages a discussion that is possible and impossible at the same time. One might conclude here that he simply invited the wrong guest, that the whole discussion rambles, that he favored Segers heavily over Pala, but on the other hand, Pauw did stage a fundamentalist who speaks our language and takes part in the discussion in a self-controlled way. By this move, Pauw did contribute to the debunking of stereotypical representations of Muslim fundamentalists in a scenario of war and absolute horror. As such he also managed to create or enforce a dissociation between Pala's appealing dream of an ideal society, a dream that is shared by all kinds of (religious) fundamentalists all through human history, and the horror that is produced when such dreams are used to warrant injustice, violence and wars. He used his professional authority to prevent Pala from setting up some "mealy-mouthed" discourse and to force him to "confess" his undemocratic ideas.

Of course, one could argue that Pauw missed the chance to work more actively with this dissociation and go into actual political questions such as the consequences of globalization, the reaction of the Western society to the growing attraction of the IS-crusades to young people that grew up in a democratic environment, and the renewal of the very concept of democracy. This is the motive of the television discussion in the first place, and this is what his target audience might be concerned about directly. But then, Pauw did take part in these important actual polemics, and his "impossible" discussion did focus on rather problematic issues. Not surprisingly, it did not prevent the debate from continuing. On the contrary, it was picked up in its turn by *De Correspondent*, a Dutch online news medium that published Okay Pala's opinion one week later, in a piece called: "This is what I wanted to say in *Pauw*". Pala deplores Pauw's stereotypical questions on Islam and the low quality of the debate in general, and he calls for an open discussion about two different ideologies, as he puts it, stressing the fairness and generosity of Islam ideology. Finally he formulates his arguments against Opstelten's proposed measures[1].

6. Conclusion

Chantal Mouffe presents her *agonistic pluralism* as an alternative to the deliberative model. It is important to realize that politics, which is the ensemble of practices, discourses and institutions that organize human coexistence, is always affected by the dimension of human antagonism (the political). The aim of democratic politics is to construct the "them" in such a way that it is no longer perceived as an enemy to be destroyed but as an "adversary," or a "legitimate opponent," that is, somebody whose ideas we combat but whose right to defend those ideas we do not put into question. (Mouffe 2000, p. 102) The consensus that is reached can be defined as a "conflictual consensus," ideally staged around the diverse conceptions of citizenship that propose their own interpretation of the "common good": "We have to accept that every consensus exists as a temporary result of a provisional hegemony, as a stabilization of power, and that it always entails some form of exclusion. The ideas that power could be dissolved through a rational debate and that legitimacy could be based on pure rationality are illusions which can endanger democratic institutions." (Mouffe 2000, p. 104)

Polemic discourse that takes place within the structures and rituals of the media cannot simply be rejected for its questionable argumentation. It is one of the forms that make it possible for dissensus to exist and find a place. It is important to determine norms for reasonable discussions that aim towards consensus, but it is equally important to study the form and function of polemics that bring dissensus to the fore. In this case, it is interesting to see how the journalist, in the name of democratic values, tries to stage an "impossible" discussion with a fundamentalist, and uses different tricks to discuss and evoke the gap between them at the same time. As such, Pauw embodies the paradoxical situation of debating with people who take part in the Western democracy and use the right of free speech in order

---

1   1) Asking citizens to report on one another splits Dutch society. 2) The word 'radical' is not specified. 3) They enable situations where Muslims are arrested without any juridical motivation. 4) It shows how the government focuses on Jihad-warriors while it looks away from other forms of extremist violence, such as Israel-warriors.

to defend a society without free speech. While Gert-Jan Segers gets a chance to formulate justly and very eloquently once again the principles of democracy and rule of law, it is Jeroen Pauw who energizes the polemic discourse. He plays with rules, changes positions between the authority of the professional objective journalist representing knowledge, relevance, truth, balance and neutrality, and the involvement of the subjective engaged journalist/polemicist who takes part in the never-ending dissensus by which our public life is defined. Whereas polemic discourse is defined by brutal dichotomies and strategies, it is marked by more subtle processes as well. In the *Pauw* case, it is the journalist's power strategy that reveals a paradoxical situation that comes to the fore.

References

Amossy, Ruth: *Apologie de la polémique*. Puf: Paris 2014.

Angenot, Marc: *La parole pamphlétaire. Typologie des discours modernes*. Paris: Payot 1982.

Angenot Marc: *Dialogues de sourds. Traité de rhétorique antilogique*. Mille et une nuits (Fayard): Paris 2008.

Broersma, Marcel: "The Unbearable Limitations of Journalism. On Press Critique and Journalisms' Claim to Truth". *The International Gazette* 72 (1), 2010, pp. 21–33.

Carpentier, Nico: "Identity, Contingency and Rigidity. The (Counter-)hegemonic Constructions of the Identity of the Media Professional". *Journalism* 6 (2), 2005, pp. 199–219.

Jasinski, James: "Enemy Construction". In: Jasinski, J. (ed.): *Sourcebook on Rhetoric. Key Concepts in Contemporary Rhetorical Studies*. Sage Publications: Thousand Oaks, CA 2001.

McGoldrick, Annabel: "War Journalism and 'Objectivity'". *Conflict and Communication online* 5 (2), 2006.

Mouffe, Chantal: *The Democratic Paradox*. London/New York: Verso 2000.

PAUW: http://pauw.vara.nl/media/319795 (retrieved June 17, 2015).

Peleg, Samuel: "Peace Journalism through the Lens of Conflict Theory: Analysis and Practice". *Conflict & Communication online* 5 (2), 2006.

Phillips, Kendall R.: "A Rhetoric of Controversy", *Communication Monographs* 63 (4), 1996, pp. 231–248.

Ludmilla A'Beckett

University of the Free State

Stigmatizing female oppositionists in Russia: Stances toward comparisons with Joan of Arc

1. Introduction

Rhetorical analysis traditionally looks into how people act through language to influence and change other people's attitudes and beliefs. (cf. Kjeldsen, Jens E.: "Speaking to Europe: A Rhetorical Approach to Prime Minister Tony Blair's Speech to the EU Parliament". In: Flottum, Kjersti (ed.): *Speaking of Europe*. John Benjamins: Amsterdam et al. 2013, p. 24; Lennon, Paul: *Allusions in the Press: An Applied Linguistic Study*. Mouton de Gruyter: Berlin 2004, p. 83) Unfortunately, the impact of rhetorical performance on the mind of the discourse community has been usually reconstructed as the reactions of a hypothetical or implied audience. (Perelman, Chaim/ Olbrechts-Tyteca, Lucie: *The New Rhetoric. A Treatise on Argumentation*. University of Notre Dame Press: London. 1969; Charland, Maurice: "Constitutive Rhetoric: The Case of the Peuple Quebecois". *Quarterly Journal of Speech* 71, 1987, pp. 133–150, McGee, Michael C.: "Text, Context and the Fragmentation of Contemporary Culture". *Western Journal of Communication* 54, 1990, pp. 274–289; Wander, Philip: "The Third Persona: An Ideological Turn in Rhetorical Theory". In: Lucaites, John L./ Condit, Celeste M./ Caudill, Sally (eds.): *Contemporary Rhetorical Theory. A Reader*. Guildford Press: New York et al. 1991, pp. 357–379) Most rhetorical studies have been speaker- or text-oriented. (cf. Kjeldsen 2013, p. 25)

Nevertheless, advantages of the knowledge society include the rapid growth of information technology (Valimaa, Jussi/ Hoffman, David: "Knowledge Society Discourse and Higher Education". *Higher Education*, 56 (3), 2008, p. 278) and, hence, public reaction can also be examined. Correspondingly, this paper seeks to compare the envisaged effect of utterances, i.e. the effects which have been theoretically assigned to the texts, with the revealed reaction of newspaper readers.

The knowledge society, which promotes the implementation of interdisciplinary methods or interconnectedness, contributes to sharpening the tools of rhetorical analysis. Methods of discourse studies and cognitive linguistic approaches enable rhetoric scholars to enrich their understanding of language facts and to enhance their research tools. Novel approaches in discourse analysis go hand in hand with the traditional assessment of rhetorical performance in terms of *logos*, *pathos* and *ethos*. (Aristotle/ Trans. Kennedy, George A.: *On Rhetoric: A Theory of Civic Discourse*. Oxford University Press: New York 1991)

One of the characteristic features of modern society is the diversity of the discourse community and a mosaic of public knowledge and expectations (Kjeldsen 2013, p. 22). Historical events of the remote past as well as modern political analysis no longer enjoy the privilege of uniform canonical interpretation. The advent of popular culture (cf. Brummett, Barry: *Rhetorical Dimensions of Popular Culture*. University of Alabama Press: Tuscaloosa 1991) produces multifaceted versions of salient historical episodes. This heterogeneous knowledge of past events and their evaluation have been re-distributed among the language community and incorporated into the media stories about modern politics. Contemporary rhetoricians have to take into account multiple stands of the discourse community toward the same phenomenon. (Kjeldsen 2013, p. 23) This paper pursues the goal of explaining how a diverse perception of some past events has been adapted as a dissuading strategy and how stigmatizing has been disguised as a compliment.

This paper investigates how unflattering opinions about female public figures has been formed and reinforced in selected Russian newspapers. This case study is concerned with a particular lexical choice, i.e. the name "Joan of Arc" in the context of inviting negative judgements. In traditional rhetorical understanding, the dissuading technique could be studied within the category of pathos which Aristotle (1991, pp. 2–3) defined as "awakening emotion (pathos) in the audience so as to induce them to make the judgment desired." The dissuasive technique under study relates to the fact that authors have attempted to invoke disapproval, condemnation and disdain. Paradoxically, metaphors and similes triggering parallels with the legendary French heroine Joan of Arc have been used for this purpose.

The main objective of this paper is to show how the allusion to the legendary heroine has contributed to discrediting some public figures. The paper investigates how readers assent to the conceptual schema and the communicative frame for finding faults and expressing discontent with political personages and their actions. Ultimately the so-called "flattering categorization or comparison" flags disapproval of a political cause in which the celebrity has been involved.

Since metaphor and simile have been used for creating persuasive statements, modern approaches of appraisal theory (cf. Martin, J. R./ White, Peter R. R.: *The Language of Evaluation: Appraisal in English*. Palgrave: New York, NY 2005) and discourse dynamics framework for metaphor (cf. Cameron, Lynne: "The Discourse Dynamics Framework for Metaphor". In: Cameron, Lynne/ Maslen, Robert (eds.): *Metaphor Analysis*. Equinox: London 2010, pp. 77–94; A'Beckett,

Ludmilla: "Cameron, L. /Maslen, R. (eds.) (2010) *Metaphor Analysis: Research Practice in Applied Linguistic, Social Sciences and the Humanities*. Book Review". *Metaphor and the Social World* 4 (1), 2014, pp. 127–138) have been adopted as research tools in rhetorical analysis. References to Joan of Arc in Russian public discourse have been compiled to check the evaluative responses invited by the trope. Some female celebrities came to public attention when they participated in actions challenging the Russian political elite. Female politicians and journalists were named "Joan of Arc" after protesting against Putin's rulings or questioning his decisions. Members of the Russian government have openly condemned the activities of these women. (cf. Sperling, Valerie: *Sex, Politics and Putin. Political Legitimacy in Russia*. Oxford University Press: Oxford et al. 2015, pp. 192–194) The media coverage of the events and the engagement of the general public with the contents of publications have constituted another interesting aspect of these cases.

2. Data, terminology and procedures

At the first stage of this research, 200 examples of allusive naming "Joan of Arc" have been collected from the two most popular Russian newspapers *Argumenty i fakty* (AiF) and *Komsomolskaya Pravda* (KP), whose profiles have been discussed in A'Beckett. (A'Beckett, Ludmilla: "Cross-cultural Allusions in the Russian Press: Parallels between Joan of Arc and the Former Ukrainian Prime Minister Yulia Tymoshenko". *Foreign Language Studies* 19, 2013, pp. 135–136; A'Beckett, Ludmilla: "Strategies to Discredit Opponents: Russian Presentations of Events in Countries of the Former Soviet Union". *Psychology of Language and Communication* 17 (2), 2013, pp. 103–104) The time frame covers approximately the period 2004 to 2013 (with the exception of examples on Tymoshenko explained in Section 3). Several defamatory statements by Russian public figures such as examples 5 and 10 were published in various media outlets simultaneously. For the purpose of this paper, the database has been expanded to include examples from Russophone discussion blogs. The collected examples represent a phenomenon known as "onomastic allusion," which is defined as the use of a proper name for the purpose of passing strong associations. Lennon (2004, p. 128) suggests:

> Allusive naming involves the re-using of names to communicate indirectly semantic information associated with the original referent. Decisive for allusive use of a name is that the writer intends (and thereafter understands) the name to refer to a particular person, place or event, but this referential meaning of the name is of secondary or minor importance, while the associative meaning bound up with this instantiation is of primary or major importance.

Technically speaking, many indirect uses of the name of Joan of Arc can be considered as a type of metaphor, where one thing, i.e., a contemporary public figure, is understood in terms of another, i.e. the French heroine Joan of Arc. (cf. Lakoff, George/ Johnson, Mark: *Metaphors We Live by*. Chicago University Press: Chicago, IL. 1980, p. 5; Cameron, Lynne: "What Is Metaphor and Why Does it Matter?" In: Cameron, Lynne/ Maslen, Robert (eds.), *Metaphor Analysis*. Equinox: London 2010, p. 3; Kövecses, Zoltan: *Metaphor: A Practical introduction*. Oxford University Press: Oxford 2002, p. 4) Some messages deploy the structure "A is B", such as "Tymoshenko is Joan of Arc" or "Sobchak is Joan of Arc." Other fragments adopt the scheme "A takes the role of B" or "A performs B," e.g. "Khakamada plays the role of Joan of Arc" or "Tymoshenko assumes the role of Joan of Arc." Since the emulators of Joan of Arc are not actresses, such statements have also been treated as metaphors.

Explicit comparisons, known as similes, have also featured in the compiled corpus. Although some research approaches highlight conceptual differences between metaphors and similes (cf. Chiappe, Dan L./ Kennedy, John M.: "Literal Bases for Metaphor and Simile." *Metaphor and Symbol* 16, 2001, pp. 249–279), these discrepancies have been ignored here. It has been found that explicit and implicit parallels with Joan of Arc are often interchangeable in extended contexts and that they carry identical pragmatic functions.

Finding terminological overlaps and discrepancies is of importance for this study since the adoption of given terms entails the use of a particular methodology. If the language choice representing a figure of speech has been identified as a metaphor, then multiple certified techniques of conceptual analysis and linking between individual choice and community values become available. (cf. Cameron 2010b) If the lexical choice has been identified as the use of a historical name then the research is bound in with the revision of history, rather than with establishing connections between ideas, beliefs and attitudes.

Since the construed analogies can be covered by the term *metaphor*, then some guidance of discourse dynamic research for metaphors can be used. The framework "is designed to apply to metaphor in language use in social interaction and builds explanatory theory that accounts for what we know about discourse." (Cameron 2010a, p. 78) Discourse, on the one hand, is a totality of texts (cf. Koller, Veronica: *Metaphor and Gender in Business Media Discourse: A Critical Cognitive Study*. Palgrave Macmillan: New York, NY 2004, p. 18) that invokes a characterization of female politicians and, on the other hand, reproduces "the virtual conversation within and between communities." (Musolff, Andreas: *Metaphor and Political Discourse*. Palgrave: Basingstoke 2004, p. 5) The interactive aspect of the collected texts has been evident in readers' remarks and the exchanges between readers extracted from comments sections of the newspapers.

The discourse dynamic framework for metaphors does not treat metaphor as a mental store of static and fixed mappings and, correspondingly, ideas. This approach explains the connection between discourse context and metaphor use. It accounts for changes of the conceptual underpinnings of metaphors. The adoption of the methodological postulates of the discourse dynamic framework for metaphors has allowed this paper to re-produce the cline of variations in the perception of Joan of Arc's image. Hence, 100 examples were a subject to a quantitative study which reconstructed the Russian prototype of Joan of Arc and unearthed associative meanings of this name. The quantitative analysis has recreated the distribution of salient features evoked by the name in discourse, e.g. the ones which are at the forefront due to its conventionality, familiarity, frequency and prototypicality. (cf. Giora, Rachel: *On Our Mind: Salience, Context and Figurative Language.* Oxford: University Press: Oxford 2003, pp. 15–17)

The next stage of the analysis involved assessing attitudes toward the parallels between Joan of Arc and her emulators. Attitude is understood as "emotional reactions, judgements of behavior and evaluation of things." (Martin/ White 2005, p. 35) Appraisal theory has been used here to conjecture readers' reactions which can be located along the axes appropriateness-inappropriateness and approval-disapproval. Critical cues in metaphor contexts have been taken as evidence of authorial negative perception of the analogies suggested. The interaction between the metaphor/analogy and its contextual environment has induced other tropes, such as irony and sarcasm (cf. Gibbs, Raymond W.: *The Poetics of Mind: Figurative Thought, Language and Understanding.* Cambridge University Press: Cambridge, MA 1994, pp. 359–397) as well as an implicit antithesis. The appearance of these figures of speech has been taken as evidence of the negative evaluation of the topic, i.e. the incongruity in juxtaposition of Joan of Arc and contemporary political personages.

The repetitive patterns of the interaction between contexts and the metaphor/allusion have been catalogued to recreate dialogic engagement in this public discourse. According to Martin and White (2005, p. 35), "engagement deals with sourcing attitudes and the play of voices around opinions." Thus, the authorial voices offering a genuine parallel between the contemporary women and Joan of Arc would present a contrast with the voices who underscore their incongruence. However, the promoters of the resemblance between the past and the present could differ in their understanding of contemporary demands for exhibited traits. Hence, the differences in assessment of the offered analogy have created heteroglossia. (cf. Bakhtin, Mikhail/ Trans. Emerson, Caryl/ Holquist, Michael: *The Dialogic Imagination*. University of Texas Press: Austin 1981; A'Beckett, Ludmilla: "The Play of Voices in Metaphor Discourse: A Case Study of 'NATIONS ARE BROTHERS'". *Metaphor and Symbol* 27 (2), 2012, pp. 171–194)

The last stage of the investigation has attended to readers' responses to the naming. Discussion blogs and comment sections following publication about new "Joans of Arc" have been searched for various indications of audience reaction to the comparison. Readers' reactions have been studied to compare to predictions and to analyze the audience's ways of engagement with the analogy.

3. Targets of "Joan of Arc" label in the Russian press

The linguistic analysis of the collected data could be misleading without a brief characterization of the women "inspiring" the analogy with Joan of Arc. The "emulators" of the French heroine are of different ages, and ethnic and social backgrounds. However, most of them share one common trait – they have been perceived as a threat to Putin's regime. The group of "discredited Joans of Arc" in the Russian press consists mainly of journalists and politicians. The subgroup of political women include former Ukrainian Prime Minister Yulia Tymoshenko and the former leader of the former Russian party "Right forces" Irina Khakamada, Xenia Sobchak and Bozhena Rynska could be identified as the journalists who pursued political ambitions and participated in protests against unfair elections. A socialite and TV presenter Tina Kandelaki was also named Joan of Arc several times since she was mistakenly identified as an oppositionist to the government.

The first mentioning of Tymoshenko - Joan of Arc can be traced back to her imprisonment in 2001 on charges fabricated by the administration of Ukraine's President Leonid Kuchma, who was chiefly viewed by the Russian government as a friendly leader of a neighboring state. After the Orange Revolution in 2004 the negative circulation of the nickname for Tymoshenko as a Joan of Arc of Ukraine increased. The Orange Revolution was viewed by Putin's regime as a mutiny which toppled their Russian choice, Victor Yanukovych. (cf. Horvath, Robert: "Putin's 'Preventive Counter-revolution': Post-Soviet Authoritarianism and the Spectre of Velvet Revolution". *Europe-Asia Studies* 63 (1), 2011, pp. 1–25) Tymoshenko received bad publicity in Russia since she was the one who energized the protests against unfair elections in 2004. Later, her disagreements with President Victor Yushchenko in the Orange coalition came into focus in the media. The Russian press relished the squabbles between President and Prime Minister, since the disagreements corroborated its perception of the Orange Ukraine as a historic mistake for which Ukrainian people and neighboring countries would pay dearly. The defamation campaign sponsored by Ukrainian tycoons, Victor Yanukovych's supporters, Yushchenko's administration and Russian tabloids, in both Russian and Ukrainian language, contributed to Tymoshenko's defeat by Yanukovych in a close presidential election of 2010. (*The Economist*: "Ukrainian Justice: Don't Cross Viktor". 13.08.2011, Web) After Yanukovych's victory, several criminal cases were opened against Tymoshenko, who was eventually convicted on charges which were not internationally recognized. (Amnesty International: "Jailed Former Ukrainian Prime Minister Must Be Released", Web) The All Ukrainian "Fatherland" party led by Yulia Tymoshenko remains one of the most influential forces in the Ukrainian political scene though her personal popularity is relatively low upon her release from prison following the Ukrainian Revolution of 2014. Subsequently, Tymoshenko lost a second presidential race to Petro Poroshenko by a large margin.

In 2004 Irina Khakamada was also named "Joan of Arc" or "a Joan of Arc of Russian and Japanese origin." Khakamada was a leader of the Democratic Union "Right forces" which strongly opposed to authoritarian policies of Vladimir Putin. She ran for presidency in the 2004 presidential elections and lost with 3.7 per cent of votes. In March 2008, Khakamada announced to be out of political activity though she still provides her opinion in the capacity of an expert. The naming of Khakamada as a "Joan of Arc" contained the prediction of the election being a tragic show, with Khakamada as the ultimate loser in the struggle with Putin or as an inadequate public figure.

In December 2010 other Joans of Arc appeared in the Russian press after popular female journalists and socialite Xenia Sobchak and Bozhena Rynska participated in the events known as the Snow Revolutions. The demonstrations were organized to protest the 2011 Russian legislative election process, which many Russians and foreign representatives regarded as flawed. (Sperling, 2015, pp. 258–59) The December rallies evolved into protests against the third election of President Putin in May 2012. Overall, 27 people were arrested and accused after the protest, known as the Bolotnaya Square rally, for causing the "social unrest."

Bozhena Rynska, a socialite and famous gossip columnist, was also baptized "Joan of Arc" after attending a protest in December and upon her subsequent detainment by the police. She used to work as a lingerie model and was rumored to express political judgments when she could benefit from them. At the beginning of the Snow Revolution she was transformed from glamour girl to Putin's opponent. Reportedly she explained her transformation as follows: "Then I woke up because the Kremlin is in the process of destroying Russia." (*Spiegel Online International*: "Putin's Famous Enemy: Opposition in Russia Gaining High Profile Support". 11.07.2012, Web) After her detention she posted in her blog: "Next time, maybe I'll take along a nail and scratch out the cop's eyes," adding that anyone who messed with her would be torn apart "as if by an attack dog." (*Spiegel*) However, her political determination seemed to be short-lived.

The most genuine and persistent among the other Russian Joans of Arc was Xenia Sobchak who became a prominent female oppositionist of the new generation. Sobchak's father, Anatoly Sobchak, was a renowned politician with democratic credentials. He maintained a very close relationship with Putin. (cf. Meier, Andrew: "Xenia Sobchak, the Stiletto in Putin's Side". *The New York Times* 2015, pp. 114–117, 192–194) She was rumored to enjoy privileged status because of the family ties with Putin. As Rynska she was a socialite and a media celebrity known as "Russia's Paris Hilton." Pavel Gusev, the editor in chief of Moskovsky Komsomolets, one of the most popular newspapers in Russia, said about Sobchak that she was "not just a socialite… but one with a terrible image – after her trailed a long string of scandals. Some were vulgar… She has realized, just in time, she must change her image. She understood that a Joan of Arc is in great demand." (cited from Meier 2012) In 2011, she openly defied Putin, her father's friend, when she joined the protest rallies against fraudulent parliamentary elections. Sobchak is still a TV hostess at the independent TV channel "Dozhd" though after the assassination of the Russian oppositionist Boris Nemtsov she tries to keep a lower political profile.

The portrayal of the women known in Russia as "Joans of Arc" demonstrates that any resemblance between them is very casual and superficial. The participants in the Snow Revolutions were and are socialites. Although the social climbing of Tymoshenko and Khakamada was not as scandalous as in case of Sobchak and Rynska, rumors magnify their thirst for public attention. The fame of the female journalists participating in the Snow Revolution, in rough terms, can be compared to that of the pop singer Madonna. The conversion of Madonna into a figure of Joan of Arc standing is unlikely to be accepted as a genuine passion for democratic values without reservations. This parallel with Jon of Arc entails controversy and public skepticism.

4. Conceptual and semantic variations in perception of the historical prototype

Since the modern discourse community consists of fragmented groups, the historical prototype is unlikely to enjoy a uniform perception. In the contemporary Russian press there is an ostensible "heteroglossia" (Bakhtin 1981), e.g. a variety of opinions and evaluative stances expressed toward the same phenomenon. However, some voices and views have gained dominance. The naming "Joan of

Arc" functions as a characterization frame which attributes either negative or positive features to a person and may significantly differ from how the others view them. (cf. Kaufman, Sandra/ Elliot, Michael/ Shmueli, Deborah: "Frames, Framing and Reframing". In: Burgess, Guy/ Burgess, Heidi (eds.): *Beyond Intractability*. University of Colorado: Boulder 2013) But which traits does this name attribute to its new referent? Which salient associations entail the use of this name? The analysis of contextual information accompanying the name has been undertaken to catalogue its associative meanings.

The examinations of contexts has revealed that the allusion to Joan of Arc in the Russian press has promulgated different role models such as martyr, female warrior/soldier, ascetic, strong and decisive personality, widely accepted celebrity, an example of self-denial, mental disorders and so on. The sample of 100 Joan of Arc contexts has been classified according to the major topics they allude to. The term *topic* is understood as a referent (Cameron 2010b, p. 13) but also as a basis for comparison between two personalities connected by the metaphor/allusion. The discrepancies between the naming of a particular person and an attribute of the prototype (e.g. "Joan of Arc's hairstyle") have been attended to. Sometimes the personal reference has been followed by elaboration of the resemblance between the women. As a result, the total counting of topics exceeds one hundred.

The major group of the name users was a group of female politicians (35 references); journalists were named "Joan of Arc" 13 times. Among journalists and politicians frequently compared with Joan of Arc were Tymoshenko (30), Sobchak (7), Khakamada (3), Kandelaki (3), and Rynska (3). Actresses and artistic personalities (e.g. singers, models and dancers) have attracted the name nine times. These women have often been compared with Joan of Arc because they might have played this role in a film or theatrical production or they may have chosen an attribute associated with Joan of Arc as a fashion accessory. A certain similarity between actresses and the French heroine was a common prerequisite for such a parallel, though the ground for comparison was not always unquestionably positive. The highlighted commonalities included disobedience, disrespect for authorities, witchcraft and pugnacity. The latter was also categorized as an instance of aggression. The last occupational group enjoying the "privilege" of the naming was represented by heroines of WWI, WWII and female insurgents (5).

When the name resonated with some aspects of the French heroine's story, it was assigned to the categories representing a specific fragment of Joan of Arc's life or a characterization. In such instances, the writer could refer to his or her own experience or discuss banal situations rather than address a particular emulator. Heroic deeds and personalities have been marked by the use of the name eleven times. In such instances the naming could be ironic or involve negation (e.g., "she was not a Joan of Arc"). Costumes and hairstyles "a la Joan of Arc" have been mentioned 7 times though the vision of this style is dissimilar among different authors. An episode of imprisonment has provided a serious chance to be Joan of Arc and has been mentioned eleven times. Insanity or paranormal skills such as an intuition and witchcraft have been recalled 8 times. Aggression and pugnacity have also become a pre-requisite for the naming and scored six references. Ordeal by fire or exposure to heat has been mentioned five times. The same score has been allocated to instances of betrayal by allies. The rare representations (only one reference each) gained the following traits: disobedience, religious beliefs, and disrespect for authorities.

The naming "Joan of Arc" rendered 46 negative or mocking instances out of total 62 references to a person. The negative traits introduced through this name include hallucinations, Morris' syndrome (testicular feminization syndrome), schizophrenia, hysteria, witchcraft, epilepsy and instances of aggressive conduct. In general, this allusion introduces a flattering portrait of women of French origin (e.g., Segolene Royal, Sarah Bernhardt, Edith Piaf, and Fanny Ardant).

The distribution of salient traits has revealed that the public perception of Joan of Arc is fluid. As was mentioned earlier, there is no uniformity even in the perception of her hairstyle or attire. Moreover, there is a noticeable tendency to view the French heroine as an odd and troublesome woman. Compare the examples[1]:

1) We have too many of Joans of Arc but are experiencing shortage of Josephines. (AiF, 16.08.2006)
2) Try to attract male attention by all available means but do not play a Joan of Arc. (AiF, 28.12.2004)

There was public discussion of whether the French heroine is a woman that one would be happy to live with. (cf. Erofeev, Viktor: "Zhenit'sya na Zhanne d'Ark?" [To marry Joan of Arc?]. KP, 6.01. 2012, Web) It has demonstrated that the traits and circumstances comprising the heroic prototype can invoke bipolar reactions within the same community. The evaluative patterns triggered by the name diverge. For instance, in the previously mentioned article by Erofeev (2012) the paranormal skills of Joan of Arc have been presented as "exceptional intuition" by the writer, but have then been re-cast as "madness" and "perversion" by his interviewer. It is interesting that the fluidity of imaginative features and interpretative categories allows for extending some positive characteristics into their negative analogues.

---

1 My own translation of passages in Russian newspapers.

For instance, a fighting spirit can be viewed as unnecessary violence and masculinity, non-conformism as disobedience, conviction as wrong-headedness and fanaticism, intuition as witchcraft and delusions. The Russian press exploits both sides of this spectrum and, through allusions, manufactures positive and negative identities for celebrities. (cf. Ponton, Douglas: "The Female Political Leader: A Study of Gender Identity in the Case of Margaret Thatcher". *Journal of Language and Politics* 9 (2), 2010, pp. 195–218, on fomenting identities of political personages in discourse processes)

5. Possible impact on the audience

It is possible to suggest that the readers' attention to the message has been intensified by several captivating components of its content. First of all, authors have utilized a dramatic way (cf. Kjeldsen 2013, p. 24–32 and Svensson, Peter/ Stenvoll, Dag: "Risky Readings: The Virtue of Overinterpretations and Speculations in Political Discourse Analysis". In: Flottum, Kjersti (ed.): *Speaking of Europe*. John Benjamins: Amsterdam 2013, pp. 171–189, p. 178) for the characterization of contemporary celebrities which captures the reader's mind and provokes excessive interpretations beyond the spontaneous and immediate understanding of the text. See examples below:

3) Special Forces carried Tymoshenko on their shields. Joan of Arc of Ukraine orders revolutionary soldiers to form two columns and "watch over the administration" (KP, 24.11.2004)
4) At the vanguard there is Xenia Sobchak … Joanne of Arc of our democracy with fluttering banner and naked breasts. While Chubais [a former Russian democrat and a designer of privatizing schemes of state properties] will be handing over cartridges from a Xerox box (KP, 12.06.2012)

Second, the omnipresence of jocularity and censure attached to the comparisons creates a perception that the society as a whole, except for some extravagant exceptions, rejects the contemporary reincarnations of the female freedom fighter and denounces movements embodied in this symbolic manifestation. Ironic prompts and stigmatization of positive opinion holders such as "a tiny flock of elderly ladies" (example 7), "our democracy" (example 4) and "Vladimir Zhirinovsky" (example 5) create a common bond between members of the discourse community who believe in defending moral standards and fighting delusions and irrationality. Readers have been aligned with the community of shared values and beliefs (cf. Martin/ White 2005, p. 35) as they have a common object for criticism and recognize the legality of the critical approach. See examples below:

5) Vladimir Zhirinovsky [a scandalous Russian politician]: "Sobchak is thrilled when she is grabbed by the riot police. She needs strong male hands to catch, hold and molest her. She enjoys it! To be behind the bars, here she is – the Joan of Arc!" (KP,15.05.2012, AiF,15.05.2012, cf. also rbc.ru, 15.05.2012, metronews.ru 15.052012, eg.ru, 15.05.2012 and others)

6) Here is Bozhena Rynska - the glamorous chronicler of New Russian parties - imbued with revolutionary flame like our Joan of Arc though in a fur coat yells at the riot police: "I will bust your mouth. I am Bozhena!" (KP, 6.12.2011)

In addition to it, the authors distance themselves from the comparison and accredit dubious sources with the expression of the flattering parallels. The source factor has been described as an influential constituent in persuasive communication: a negatively valenced source often yields to a rejection of the argument. (Martin/ White 2005, p. 111–118) Hence, it is the third factor in communicating a negative attitude toward the positive proposition. See example 7:

7) Yulia Tymoshenko (against whom criminal charges have again been raised) and a tiny flock of old ladies are marching with placards [reading] "Yulia! You are our Joan of Arc!" in front of TV cameras. (AiF, 25.09.2002)

Fourth, readers' attitudes can be affected by the vivid demonstration of quirky behavioral patterns. The audience has been encouraged to co-operate with the author in the meaning construction, the selection of relevant social norms and the making of the final judgment. The identification of modern women through the reference to Joan of Arc amplifies improbable connections and incongruity between the legendary past and the undetermined present. On the one hand, over-indulgence of some contemporary Joans of Arc, their vanity and attention-seeking manners (examples 6, 5, 4) clash with the features of the prototypical Joan of Arc. The Russian media portray the discrepancies between female politicians and Joan of Arc to repudiate the comparison: Joan of Arc was poor but her emulators came to politics as wealthy women; Joan of Arc was an ascetic female soldier while Tymoshenko and the participants in the Snow Revolution indulged themselves in elaborate fashionable clothing; Joan of Arc was burnt at the stake while Tymoshenko changed her allegiance and Khakamada dishonorably lost her political battle. The contrast has been as often used for misrepresentation as the comparative frame has been skillfully controlled. This comparative frame has been imbued with a negative judgement of contemporary women. Authors have exploited the constructed incongruity to prod their readers toward a dislike of the displayed conduct. On the other hand, the similarities between the women and the prototype often come out as negative features: e.g., insanity, witchcraft, ominous fate (example 9) and excessive aggression (example 8, 3).

8) [F]or [Tymoshenko] restrictions and barriers do not exist. She is as dangerous in any battle as a nuclear bomb. She cultivates the image of Joan of Arc. [...] She rushes to gain absolute power. (AiF, 28.05.2008)

9) [Khakamada] took the risky but extravagant role of a democratic Joan of Arc who challenged the antidemocratic Chief Character [...]. It is evident that Khakamada's personage will end her life at the political stake, according to this scenario, and will receive rare and brief applause. (KP, 22.01.2004)

Fifth, even when the ridiculous incongruity between the women has not been in evidence, the chosen prototype clashes with beliefs on the capacity of women to become national leaders. Casting female oppositionists as political fighters rather than devoted mothers and caring wives also provokes negative judgements from conservative readers. Authorial prompts cause the activation of social stereotypes whose relevance the audience is inclined to test. According to Pettey and Perloff, (Pettey, Gary R./ Perloff, Richard M.: "Creating a Climate of Safer Sex: Making Efficacious Actions Possible". In: Swanepoel, Piet/ Hocken, Hans (eds.): *Adapting Cultural Communication to Cultural Needs*. John Benjamins: Amsterdam 2008, pp. 31–49) members of the discourse community can be engaged in the constructing of an evaluative frame when beliefs and stereotypes of the target audience have been tested by the content of the message. See the following example:

10) [Tymoshenko] should have swapped the role of Joan of Arc for the role of Mother Theresa. She should be humble. Only after her conversion to a humble person could people follow her again. But she chose a different way. [Berezovsky] (AiF, 22.01.2011, cf. also gazeta.ru 22.01.2011,news.mail.ru, 22.01.2011)

Finally, authors apply an interpersonal approach when they organize the play of voices around the comparison in such a manner that the reader can perceive peer-pressure and dependence on the collective choice of the discourse community while making an evaluative decision. A reader faces problems with constructing alternative characterizations if any deviation from the mass view has been persistently marked as peculiar and by and large dismissed. Weaker supporters can feel threatened by constant ridiculing. The flow of sarcastic statements causes embarrassment to those who were inclined to believe in the value of the political position represented by a "Joan of Arc." This emotional pressure can cause retraction from standpoints previously solicited. See the following example:

11) Joke: I have heard that Tymoshenko has been named "Joan of Arc." I wonder when inquisitors can set up the stake to burn her. (from http://forum.3dnews.ru/printthread.php?t=166&pp=15&page=84, 08.12.2004, see also http://rmonline.ru/forum/archive/index.php/t-13171.html, 15.02.2010)

Hence, the predicted reactions of readers may evolve around expressions of inappropriateness of the comparison, endorsement of ironic claims, (i.e. the covert negation of the proposition cf. Giora 2003, p. 72) expressions of aversion toward Joan of Arc's emulators and explanations of the unsuitability of the role model.

6. Readers' reactions

Judging from comment sections in the studied newspapers, most participants in discussions of the articles continue using the name "Joan of Arc" in a pejorative sense. Although several readers have claimed their appreciation of female politicians and stressed the comparison between contemporary women and Joan of Arc, the view prevailed that the public figures under discussion represent a parody of the French heroine or do not deserve to be named after her. At the same time the supporters of the analogy have been mocked and criticized for their inadequacy.

Several modes of discourse engagement with the allusive naming emerged in discussions. Among them there have been objections to the heroic role model and disputes over the appropriateness of the paragon. Another mode of dialogical engagement has included demonstration of incompatibilities in the biography of Joan of Arc and her emulators. Such revelations commonly lead to dismissing the validity of comparison (examples 12, 13). The discussion of inappropriate naming entails the contesting of the common sense and sincerity of the name givers. The devotees of the "usurpers" have been cast as dishonest, delusional and irrational or pragmatic. Compare the following examples:

12) The comparison of Tymoshenko with Joan of Arc is intolerable! What insolence! Let her make her own name rather than exploit those of others. (Comment section of KP, 22.02.2010)
13) When the daughter of high ranked parents [Sobchak] has been called "Joan of Arc"—I disagree. In my view, it is inconsistent, to be more precise it is boorishness!!! (Comment section of KP, 09.04.2012)

In example 13, the credibility of the "ideologists" building the comparison and venerating the emulators has been challenged. The parallel has been dismissed as a contrived creation of confused minds. It should be noted that the provenance of the name-giving is unknown. It has also been reported that Tymoshenko constantly expresses objection to her comparison with Joan of Arc. (A'Beckett 2013a, p. 127)

The readers, as much as the authors of narratives, like to enhance the ridiculous incongruity between the paragon and the emulators. They elaborate jocular narratives and add more comic details. The samples supplied by the media have been taken up and further developed. Bloggers have used the opportunity to generate more jokes following ready-to-use patterns. Compare the following examples.

14) It's time to imprison Navalny and Sobchak. Thus, we will have our own Nelson Mandela and our own Joan of Arc. (Comment section of KP, 18.06.2012)
15) What is the difference between Joan of Arc and Yulia Tymoshenko? No difference. Although there is a petit "but"—Joan of Arc not being interested in the Nikopol plant of ferroalloys. (Comment section of KP, 17.05.2008, http://www.spbgu.ru/forums/index.php?showtopic=12225&st=210, 16.08.2006)

Example 14 stresses that Russia is different from the South African Republic in the time of apartheid and medieval France. Prisoners in contemporary Russia are not freedom fighters but twerps. Example 15 elaborates on the topic of the alleged egocentricity of Tymoshenko. The author of the comment acknowledges that Tymoshenko has a fighting spirit similar to Joan of Arc but she uses it for self-profit.

In addition to the aforementioned trends, commenters frequently use the nickname "Joan of Arc" for Tymoshenko and Sobchak, but it is evident that the name is negatively charged. The name does not signal adulation. The bloggers do not joke but show their contempt for these public figures.

16) Don't vote for Joan of Arc of Ukraine! (Comment section of KP 25.08.2009, cf. also http://dumskaya.net/user/Korol_Artur/ 11.11.2009; sevastopol.su/news.php?id= 174136 30.12.2009)
17) The Moscow hippy trash in their disgust toward the rest of Russia, rushed to defend their Joan of Arc [Sobchak]. They defended her according to their abilities, their education, cultural views and upbringing. It is not surprising – the Joan of Arc merits her defenders. They can only shit near monuments and in Twitter feeds. (from http://www.forum-tvs.ru/lofiversion/index.php/t93393.html 13.05.2012; cf. also http://oleg-dubov.livejournal.com/317194.html 13.05.2012)

At the same time, participants in discussion blogs can positively evaluate the personality of female politicians but they refuse to endorse professional and social achievements when the traditional gender roles have been abandoned. Compare the statements of some discussants in the social media:

18) Xenia [Sobchak] —you are a warrior. I understand and support your ambitions. But if the noble woman Morozova and Joan of Arc were burnt at the stake then why do you need it all? In your Russia, and here in Ukraine, the last female ruler was Catherine the Great. Hence I think it is unnecessary to shoot yourself in your own foot and risk the lives of your relatives for the sake of your ambitions. Live long, happy, smart and in love!!!! (Comment section of KP, 21.07.2012)

The reader's reaction in example 18 demonstrates that Sobchak has drawn sympathy from the discourse community; however, the chosen role model has not been commensurate with the expectations for pretty and intelligent women in Russia and Ukraine. A similar comment has been found regarding Tymoshenko.

To summarize, the modes of interplay between authors and secondary users of the name have illuminated the following readers' reactions: (1) objections to the relevance of the prototype in modern conditions; (2) repudiation of the similarity between contemporary public figures and the French heroine; (3) elaboration on the grotesque mismatches of the comparison; (4) adoption of the nickname as a sign of disdain.

7. Concluding remarks

This paper has aimed to explain the functions of traditional rhetoric through the application of some contemporary tools of discourse analysis. It has been also an experiment in the comparison of theoretical predictions of readers' reactions with the attitudes exhibited among members of the audience.

It has revealed that the allusion to Joan of Arc is an effective technique for denigrating contemporary female politicians in the Russian press. The memorability of the scheme, contrasting techniques, ironic cues, and the dialogic engagement around the topic contributed to the success of this dissuasive strategy. The audience has been engaged in the construction of the negative characterization and in substantiating the authorial viewpoint with their commonplace observations. The readers have retained the disparaging blocks of information: they have utilized and modified the authorial conceptual slots and argumentative patterns for communicating their own preferences.

The investigation of multiple factors contributing to the success of the rhetorical device enables us to see how different groups of the fragmented discourse community can be affected in a negative way through a similar organization of a message with allusive naming. It allows us to make predictions about potential targets of dissuasion and substantiate claims that victimization and vilification have been attempted. Kjeldsen (2013, p. 23) claims that the examination of the discourse environment in which contemporary rhetoric functions enables scholars to make new practical suggestions and predict certain forms of rhetoric depending on the situation: "We will also be able to approach a diagnosis of the rhetorical use of language and create a prognosis for how we may expect this to develop in certain types of circumstances and situations."

In fact, recently a new wave of alluding to Joan of Arc has emerged in the Russian press. The Ukrainian singer and Eurovision Song Contest winning artist Ruslana Lyzhychko became a new target of ridicule in the Russian press following her commitment to the Euromaidan movement which toppled Ukrainian President Yanukovych. While many international publications acclaimed her role in the process of Ukrainian European integration and the Spanish newspaper *El Mundo* compared Ruslana to Joan of Arc, (cf. Colás, Xavier: "Ruslana, una indígena ucraniana por Europa". *El Mundo*. 9.12.2013, Web) the Russian publications predictably used this comparison to mock her. Similarly, Nadia Savchenko, a first lieutenant in the Ukrainian ground forces and the only female aviator to pilot Sukhoi Su-24 bombers and Mil Mi-24 helicopters who was captured by pro-Russian rebels in Eastern Ukraine and handed over to Russia, opened another Joan of Arc theme in the Russian press. Savchenko is a prisoner of war, nevertheless, she is held and being prosecuted in Russia on charges of killing two Russian journalists despite the fact that she was captured one hour before their death. The Russian press stigmatizes Savchenko using the label Joan of Arc and highlighting either discrepancies between Savchenko's "brutality" and humanitarian mission of Joan of Arc or parading the aggression, martial spirit and callousness of both women. Both Ruslana Lyzhychko and Nadia Savchenko represent the Ukrainian movement for European integration and independence from Russian political dominance, which is traditionally perceived as a threat to Russian revanchist plans. They both match the profile of contemporary emulators of Joan of Arc – combining an artistic personality (Savchenko used to be a fashion designer) with strong will in politics.

It can be concluded that the combination of text-oriented and reception-oriented analysis of the studied parallel has assisted in revealing fragments of social knowledge and argumentative techniques that became building blocks for covert stigmatization. It has been a helpful exercise on testing possibilities for further deployment of this dissuasive strategy.

References

A'Beckett, Ludmilla: "Cameron, L. /Maslen, R. (eds.) (2010) *Metaphor Analysis: Research Practice in Applied Linguistic, Social Sciences and the Humanities.* Book review". *Metaphor and the Social World* 4 (1), 2014, pp. 127–138.

A'Beckett, Ludmilla: "Cross-cultural Allusions in the Russian Press: Parallels between Joan of Arc and the Former Ukrainian Prime Minister Yulia Tymoshenko". *Foreign Language Studies* 19, 2013a, pp. 101–132.

A'Beckett, Ludmilla: "Strategies to Discredit Opponents: Russian Presentations of Events in Countries of the Former Soviet Union". *Psychology of Language and Communication* 17 (2), 2013b, pp. 133–156.

A'Beckett, Ludmilla: "The Play of Voices in Metaphor Discourse: A Case Study of 'NATIONS ARE BROTHERS'". *Metaphor and Symbol* 27 (2), 2012, pp. 171–194.

Amnesty International: "Jailed Former Ukrainian Prime Minister Must Be Released", retrieved 11.10.2011 from http://www.amnestyusa.org/news/news-item/jailed-former-ukraine-prime-minister-must-be-released.

Aristotle/ Trans. Kennedy, George A.: *On Rhetoric: A Theory of Civic Discourse*. Oxford University Press: New York 1991.

Bakhtin, Mikhail/ Trans. Emerson, Caryl/ Holquist, Michael: *The Dialogic Imagination*. University of Texas Press: Austin 1981.

Brummett, Barry: *Rhetorical Dimensions of Popular Culture*. University of Alabama Press: Tuscaloosa 1991.

Cameron, Lynne: "The Discourse Dynamics Framework for Metaphor". In: Cameron, Lynne/ Maslen, Robert (eds.): *Metaphor Analysis*. Equinox: London 2010a, pp. 77–94.

Cameron, Lynne: "What Is Metaphor and Why Does it Matter?". In: Cameron, Lynne/ Maslen, Robert (eds.), *Metaphor Analysis*. Equinox: London 2010b, pp. 3–26.

Charland, Maurice: "Constitutive Rhetoric: The Case of the Peuple Quebecois". *Quarterly Journal of Speech* 71, 1987, pp. 133–150.

Chiappe, Dan L./ Kennedy, John M.: "Literal Bases for Metaphor and Simile". *Metaphor and Symbol* 16, 2001, pp. 249–279.

Colás, Xavier: "Ruslana, una indígena ucraniana por Europa". *El Mundo*. 9.12.2013, retrieved 9.12.2013, from http://www.elmundo.es/loc/2013/12/09/52a2257e63fd3deb448b457e.html.

Erofeev, Viktor: "Zhenit'sya na Zhanne d'Ark?"[To marry Joan of Arc?]. *Komsomolskaia pravda*, 6.01.2012, retrieved 6.01.2012 from http://www.kp.ru/daily/25814.3/2792986/.

Gibbs, Raymond W.: *The Poetics of Mind: Figurative Thought, Language and Understanding*. Cambridge University Press: Cambridge, MA 1994.

Giora, Rachel: *On Our Mind: Salience, Context and Figurative Language*. Oxford University Press: Oxford 2003.

Horvath, Robert: "Putin's 'Preventive Counter-revolution': Post-Soviet Authoritarianism and the Spectre of Velvet Revolution". *Europe-Asia Studies* 63 (1), 2011, pp. 1–25.

Kaufman, Sandra/ Elliot, Michael/ Shmueli, Deborah: "Frames, Framing and Reframing". In: Burgess, Guy/ Burgess, Heidi (eds.) *Beyond Intractability*. University of Colorado: Boulder, Colorado 2013.

Kjeldsen, Jens. E.: "Speaking to Europe: A Rhetorical Approach to Prime Minister Tony Blair's speech to the EU Parliament". In: Flottum, Kjersti (ed.) *Speaking of Europe*. John Benjamins: Amsterdam 2013, pp. 19–43.

Koller, Veronica: *Metaphor and Gender in Business Media Discourse: A Critical Cognitive Study*. Palgrave Macmillan: New York 2004.

Kövecses, Zoltan: *Metaphor: A Practical Introduction*. Oxford University Press: Oxford 2002.

Lakoff, George/ Johnson, Mark: *Metaphors We Live by*. Chicago University Press: Chicago, IL. 1980.

Lennon, Paul: *Allusions in the Press: An Applied Linguistic Study*. Mouton de Gruyter: Berlin 2004.

Martin, J. R.,/ White, Peter R. R.: *The Language of Evaluation: Appraisal in English*. Palgrave: New York 2005.

McGee, Michael C.: "Text, Context and the Fragmentation of Contemporary Culture". *Western Journal of Communication* 54, 1990, pp. 274–289.

Meier, Andrew: "Xenia Sobchak, The Stiletto in Putin's Side". *The New York Times*, 3.7.2012, retrieved 3.7.2012, from http://www.nytimes.com/2012/07/08/magazine/ksenia-sobchak-the-stiletto-in-putins-side.html?_r=0.

Musolff, Andreas: *Metaphor and Political Discourse*. Palgrave: Basingstoke 2004.

Perelman, Chaim/ Olbrechts-Tyteca, Lucie: *The New Rhetoric. A Treatise on Argumentation*. University of Notre Dame Press: London 1969.

Pettey, Gary R./ Perloff, Richard M.: "Creating a Climate of Safer Sex: Making Efficacious Actions Possible". In: Swanepoel, Piet/ Hocken, Hans (eds.): *Adapting Cultural Communication to Cultural Needs*. John Benjamins: Amsterdam 2008, pp. 31–49.

Ponton, Douglas: "The Female Political Leader: A Study of Gender Identity in the Case of Margaret Thatcher". *Journal of Language and Politics* 9 (2), 2010, pp. 195–218.

Sperling, Valerie: *Sex, Politics and Putin. Political Legitimacy in Russia*. Oxford University Press: Oxford 2015.

Spiegel Online International: "Putin's Famous Enemy: Opposition in Russia Gaining High Profile Support". 11.07.2012. Retrieved 11.07.2012, from http://www.

spiegel.de/international/europe/moscow-socialite-bozhena-rynska-joins-fight-against-putin-regime-a-838095.html.

Svensson, Peter/ Stenvoll, Dag: "Risky Readings: The Virtue of Overinterpretations and Speculations in Political Discourse Analysis". In: Flottum, Kjersti (ed.): *Speaking of Europe*. John Benjamins: Amsterdam 2013, pp. 171–189.

The Economist: "Ukrainian Justice: Don't Cross Viktor". 13.08.2011, retrieved 13.08.2013, from http://www.economist.com/node/21525974.

Valimaa, Jussi/ Hoffman, David: "Knowledge Society Discourse and Higher Education". *Higher Education* 56 (3), 2008, pp. 265–285.

Wander, Philip: "The Third Persona: An Ideological Turn in Rhetorical Theory". In: Lucaites, John L./Condit, Celeste M./ Caudill, Sally (eds.): *Contemporary Rhetorical Theory. A Reader*. Guildford Press: New York et al. 1991, pp. 357–379.

Part Four:
Rhetoric, pedagogy and production of knowledge for democratic citizenship

Maureen Daly Goggin

Arizona State University

Preparing students for the emergent knowledge society: Rethinking learning and pedagogy in rhetoric

1. Introduction

The twenty-first century convergence of *the emergent knowledge society, accelerating change,* and *globalization* calls for a new paradigm of pedagogy – what and how we teach and what students learn and how they learn – in higher education. This new paradigm will need to take into account shifting epistemes as earlier systems of knowledge production and dissemination are becoming quickly obsolete as knowledge is growing at an exponential rate. As Neubauer points out, "the amount of information produced in the world in the coming year will exceed all of that produced in the past 5,000 years,… [and] one half of what an undergraduate in a science or technology field learns will be obsolete within 18 months." (Neubauer, Deane E: "Introduction". In: Neubauer, Deane E. (ed.): *The Emergent Knowledge Society and the Future of Higher Education. Asian Perspective.* Routledge: New York et al. 2011, p. 2) The latter calls into question what should constitute content in teaching and learning. The former is reconstructing knowledge – how we make it, how we store it, how we circulate it. That is, the acceleration in knowledge and globalized technologies has changed the face of knowledge production, distribution, and preservation. In the words of Neubauer, the "three key functions of universities – *knowledge creation* through research, *knowledge dissemination* through teaching, [publications], and service, and *knowledge conservation* through libraries [as well as] the disciplinary structuring of knowledge… are increasingly being carried out much more widely outside universities in the new 'knowledge society." (Neubauer, Deane E. "The End of the University as We Know It". In: Neubauer, Deane E. (ed.): *The Emergent Knowledge Society and the Future of Higher Education. Asian Perspective.* Routledge: New York et al. 2011, p. 224) Given this new (re)turn[1] in relation to knowledge creation, distribution, and preservation,

---

1   I say "(re)turn" here because this is not a new knowledge arrangement in relation to higher education as I show in the next section. Up until the late nineteenth century,

higher education must accommodate itself to the emerging shifts in thought, beliefs, priorities and practices in regard to education in society.

These new patterns of knowledge are forming to harness and manage the chaos, indeterminacy, and complex relationships of the postmodern era. Because we all are currently in the midst of this chaos, we have an opportunity to and *must* reinvent what it is we teach and how we teach it. Questions, thus, emerge. How do we construct higher education in new ways that are relevant to our post-Ford, post-industrial, globalized emergent and accelerating knowledge society? More specifically, how do we construct our rhetoric courses and alter our pedagogies to best engage students in knowledge-making activities that will prepare them for the emergent knowledge society? I cannot offer complete answers to these questions – I do not know that anyone can yet – but I take them up in this paper as a way to get us all thinking about changes we as educators need to undertake.

In what follows, I offer a brief history of the higher education in the United States, a discussion of the shifting paradigms and metaphors for higher education in light of the new economic structures, and a description of a new undergraduate major in rhetoric designed to address these current shifts.

2. Brief history of higher education in the US

Higher education has evolved over time to meet the needs of changing social and economic circumstances; various paradigms, forms, and functions have arisen and co-existed, eventually displacing or radicalizing older ones. In other words, radical efforts in higher education transpire to accommodate the socio-economic and political demands placed on it. Granted, these changes have occurred slowly until now, but today the changes will have to occur with increasing speed as socio-economic systems have transformed in a short period of time. Let me offer a brief sketch of the history of higher education in the United States to demonstrate what I mean.

In early days of pre-industrial, agrarian society in the US, tertiary education borrowed its model from Europe. During the seventeenth, eighteenth and much of the nineteenth century, like European higher education, it sought to serve pulpit, bar and politics to ensure that morals, laws, and government were firmly grounded for the country. The goal for faculty at that time was to instill knowledge, morality, values and piety. The goal for students was to demonstrate they had attained these

---

knowledge creation, dissemination, and preservation occurred outside institutions of higher education in homes, in labs at home or work as it is now occurring today, especially given the internet.

ends. The pedagogy was recitation; students recited what they had memorized to demonstrate they knew what they were supposed to know. Thus, the role of education was to *pass on* but not to *create* knowledge. Creation and dissemination happened elsewhere on land and sea, in people's homes or in labs built in their homes or work. Indeed, the concept of credentialism – the reliance on academic and other formal qualifications as a measure of a person's intelligence or ability to do a particular job – did not emerge until the late nineteenth century when for the first time high school and higher education degrees offered the credentials necessary for a particular profession. (Bledstein, Burton: *The Culture of Professionalism: The Middle Class and the Development of Higher Education in America*. Norton: New York 1976; Collins, Randall: *The Credential Society: An Historical Sociology of Education and Stratification*. Academic Press: Orlando 1979)

In the later part of the nineteenth century, there was a radical paradigm shift in higher education in response to the rise of industrialization that created the system we have today. Under industrialization, following a Fordist-model, higher education was divided into disciplines (intellectual spaces), departments (physical spaces) while classes were divided by time (into years and class periods) and space (classrooms) for efficiency. And thus was the beginning of intellectual, physical and social silos in tertiary education. Modern higher education, as Veysey (Veysey, Laurence R.: *The Emergence of the American University*. University of Chicago Press: Chicago 1965) has noted, then emerged as three distinct entities that are still with us but are being challenged today: the first is the Research Ideal. Here the goal is to *create* knowledge, and pedagogy is primarily lecture and lab. The second is the Liberal Culture Ideal. Here the goal is to *preserve* knowledge; pedagogy is primarily recitation and lecture. And finally, the Utility Ideal. Here the goal is to *use* knowledge; pedagogy is primarily lecture, lab, and field work. Although today no one institution of higher education is limited by one of these ideals, the focus of schools differs according to these ideals. Thus, for research universities, the goal is to create knowledge; for liberal arts colleges, to preserve knowledge; and for comprehensive and technical universities, to use knowledge. Yet these ideals are now under fire and cracks are forming in the intellectual, physical, and social silos.

This is mainly because since the mid-1990s, there has been a post-industrial shift in job skills matrix – what it is workers (e.g. students) need to know in order to have a successful career – whether in manual or cognitive fields. During the nineteenth and most of twentieth century, necessary skills were routine for both manual jobs that had well-defined physical tasks and cognitive jobs that had well-defined mental tasks. But in the late twentieth and twenty-first centuries, careers have become increasingly non-routine and ill-defined whether manual or cognitive. Moreover, complex communication is becoming critical in virtually *every* career. In their analysis of job skills, Albanesi, et al. (Albanesi, Stefania et al.: "Is Job Polarization Holding Back the Labor Market". *Federal Reserve Bank of New York*. 27 March 2013) found that routine occupations accounted for over 60 percent of the jobs in 1975 and dropped to less than 40 percent by 2010 while the reverse is true for non-routine occupations. These non-routine career paths call for ongoing knowledge creation efficiently and effectively in the workplace. These jobs also challenge universities as the only sites for knowledge creation, dissemination, and preservation.

3. Shifting paradigms and metaphors for education

What does this economic shift mean for universities, and, more specifically, for rhetoric? Too many degree courses are still founded on a passive model of undergraduate education where a student is supposed to receive information, then process it somehow, and demonstrate it back to the teacher. Knowledge here is a thing or a commodity to be distributed to and possessed by the individual. This perspective is captured well by the metaphor of "learning as knowledge acquisition." (Sfard, Anna: "On Two Metaphors for Learning and the Dangers of Choosing Just One". *Educational Research* 27 (2), 1998, pp. 4–13) As Sfard points out, "The language of the 'knowledge acquisition' and 'concept development' makes us think about the human mind as a container to be filled with certain materials and about the learner as becoming an owner of these materials." (1998, p. 5) The second dominant metaphor for learning theories, the one meant to displace the acquisition metaphor, is the metaphor of "learning as participation." Sfard notes, "in the image of learning that emerges from this linguistics turn [to a metaphor of participation], the permanence of having gives way to the constant flux of *doing*." (1998, p. 6) Within this perspective, learning is "conceived of as a process of becoming a member of a certain community" and calls for collaboration and sharing. It is a social view. Under this view in the latter part of the twentieth century, student-centered, activity-based learning models emerged and were propagated. Sfard offers a useful table for these two metaphors.

Fig. 11.1: The metaphorical mapping of acquisition and participation metaphors

Acquisition Metaphor		Participation Metaphor
Individual enrichment	Goal of learning	Community building
Acquisition of something	Learning	Becoming a participant
Recipient (consumer), (re-)constructor	Student	Peripheral participant, apprentice
Provider, facilitator, mediator	Teacher	Expert participant, preserver of practice/discourse
Property, possession, commodity	Knowledge, concept	Aspect of practice/discourse /activity
Having, possessing	Knowing	Belonging, participating, communicating

Source: Sfard, Anna: "On Two Metaphors for Learning and the Dangers of Choosing Just One". *Educational Research* 27 (2), 1998, p. 7.

My purpose is not to dispute the theories under these metaphors or the metaphors themselves; indeed, these routine models may have served us well at one time. However, in our current paradigm shift, knowledge creation and innovation are the keys. Non-routine careers demand professionals who can do more than just parrot ideas or actively participate; they must be able to create knowledge as part of their workload. To achieve these ends, calls for new theories under a new metaphor of learning.

A third metaphor is coming of age today, "learning as knowledge creation". (Paavola, Sami/ Lipponen, Lasse/ Hakkarainen, Kai: "Epistemological Foundations for CSCL: A Comparison of Three Innovative Knowledge Communities." *Centre for Research on Networked Learning and Knowledge Building: Scientific Background*. 2002; Paavola, Sami/ Lipponen, Lasse/ Hakkarainen, Kai: "Development of Learning Theories". *Centre for Research on Networked Learning and Knowledge Building: Scientific Background*) Theories under this model "posit learning as a process of creating or articulating knowledge rather than just assimilating existing knowledge or participating in existing practices." (Paavola et al. "Development...", p. 2) They, thus, seek "to provide valuable guidance for restructuring school according to innovative knowledge communities through helping teachers and students work deliberately for advancing their knowledge, and supporting them in reflecting on and transforming of their communities." (Paavola et al. 2002, p. 2) Such theories help us to develop both strong professionals and strong citizens. The time is now because what and how we teach must be relevant for the twenty-first century.

In *Future Shock,* Toffler gets it right when he quotes psychologist Herbert Gerjuoy who said, "The illiterate of the 21st century will not be those who cannot read and write, but those who cannot learn, unlearn, and relearn." (Toffler, Alvin: *Future Shock*. Bantam: New York 1984, p. 384) This new vision for the meaning of literacy calls for new visions of knowledge making and management. Knowledge under this new view is not a stagnant thing that is contained in the brain of one person but an ongoing process and practice among people that has implications for the individual. That is to say, the impact of the new emergent knowledge society, according to knowledge management scholars Kumar and Gupta, means that

> Knowledge sharing and knowledge creation go hand in hand. Knowledge is created through practice, collaboration, interaction, and education, as the different knowledge types are shared and converted. Beyond this, knowledge creation is also supported by relevant information and data which can improve decisions and serve as building blocks in the creation of new knowledge. (Kumar, Shailesh/ Gupta, Sanjeev: "Role of Knowledge Management Systems (KMS) in Multinational Organization: An Overview". *International Journal of Advanced Research in Computer Science and Software Engineering* 2 (11), 2012, p. 11)

In other words, learning is both social and cognitive. It is active and requires understanding how individuals, communities, and networks participate in knowledge creation and in mechanisms of knowledge circulation. It calls into question understanding the nature of knowledge (to what extent knowledge is "in the head" or "in the world"), and calls for teaching processes of inquiry (the role of questions and theories) involved.[2] The theories under the metaphor of knowledge creation aim toward these goals. This is important as all students now need to learn how to become *knowledge creators* and how to work successfully with others so they can participate in solving ill-defined problems, completing non-routine tasks, and critically reflecting on processes. Even more importantly, beyond the workforce, as knowledge creators and disseminators, they can become well informed democratic citizens – a goal of education since rhetoric emerged in classical Greece.

To realize the ideals of democratic education, instruction in knowledge creation and sharing must create opportunities for students to integrate academic pursuits with their own interests and passions. Research, as Appadurai defines it, "is an essential capacity for democratic citizenship." (Appadurai, Arjun: "The

---

[2] It is beyond the scope of this essay to explicate in great detail the metaphor of knowledge creation. However, there are several essays that do this quite well. Cf., Carl Bereiter (Bereiter, Carl: *Education and Mind in the Knowledge Age*. Erlbaum: Hillsdale, NJ 2002); Sami Paavola, Lasse Lipponen, and Kai Hakkarainen. (Paavola et al. "Development" and "Epistemological")

Right to Research." *Globalization, Societies, and Education* 4.2, 2006, p. 176) And as Behizadeh (Behizadeh, Nadia: "Enacting Problem-Posing Education through Project-Based Learning". *English Journal* 104, 2014, pp. 99–104) argues, democratic principles demand that the issues, problems, and questions students bring to the table be at the center of the curriculum.

Thus, we need more refined questions about how to prepare students to do all that they need to do in higher education. How do we help students gain practice in innovating and creating knowledge, and learn how to collaborate, share different types of knowledges, interact as they learn different ways of learning, unlearning and relearning, and critically reflect on practices and products. In short, what pedagogies should we develop to offer new ways of learning?

4. SWIRL: Studies in writing, inquiry, rhetoric, and literacies

These are some of the questions, among many, that those of us in rhetoric at Arizona State University debated as we created a new undergraduate major that began in 2015 called SWIRL: Studies in Writing, Inquiry, Rhetoric, and Literacies. This new major is distinct and unlike any other major in rhetoric and writing that we researched. Most of those majors focus on writing such as the major of Writing and Rhetoric at Syracuse University, Professional Writing at Purdue University, the Rhetoric and Writing Program at San Diego State University, the Rhetoric Program at the University of Texas Austin, and the Writing and Rhetoric program at Stanford University; others focus on rhetoric and discourse, such as the Writing, Rhetoric and Discourse program at DePaul University; others focus on digital writing such as the Writing, Rhetoric, and Digital Studies at the University of Kentucky; still others focus on rhetoric and culture such as the Cultures, Rhetoric, and Theory major at Ohio University.[3] What makes SWIRL distinctive from these kinds of programs?

SWIRL is designed to prepare students to become life-long learners; those who are able to identify, frame, and analyze social problems; apply usable knowledge to the examination of those problems; and pose possible solutions to those problems to a wide range of audiences. The major prepares students to critically analyze pressing social issues or questions, view themselves as agents of change, and communicate (through writing and other modes) potential solutions to the problems identified

---

3   The number of undergraduate programs in writing and rhetoric in the US is growing. Most of these focus almost exclusively on writing. Others focus on rhetoric in or still others add a layer of writing to a literature degree in Departments of English. I mention just a few here. Of course, Communication Departments have long offered degrees in rhetoric; their focus tends to be on the history and theories of rhetoric only.

and examined. SWIRL teaches students strategies for inquiry – ways of posing and solving problems and the ways communication has, does, and will create knowledge and action. Students come to understand that how one asks a question is as important as what the question is. Students also learn how to draw on what they know and understand to generate new knowledge, new understandings, and new ways of communicating while engaging with those questions. Students are encouraged to use their newly acquired tools of critical inquiry to determine whether change is desirable and if so, when, why, how, and what kind of change is needed. With an inquiry-based focus on the connections among writing, rhetoric and literacy, this major is uniquely situated to pursue the relationship between theory and practice as students come to learn the theories and histories of rhetoric, literacy, and writing. SWIRL also provides a space for students to understand that communication is constructed, circulated, reacted to, and repurposed through time and place. Understanding the theories, purposes, and practices of writing, rhetoric, and literacy go a long way to reaching these goals.

SWIRL meets market demand in business, government, nonprofit, education and other settings that require citizens and employees who can create innovative knowledge and can reason, read, write, and act in robust and significant ways to understand historical influences on current questions, anticipate the future, and meet the challenges of the present. While in the SWIRL major, students take courses and do projects across the areas of rhetoric, writing, and literacy, they are encouraged to take relevant courses in other colleges, institutes, centers, schools, and departments throughout the university to help them learn how to work transdisciplinarily, for problems today are far too complex to understand through the lens of one discipline.

4.1 ENG 205 Introduction to writing, rhetoric, and literacies

In spring 2015, I taught the introduction to this major: a 200-level class that enrolled students in majors from around the university – English, Communication, Engineering, and Creative Writing. I designed the class to introduce students to the core concepts in rhetoric, literacy, and writing and to understand different ways of inquiry. Here is the description from the course:

> How do we understand the ways in which people in systems – both small and large – social, political, and economic – throughout the world use language and other symbolic resources to carry out work? Three fields of study take this kind of questioning especially seriously: studies in writing, studies in rhetoric, and studies in literacy. Inquiry – that persistent, deliberate commitment to question and to build methods sufficient to that questioning – is a generative force in each of these fields of study. This course is designed to familiarize you with such questioning traditions and to help you judge for yourself what each is good for. The goal is to strengthen your own repertoire and decision-making

power for producing and circulating work (widely defined across material, print, and digital media) that matters in our risk-ridden world. Quite simply, then, this is a course in asking good questions and in evaluating responses to situations that spur questioning.

The pedagogy for the class was designed as discussion based, with student-centered and student-led activities. Materials were presented via brief lecture, PowerPoint, and videos, all of which students discussed. Students not only worked in groups on various tasks but they also designed quizzes on the readings that they gave to each other in the class, they created evaluation rubrics to assess their multimodal projects, and they all assessed each project (they were a lot harder on each other than I was). They led discussions. They gave presentations. They were enmeshed in a number of active learning endeavors that allowed them to be innovative, create knowledge, and disseminate knowledge in unique ways. By the end of the course, they were to accomplish the following goals:

- Conduct critical inquiries and rhetorical analyses of written, spoken, visual, and digital texts.
- Use knowledge of theories and methods of writing, rhetoric, and literacy discussed in class to develop a framework for comparing the explanatory power of these theories within and across the areas of inquiry.
- Assess the relative value of available methods given the demands of a given rhetorical situation at hand or problem under investigation.
- Demonstrate understandings of disciplinary methods and practices for data-driven, theoretically informed rhetorical decision making.
- Put new knowledge to new purposes, working both collaboratively and individually – and gauge the impact of that work for various people affected by and/or participating in it.
- Contextualize the rhetorical situation in which they find themselves – historically, theoretically, and methodologically – and chart a path forward by using disciplinary tools.

The major assignments were designed with these goals in mind. They were:

- Individually composed photo-essay
- Semester-long multimodal project on cultural work (individual & group work)
- Presentation of multimodal project
- Critical reflection on multimodal project

Each had a set of sequenced assignments to help students engage in a process of progressive problem solving to construct the final product. The photo essay required students to post potential images for the assignment and for peers to analyze these photos and make recommendations about which were useful and what themes they evoked. Then students were required to generate a rough draft of the photo essay that peers reviewed and commented on. They also had to write a critical reflection on the photo essay. Critical reflection (which is also built into the next project) is a crucial tool for creating and articulating knowledge; as Taczak notes, "Reflection allows writers to recall, reframe, and relocate knowledge and practices." (Taczak, Kara: "Reflection is Critical for Writers' Development". In: Adler-Kassner, Linda/ Wardle, Elizabeth (eds.): *Naming What We Know: Threshold Concepts of Writing Studies*. Utah University Press: Logan 2015, p. 79) The group multimodal project required several progressive, sequenced assignments. First, the group had to work together to construct a socially significant topic; they then had to generate a group proposal for what the topic was and how they planned to research and execute it. Students then individually wrote up research reports in which they identified, conducted, and reported on relevant research, providing critical summaries for each other. As with the photo essay, students generated a rough draft and received peer feedback. Then they presented their multimodal project orally to the class and wrote individual critical reflections on the project. (See Appendix for sequenced assignments.)

5. Conclusion

By way of a conclusion, I share here a description of projects from two of the assignments: the photo essay and the multimodal project made by a sophomore-level class. Both assignments required research as students were to explore socially and culturally significant topics: for the photo essay they were to focus on a person, place, or thing that acts as a cultural worker; and for the multimodal, they were to focus on a socially and culturally significant issue. Rather than paper-only assignments, I wanted students to engage with and demonstrate that: they understood multiple modes of discourse as they were learning about multiple modes of rhetoric, literacy, and writing – both as producers and consumers. In short, the assignments were meant to show that they had accomplished the goals of the class. I was impressed by what these young students produced.

The first project is a Photo Essay by Katlyn Ewens. What is important about this photo essay on Piestewa Peak in Arizona, is that although Katlyn Ewens treasures hiking up this peak, she knew little about its history or specifics of the terrain or the demographics of who used the trail, so she did a good amount of research to find out facts about the peak. She also took all but one of the pictures for the essay and she compiled the layout for the photo essay. While the pictures were meaningful for her personally, the experience of compiling the photo essay was very significant, a point she clearly conveyed in her critical reflection on the project.

The second example is the Multimodal project, in this case, a feminist website titled "Empowering Women: The Time is Now," by Jennifer Pielack, Lauren Rice, and Sarah Yong that is still live today and continues to get lots of hits. The URL is http://empower-women.weebly.com/. On the site, they include five robust sections:

a. ABOUT in which they offer a mission statement, and they introduce themselves
b. MEDIA in which they offer information and graphics on women in the media as well as women-friendly media videos
c. TAKE ACTION in which they offer sites where folks can take action to help women
d. ROLE MODELS in which they offer role models for young women along with recent videos by these women
e. CONTACT in which they invite comments

All of these sections as well as the layout of the site required a considerable amount research which the students conducted admirably. I encourage readers to visit the site and to examine all of the material as it represents a substantive amount of research and refined writing skills.

From this ENG 205 class, I learned much myself – about what students, when given full reign, can accomplish and what they can teach me when I stand out of their way. What this experience also taught me is that, like the students, I have to continue to learn, unlearn, and relearn, each semester, if not each class period. And that is an exciting venture!

References

Albanesi, Stefania et al.: "Is Job Polarization Holding Back the Labor Market". *Federal Reserve Bank of New York*. 27 March 2013, retrieved 7.30.2015, from http://libertystreeteconomics.newyorkfed.org/2013/03/is-job-polarization-holding-back-the-labor-market.html#.VbvxfvlVhBc.

Appadurai, Arjun: "The Right to Research." *Globalization, Societies, and Education* 4 (2), 2006, pp. 167–77.

Behizadeh, Nadia: "Enacting Problem-Posing Education through Project-Based Learning". *English Journal* 104, 2014, pp. 99–104.

Bereiter, Carl: *Education and Mind in the Knowledge Age*. Erlbaum: Hillsdale, NJ 2002.

Bledstein, Burton: *The Culture of Professionalism: The Middle Class and the Development of Higher Education in America*. Norton: New York 1976.

Collins, Randall: *The Credential Society: An Historical Sociology of Education and Stratification*. Academic Press: Orlando 1979.

Kumar, Shailesh / Gupta, Sanjeev: "Role of Knowledge Management Systems (KMS) in Multinational Organization: An Overview". *International Journal of Advanced Research in Computer Science and Software Engineering* 2 (11), 2012, pp. 8–16.

Neubauer, Deane E: "Introduction". In: Neubauer, Deane E. (ed.): *The Emergent Knowledge Society and the Future of Higher Education. Asian Perspective*. Routledge: New York et al. 2011a.

Neubauer, Deane E. "The End of the University as We Know It". In: Neubauer, Deane E. (ed.): *The Emergent Knowledge Society and the Future of Higher Education. Asian Perspective*. Routledge: New York et al. 2011b.

Obama, Barack: "The Text of President Obama's 2015 State of the Union Address." *Washington Times*. 20 January 2015, retrieved 7.30.2015 from http://www.washingtontimes.com/news/2015/jan/20/text-president-obamas-2015-state-union-address/.

Paavola, Sami/ Lipponen, Lasse/ Hakkarainen, Kai: "Development of Learning Theories". *Centre for Research on Networked Learning and Knowledge Building: Scientific Background*, retrieved 7.30.2015, from http://www.helsinki.fi/science/networkedlearning/eng/delete.html.

Paavola, Sami/ Lipponen, Lasse/ Hakkarainen, Kai: "Epistemological Foundations for CSCL: A Comparison of Three Innovative Knowledge Communities." *Centre for Research on Networked Learning and Knowledge Building: Scientific Background*. 2002 retrieved 7.30.2015, from http://www.helsinki.fi/science/networkedlearning/texts/paavola_et_al_2002.pdf.

Sfard, Anna: "On Two Metaphors for Learning and the Dangers of Choosing Just One". *Educational Research* 27 (2), 1998, pp. 4–13.

Taczak, Kara: "Reflection is Critical for Writers' Development". In: Adler-Kassner, Linda/ Wardle, Elizabeth (eds.): *Naming What We Know: Threshold Concepts of Writing Studies*. Utah University Press: Logan 2015, pp. 78–81.

Toffler, Alvin: *Future Shock*. Bantam: New York 1984.

Veysey, Laurence R.: *The Emergence of the American University*. University of Chicago Press: Chicago 1965.

Appendix: Assignments

Fig. 11.2: Photo-essay and critical reflection assignment

ENG 205
Photo-Essay and Critical Reflection Assignment
Due: Rough Draft, Wednesday, September 28th
Due: Final Draft, Wednesday, October 5th

This assignment is made up of two parts: a photo- essay and a critical reflection. A photo-essay is made up of a collection of photographs placed in a particular order to convey an argument or narrative that is supported by words (captions and other text). World class photojournalists such as Larry Burrows, Lauren Greenfield, Joachim Ladefoged, and James Nachtwey, to name just a few, are well known for their photo-essays that reveal a progress of events, emotions, and concepts. For examples of their photos from photo-essays, see

- http://life.time.com/larry-burrows/
- http://www.laurengreenfield.com/index.php?p=VQTME4W6
- http://www.joachimladefoged.com/
- http://www.jamesnachtwey.com/

Photojournalists, however, aren't the only ones who can do photo-essays. People are creating something like them every day on Twitter, Tumblr, Facebook, Pinterest, and other social media sites. Images powerfully convey stories and arguments.

NY 2001, Collapse of South Tower, Photo by James Nachtwey

For your photo-essay assignment, you will create a one- to two-page photo-essay that combines images, captions, and text to construct an argument about a cultural worker (person(s), organization(s), place(s), thing(s)). You will need to use a minimum of

6 pictures up to 12 or so that show the kinds of cultural work that is being done. You began brainstorming on cultural worker for your first Blackboard post. Continue brainstorming to come up with a topic. Here are some things to keep in mind:

Topic and theme: Photo-essays are most dynamic when you as the photographer care deeply about the topic and the theme (the point about the topic). What cultural worker – person, organization, place, or thing – do you care most deeply about? Nail down your topic and then work on the point you want to make about it.

Research: Find out as much as you can about your topic. Who/what is it? Where does it come from? Who made it or constructed it? Why does it do what it does? For what purpose? Interview people to find out the answers to these and other questions you generate. Read what you can about the topic (both online and in the library). For instance, say you want to do a photo-essay on a graffiti artist. Speak to the artist if you can. Speak with those who have viewed the graffiti s/he does. Read about graffiti artists. Take photos of the graffiti and if possible the artist.

Find the "real story": After your research, determine the angle you want to take in your photo-essay. Is the graffiti artist from an upper, middle, or lower class? What value, idea, emotion, or belief is the artist trying to challenge and/or convey. Is the graffiti artist part of a counterculture? Why does the artist do what s/he does? And so on.

Plan your photographs: Whether you decide to sit down and extensively visualize each shot of your photo-essay or simply walk through them in your mind, think about the kinds of shots that will work best to make your argument. You might create a "shot list" for the story – a list of shots that taken together will make the argument – or a story board – a series illustrations or images displayed in a sequence to help with organizing the photo-essay sequence.

Consider the following in composing your photographs:

o   Color or B&W or some combination
o   Composition
o   Lighting (back, low, side, front)
o   Angle and distance to subject
o   Candid or posed photos?
    Consider the need for text to accompany each photograph as a caption and as an explanation or piece of the argument.

Each shot will work like a sentence in a one-paragraph story. Typically, you take many more shots than you use. In selecting your images, each shot must emphasize a different concept or emotion that can be woven together with the other images for the final draft of the argument.

Hounds of Helsinki backstage, 2014. Photographer Landon Nordeman

Organizing your photo-essay

Lead photo: should effectively draw in your readers. This is usually the most difficult photo to choose and it must follow the point you want to make. It could be an emotional portrait or an action shot but ultimately it should provoke the curiosity of the viewers.

The scene: Your second photo should set the stage and describe the scene of your argument. An overarching photo taken with a wide angle lens is often effective.

Portraits: Your photo-essay should include at least one portrait of a person, place, or thing. If you capture an emotional expression or a telling action, it can effectively humanize your argument.

For Your Critical Reflection Assignment on your photo-essay

You will write a one-page double-spaced reflection on your photo essay explaining what your argument is and how you planned the photographs you took and selected for the photo-essay. Consider what the constraints you were working with (e.g., time, access, schedules, etc.). What were the rhetorical affordances of this project (e.g., what did it allow you to do and say that another mode would have not allowed). Finally, what did you learn in doing this photo-essay project?

Fig. 11.3: Multimodal research essay assignment

ENG 205
Multimodal Research Essay Assignment

Maureen Daly Goggin   **ENG 205**

As Cheryl Ball and Colin Charlton point out, "*Multimodal* means *multiple + mode*.... [A] mode refers to a way of meaning making" (42). A multimodal research essay, then, is one that combines two or more of the following modes of communication: alpha/numeric writing, audio (e.g., speaking and/or music), visual (e.g., photographic images), drawings, and video to make an argument. Some go so far as to include gesture and tactile elements. Although it is often mistakenly assumed that a multimodal essay must include a digital component that is not always the case. Consider, for example, posters, flyers, brochures, magazines, zines, scrapbooks, reports, and so on. While some of these may be digitally produced, they are not necessarily distributed digitally – though for this assignment you will create a multimodal research project that will be delivered digitally.

For this assignment, you will work in a small group of 3 or 4 to generate a multimodal research essay to convey a scholarly argument on a topic relevant to the course (its readings or its class discussions, such as efforts of a cultural worker or examination of a social problem such as human rights) that you as a group agree on. To arrive at that argument, you will need to articulate the problem to do an inquiry on, research and document the problem, analyze what you find, and communicate the results via the multimodal research essay and the oral presentation. You will have time inside the class but you will also need to meet and work with each other outside of class.

There are several goals for this assignment:

- To practice research as systematically increasing the horizons of your current knowledge
- To practice identifying/constructing and making inquiries into a research problem
- To practice applying your analytical skills to the technical and rhetorical production of a multimodal text
- To produce a contemporary text in response to a particular rhetorical situation using multiple modes, media, and technologies
- To understand how multiple modes create a "set" that often work together
- To practice collaboration skills necessary for producing a scholarly multimodal essay
- To come to a more thorough understanding of the rhetorical situation – the relationship among the audience, the writer, and the purpose of a text – and the trajectory of your writings
- To come to a more thorough understanding of how rhetoric, writing, and literacy work alone and together as analytical and productive tools

FORMAT: you can choose as a group to do a Website-based project or a PowerPoint or a YouTube video or a Social Media site, incorporating two or more of the modes described above to make a convincing researched argument about your topic. (For your research, see Research Assignment for individual tasks.)

As a group, you will be responsible for writing a detailed proposal that contains the specifics of the project. (See Proposal Assignment as a group task.)

There are due dates for individual and group portions of this project throughout the semester. You need to all keep up with these due dates.

We will reserve the last two classes so that each group can present their multimodal research essay to the class. You will then place the **final multimodal assignment in our class Dropbox on December 2nd**. With the final project, each student needs to write a one-page critical reflection on the experience of creating the multimodal research essay. (cf. Critical Reflection Assignment) Your **critical reflection is also due on December 2nd**.

To sum up:

Group Proposal is due	October 19th
Individual Research Assignment is due	November 2nd
Multimodal Research Project is due	December 2nd
Critical Reflection on Multimodal Project	December 2nd

Fig. 11.4: Multimodal research group proposal

Multimodal Research Group Proposal
Maureen Daly Goggin	**ENG 205**

The **proposal** is a collaborative, group document that describes how the multimodal research essay project will take shape and be completed.

There are two goals for this assignment: to practice initiating collaborative group work by establishing shared discourses, conventions, and expected rules; and to convey, in writing, your multimodal project idea to an audience.

As a group, you need to write a 2-page proposal for your major project. The proposal should describe:

- What your project is about in some detail (1–2 paragraphs)
- How you plan on designing and circulating it to support your argument (website, PowerPoint, YouTube video, a social media site, or some other technique)
- Why that design is necessary to make your argument
- How your group will complete all of the components for the project
- How your group will agree to complete that work including documentation of each of your group members' roles, tasks, and responsibilities
- Your work plan for completing the project by the due date
- What research you need to accomplish

Draw up a TEAM-CONTRACT that your group negotiates and include it with your proposal. The contract should specify expectations and consequences for not meeting those expectations. Each of you needs to sign the contract.

A proposal, keep in mind, is just that. You are *proposing* to do something, which doesn't mean the proposal is written in stone but it should be concrete enough to show you have a good understanding of what needs to be accomplished in the time you have for the project. Use the proposal writing process as a way to think through in some depth what this project will look like/do and how you will get it done. If it changes slightly or even more than slightly along the way, that is to be expected as part of the writing process.

Due: Monday, October 19th

Fig. 11.5: Research assignment for multimodal project

ENG 205

Research Assignment for Multimodal Project

Maureen Daly Goggin   **Fall 2015**

Based on your project topic, *each* person in your group needs to find 2 pieces of research (at least one scholarly and one popular or two scholarly). (You may find more but the minimum is two each.) These pieces can be print based or digital.

The point is NOT to pick ANY two pieces of research; it is to select at least two pieces that will be of significant use to your project. Typically this means reading more than two to find two useful pieces.

Annotate both of these pieces for your teammates. In your annotation include:

- A written summary of the research
- A description of how the research relates to your proposed project
- A list of any important points you can use in your proposed project
- A list of any important points you think the article misses that your project will fill

Make the two research pieces available to your teammates either in print, scanned, or by a link if available.

Turn in a hard copy of your individual annotations to me **on or before Monday, November 2nd**.

Fig. 11.6: Individual critical reflection for multimodal project

ENG 205

Individual Critical Reflection for Multimodal Project

You will write a critical reflection on your multimodal research project. Here are some thoughts to keep in mind as you do so:

Framing Questions for Analytical Writing and Critical Reflections: Whenever you set out to do analytical writing and a *critical reflection* of a particular idea, you can use the following questions as a framework to guide you as you write. An analytical text and critical reflection is effective if it is written in a manner that allows the reader to answer all four of these questions satisfactorily:

- What's the point of the multimodal project? This is the **analysis/interpretation** issue, which examines the writer's (your) angle.
- Who says? This is the **validity** issues, which examines on what (data, literature, hearsay, etc.) are the claims based. (Consider the readings we have done this semester)
- What's new? This is the **value-added** issue, which explores the writer's (your) contribution to existing knowledge.
- Who cares? This is the **significance** issue (the most important issue of all—the one that subsumes all others), which asks, a) is this work worth doing; b) is this text worth reading; c) does it contribute something important?

Critical Reflections should be no more than one page (double-spaced). This means that you won't have a lot of space to say what you're trying to say well. CR's are not a place for your initial thinking. They are a place for more polished thinking that you're testing with me and with your peers. All this to say, get in the habit of writing before you write. You'll need to do some writing and talking in and out of class to make sense of what you're reading and thinking. Let the messiness of your ideas flow there. Then, go back and chase *one idea* and polish it for more public and critical discussion.

Due: Your individual critical reflection is due when you turn in multimodal group project on **Wednesday, December 2nd**.

Ove Bergersen

University of Stavanger

Kindergartens and the civic art of rhetoric: Citizens, character and knowledge

1. Introduction

The concept of rhetorical citizenship is a relatively new theoretical concept. In one of the few publications devoted to this concept, Christian Kock and Lisa S. Villadsen (Kock, Christian/ Villadsen, Lisa S.: *Rhetorical Citizenship and Public Deliberation*. Pennsylvania State University Press: University Park, PA 2012) point out that rhetorical citizenship emphasizes citizenship more as debate and deliberative practice than, for example, as a right. It is a view on citizenship in the republican tradition which "looks back to the Greek city-state." (Kock/ Villadsen 2012, p. 1) They go on to say: "We offer the concept of rhetorical citizenship as a way of conceptualizing the discursive, processual, participatory aspects of civic life." (Kock/ Villadsen 2012, p. 5) They highlight the fact that discourse in many ways is constitutive of civic engagement and not just something that precedes action.

In this chapter, I will introduce an Aristotelian perspective on rhetoric and citizens, and suggest how the concept of rhetorical citizenship can be understood in this light. I will use the theoretical discussion as a basis to analyze a kindergarten's prospectus. In this way, I will test how the concept of rhetorical citizenship relates to documents that regulate education and care for society's youngest citizens, and investigate how the concept of rhetorical citizenship can be fruitful for the rhetorical analysis of documents in education systems. As an integral part of this analysis, I will ask if rhetorical citizenship calls for a view of knowledge in society other than, for example, the concept of learning.

2. Theory

To guide me through the Aristotelian universe, I draw on the philosophical comments to Aristotle which Eugene Garver has developed over several years. (Garver, Eugene: *Aristotle's Rhetoric: An Art of Character*. University of Chicago Press: Chicago 1994; Garver, Eugene: *Confronting Aristotle's Ethics: Ancient and Modern Morality*. University of Chicago Press: Chicago 2006; Garver, Eugene: *Aristotle's Politics: Living Well and Living Together*. University of Chicago Press:

Chicago 2011) To simplify, we can say that Garver reads Aristotle's *Nicomachean Ethics* in light of his *Rhetoric* and the Aristotelian *Politics* in light of his *Ethics*. In these central works, Aristotle introduced such concepts as potency and actualization, form and function, telos and nature, and internal and external ends in art and virtue.

One main claim Garver makes is that since rhetoric has a political function, it falls into species (*eidē*). Aristotle identifies three rhetorical species or genres in which we see practical rationality: deliberative, judicial and epideictic or demonstrative rhetoric. As Garver notes, Aristotle identifies ends (*telos*) and methods characteristic for these three species:

> The end of the deliberative speaker is the expedient or harmful ... the end of the forensic speaker is the just or the unjust ... the end of those who praise and blame is the honourable and disgraceful. [...] [D]eliberation relies mostly on example, judicial rhetoric on the enthymeme, and epideixis on the more and the less. (I.9.1368a23–35) (Garver 1994, p. 54)

Deliberative rhetoric is the most central species of rhetoric, but there is a unity between the three because they are all necessary in the *polis*. Since both deliberative and judicial rhetoric have a constitutional role, let us look at how Aristotle describes the role of rhetoric in the polis.

First, we must acknowledge that Aristotle draws a sharp distinction between rhetoric on the one hand and ethics and politics on the other. For Aristotle, ethics and politics cannot be compared with such arts as for example rhetoric, because ethics and politics are based on habits and experience, whereas arts are productive activities and can be learned through instruction. Therefore, the virtue of *phronesis*, practical rationality or practical reason, which is such an important virtue for statesmen to acquire, is only loosely connected with rhetoric, which, in part, is an instrumental art. But the relation between *phronesis* and rhetoric is closer in the ideal state, so what are the characteristics of this Aristotelian ideal state?

In Book II of the *Politics*, Aristotle asks what citizens in the ideal state have in common. His answer to this question relates to the common use of private or public property. Aristotle emphasizes the role of property, partly because in *Republic* Plato claims that property must be common to ensure unity and ordered common life in his ideal state. Aristotle has no such demands, and it is an important aspect of his philosophy that he gives less weight to the technical arrangements in society than to the praxis of living well together. For Aristotle, perfection is not to be found in the *making* or in productive sciences (*techne*), but in the *doing* and in the political activity of practical wisdom (*phronesis*). What is important is that the use of what is produced at somebody's property is a task for the state. This implies that for Aristotle there is a distinction between possession and use which complies with the distinction between first and second *energeia*. (cf. Garver 2006, p. 232; 2011, p. 50)

For Garver, the argument concerning property points to a broader claim concerning education and rhetoric. He considers this quote from Aristotle: "It is the special business (*ergon idion*) of the legislator to create in men the disposition to use private property in common (1263a 39–40)." (Garver 2011, p. 53) To create a disposition in men involves civic education. Garver's claim is therefore that education is the means to unity and community in the ideal state, and the kind of education needed is characterised in the following way: "Education here must mean habituation toward the virtue of using property in common and for common purposes." (Garver 2011, p. 52) Through the laws in a society, the citizens are educated through habituation towards life in the ideal state. As citizens, they can contribute to making laws concerning the common use of available recourses through rhetorical practice. Therefore, Aristotle places deliberation at the centre of civic participation.

The Aristotelian approach to political practice, citizenship and constitution is, according to Garver, more challenging when it comes to values. He writes:

> Currently we assume a plurality of ways of living well, with the function of politics to coordinate these differences by a modus vivendi, overlapping consensus, neutral framework, or public reason. In the *Ethics* Aristotle presents a single good practical life, while the *Politics* offers a diversity of possible ways communities can organize themselves to live well. (Garver 2011, p. 66)

For Aristotle, the *Ethics* defines a common goal everybody can agree upon, whereas the *Politics* describes imperfect and ideal constitutions and ways of living together. By contrast, modern thinkers such as John Rawls write about "the fact of pluralism" in our societies, and question "justice as fairness prior to settling issues of the good life because a just society must admit plural and incompatible conceptions of good ways of living." (Garver 2011, p. 67) Aristotle, according to Garver, does exactly the opposite in Book IV of the *Politics*, assuming that we must know the nature of the best life before we can know what a good constitution is. (Garver 2011, p. 67) The challenge is, as Garver points out, that Book III does not fit in this pattern. In one way, ethics is prior to politics because the good life is led by individuals, but on the other hand, as in Book III, politics is prior to ethics because man is a political animal by nature. This duality implies that Aristotle can draw up a third possibility between liberalism and totalitarianism. Aristotle's answer limits the role of the ethics: "The common *function* of citizens [...] is preserving the constitution, not virtue, even though the *end* of the state is the good life rather than stability." (Garver 2011, p. 72) Since there is no cause that regulates the form of the constitution even though the end is defined, there is plenty of room for deliberation in the ideal state because the constitution develops through deliberation. Therefore, whereas the ethics defines the end of the polis, it is only through citizens' deliberation and law-making that the constitution finds its form. The normative in Aristotle is incomplete; deliberation and argument are therefore possible and necessary. Depending on the circumstances, the statesman gives weight to different considerations. By doing so, he shows character, ethos, and takes argument beyond logos and rationality into the ethical and concrete political situation. (Garver 2011, p. 105)

To summarize, we can say that Aristotle defines a civic art of rhetoric by limiting the agency of this rhetoric to activities aimed at preserving the constitution by deliberating over the use of common goods. Arguments concerning what to choose in practical situations of political relevance (e.g., how to use common resources) become central for these conceptualizations of rhetoric and citizenship. This Aristotelian view on rhetoric and citizenship presents us with an ideal where the rational dispositions in man fulfil a civic function. This civic or practical rationality, which demonstrates character, is the most important type of rationality, even though it is not the highest form. Our moral and rational virtues display themselves most completely when used to support a community in its decision-making.

The question is how these conceptualizations of rhetoric, virtue and society can deepen our understanding of modern texts. In the following sections I will offer a possible answer to this question, taking the above conceptualization of rhetorical citizenship as my point of departure. The type of text I would like to discuss is the annual curriculum or prospectus for kindergartens and crèches. Such an enterprise is relevant for several reasons. First, such documents are publicly available and therefore contribute to giving the public sphere its characteristics. Second, early childhood education and care (ECEC) is an important part of a country's educational system, and it is thus important to understand how linguistic and cultural diversity is negotiated and to what kind of citizenship children are habituated. Third, civic education is important for the functioning of our societies, and it is therefore important to take a closer look at how character and learning are constructed in these institutions. My aim is not to provide a fully-fledged document analysis, but rather to show some of the possibilities a reading based on the concept of rhetorical citizenship can have.

3. Method

There are no fixed methods for document analysis from the perspective of rhetorical citizenship, but based on the theory developed above, we can highlight some important questions. The first question is how the ECEC institution positions the use of common recourses. The second question deals with the three species in rhetoric: deliberative, judicial and epideictic rhetoric. I ask whether there are traces of the three types of rhetoric, which Aristotle singles out as the most important in a civic art of rhetoric. A follow-up question would be to ask whether there is any unity between the three species. By asking these three questions, I will be able to say something about the overall goals or ends (*telos*) in the described activities, and about the role of the document and its institution in society. The next analytical move will be to ask what kind of character constructions (*ethos*) we find in the document and in what ways that character is used to legitimate decisions. I will focus mainly on the character construction of the child and the character construction of the adult in the kindergarten. Finally, I would like to examine how the document demonstrates practical reason or judgement (*phronesis*). In line with this, I would like to ask whether knowledge is positioned as something which citizens can acquire simply by virtue of being citizens, or as specialist knowledge which needs to be taught. In this way, I will be able to discuss what kind of knowledge the concept of rhetorical citizenship calls for. In sum, these questions will help me to find out more about how the document positions the institution's role in the functioning of society, how rhetorical argumentation offers citizens different participation roles, and what functions practical reason and knowledge have in society.

To find a suitable example to analyze, a search based on the keywords "kindergarten" and "community" was conducted in Google. By searching for "community," I was hoping to single out documents in which this word was central. This was motivated by my interest in finding out how linguistic and cultural diversity is negotiated in a community with certain characteristics. Arguments concerning linguistic and cultural practice can be a first step towards deliberating over means to a common good, and a way for a kindergarten to position itself in the context of a wider community.

One of the top ten results from this internet search was a website that led to the prospectus for Sandgate Brighton Childcare and Kindergarten Association in Australia. (Sandgate Kindergarten: *Sandgate Kindergarten Prospectus 2015*) This is a programmatic document regulating the relationship between the kindergarten and the parents for a community-based, non-profit organization managing crèches (day-care centres for children from 0–3) and kindergartens (children aged 4–5) in Queensland, Australia. Australia is an interesting case, because the country's current Early Years Learning Framework emphasizes education for citizenship by referring to the Melbourne Declaration on Educational Goals for Young

Australians and the goal that all young Australians should become "successful learners, confident and creative individuals, and active and informed citizens." (MCEECDYA - Ministerial Council for Education, Early Childhood Development and Youth Affairs 2008. Melbourne Declaration on Educational Goals for Young Australians. p. 8–9) In the case of the Sandgate Association, the prospectus defines the institution's overall goals and states its regulations, whereas the national Early Years Learning Framework and the C&K Building Waterfalls curriculum framework define the learning activities in more detail.

4. Analysis

4.1 The kindergarten's use of common resources and its role in society

The Aristotelian reflections concerning property outlined above may seem distant to the world of kindergartens, but in this prospectus we find several passages which can be related to the question of how common recourses are used. After the first page and table of contents, the document contains a statement positioning the kindergarten as located on aboriginal land:

> We acknowledge the traditional custodians of this land and offer our respects to the Aboriginal elders both past and present. We remember that our kindergarten is built on traditional Aboriginal land (Turrbul People) and support, acknowledge, recognise and respect Aboriginal and Torres Strait people, heritage and culture (from *Acknowledgment of Country*).

We find other references to aboriginal land and culture in the sections entitled "Mission Statement" and "Our Philosophy." In the latter section, the kindergarten explicitly states its intentions to integrate aboriginal perspectives into the kindergarten's teaching practices. However, these references are not elaborated elsewhere in the document. Nonetheless, these formulations show how the kindergarten wants to pay its respects to the original inhabitants of the land and to the traditions in which it is situated. If we look at other pages on the kindergarten's website, we learn that they take part in a local annual festival called the Einbunpin Festival that celebrates aboriginal myths and legends.[1] This shows that the kindergarten wants to take an active part in society and to steer its community in a certain direction. In other words, the kindergarten not only orients itself towards a present or future society, but acknowledges the traditions it is a part of, and the diversity that is an inseparable part of the history of the land. Thus, diversity emerging

---

1 Cf. www.einbunpinfestival.org.au.

from history becomes an integrated part of the rhetorical citizenship which the kindergarten wants to create.

The kindergarten's respect for the land and history is partly connected to the broader theme of the Early Years Learning Framework for Australia, which is organised around the elements of "Belonging, Being and Becoming." (Australian Government Department of Education, Employment and Workplace Relations 2009) In line with this framework, *becoming* is in the prospectus partly based on *belonging* to a common set of recourses, on the use of these recourses with respect, and on a sustainable lifestyle. Thus, the programmatic statements in the document position the kindergarten and its practices as an integral part of a wider society, a society with a long history and with a future that should be based on this history.

The second question I ask in this section in order to find out how rhetorical citizenship is constructed in the text concerns the rhetorical species. I ask if we find deliberation, judgement and praise in this text.

The prospectus seems to be characterised by two different lines of discourse. The introduction outlines the overall ends or goods concerning the activities of the kindergarten as follows:

> Our program is based on play as we believe it is an essential part of the lives of young children and how they learn about themselves, others and the world around them. [...] They [the curriculums] invite children and adults to take part in a journey that requires a commitment to potentials, possibilities, aspirations and inspirations.

The prospectus contains many statements concerning ends – what the kindergarten wants to achieve. But as we know, only epideictic rhetoric concerns ends (when praising or blaming), and, according to Aristotle, we deliberate about means to an end. (Garver 1994, pp. 65, 69) In our document, the means to the formulated ends are not explicitly discussed. Instead, we find many statements concerning regulations in the kindergarten:

> On arrival, please sign your child in at the sign in table with the correct time ensuring your fill in the drop off time and sunscreen application time. If at this time, you are aware of any variances to pick up time, please write this in on the sheet and notify the teacher. After signing your child in, please encourage your child to unpack their bag putting their snack, morning tea and lunch in the appropriate baskets and esky. Their drink bottles are to go on the trolley, sheets in the sheet bag and shoes removed and placed on the shoe rack. Once all the jobs have been completed, your child must wash their hands in the bathroom before reading a book on the mat (from *Attendance*).

The contrast between play and inspiration for children on the one hand and detailed instructions and requirements for parents on the other in these two excerpts is striking, which illustrates the different expectations to institutional participation placed on children and parents respectively. Learning, play and civic participation seem therefore to be understood in individualistic terms. The second excerpt indicates that in ECEC practices the need to regulate behaviour and to facilitate an organized environment in which learning and play can take place is dominant. Such an environment allows less scope for discussions about right and wrong or discussions about how the ECEC institutions are supposed to achieve their ends.

When we consider all these three excerpts together, we can say that the moral, civil and collective lines of discourse exist side-by-side with a line of discourse concerning individual actions, regulations for behaviour and individual self-realization. When the document refers to a wider society, this is a part of deliberation, but one that is done through epideictic rhetoric. Although this document serves as a kind of constitution for the kindergarten, it makes only rudimentary references to deliberative and forensic reflections about the role the kindergarten can play in society. It is therefore difficult to speak about any unity between the rhetorical species here. This of course does not preclude the existence of such a unity in the actual practices experienced by the children and their parents. All the same, the epideictic rhetoric seems to be the dominant one.

4.2 Argumentation through character construction

I this section I pay special attention to how children are constructed as textual characters and how this character construction is an integral part of the kindergarten's ethos and, thus, rhetorical citizenship.

The kindergarten's prospectus contains formulations concerning children and character construction. In the section entitled "Our Curriculum," the kindergarten claims it wants to nurture "in children, strong qualities of character." What this implies is not discussed in more detail, but in one of the very first sections in the document we find some claims concerning character, experience and the wider community:

> Our philosophy and mission statement encompasses our staff's beliefs in relation to children, their families and our wider community being on a holistic journey together, as young children's experiences have a profound effect on their future. (from *Welcome to our Centre*)

This paragraph, concerning the effects that experiences in the kindergarten can have on children, is more oriented towards the future than the section entitled "Acknowledgment of Country." The kindergarten claims to promote a holistic approach towards change in children, and uses the metaphor of a journey to describe these changes or movements. As we shall see in the next section, this metaphor is also used to describe learning. In this context however, the metaphor of a journey implies that the character construction is not so much a matter of model learning or a result of theoretical insight, but rather something that emerges from experiences and rich impressions from the surroundings. In the document, the kindergarten is positioned as an institution capable of providing such a rich environment. On the other hand, the character construction of other persons relevant to the children is not thematized. This leads us to the conclusion that children are the ones who are positioned as characters undergoing changes. Furthermore, these changes are linked to the learning processes the children undergo, and the kindergarten wants to enhance their appreciation of such changes:

> Our mission is to promote in young children a love of learning in a safe, caring and challenging environment. We believe this enables optimal development and learning, encouraging children to make decisions, take responsibility for their own behaviour and to share and actively participate in their own learning. (from *Mission Statement*)

By developing a love of learning in a challenging environment, the children can optimize their development. The love for learning is thus a valuable state of mind because it has positive effects. However, in this document the journey is positioned as a life-long activity: "Life is one long journey and we cannot wait to share this part of it with you." (final sentence in document) One consequence of describing learning in this way is that the children will go through changes throughout their lives, and that this process is therefore more a state than a defined process. An important characteristic is that this life-long journey is only related to the children. The kindergarten teachers are, on the other hand, more stable characters providing the needed context and experiences for learning. Analyzing the document, we also see that the changes the children undergo are all described as positive. Aristotle writes about communities in line with Plato as a community of pleasure and pain. (Garver 1994, p. 132) The studied document seems only to describe the pleasurable aspects of this community.

Nevertheless, other parts of the document contain paragraphs where the children are not only receivers of knowledge, but where they more actively take part in knowledge construction:

> We believe children are active participants in building knowledge together by engaging, connecting and collaborating in the learning process with others by being a co-participant, co-learner and co-creator. Children will be supported to investigate, engage and reflect on their own ideas, experiences and decisions through informal, individual and group exchanges. (*Our Philosophy*)

This view of children as co-constructors of knowledge in interactions is followed in the paragraph concerning the yarning circle. The yarning circle is an opportunity for the children to bring an object to the kindergarten and to tell others about it. In the document, the activity is described as "an opportunity for all children to have their voice heard during the day." (*Yarning Circle*)

Based on these extracts, the document can be said to position the kindergarten as an institution offering children many possibilities for positive change which the children can love and actively participate in, both as individuals and as members of their group. The teachers in the kindergarten should travel with the children on this journey, but are not described in the same way as characters undergoing much change. Only their professional practices are supposed to change. (cf. section *Professional Development*) This implies that the values employed in decisions on this journey are fixed when it comes to teachers and transient when it comes to children. The rhetorical citizenship following this ethos construction can thus be described as hierarchical, with professional teachers as figures with stable characters in a transient world.

There are other conflicting discourses when it comes to character construction. When we analyze how children's language is represented in the document, we see that it only happens through pictures of children in activity, of what children have made or of objects which they are likely to play with. These pictures are not commented on or thematized in the text. This creates some interesting contrasts between the colourful pictures of play-based themes and the sometimes highly instructive text.[2] The text and the images constitute two different discourses that characterize the practices of the kindergarten: on the one hand, practicalities and regulations, and on the other hand, creativity and openness. This implies that the rhetorical citizenship the kindergarten offers is characterized by sometimes opposing and conflicting modes of being together. An important element of the journey the characters undergo seems to be compliance with the rules regulating the practices. Only in this way can creativity and participation in community flourish.

4.3 Practical reason vs. specialized knowledge

The document contains several references to learning. The word "learning" is mentioned 22 times in the document as a whole. In the section entitled "Educational Curriculum," learning is linked to play:

> Your child's curiosity, enthusiasm and love of learning will continually be encouraged by staff. As teachers and children engage in inquiry together, children are learning to observe, ask questions, reflect on their actions, and engage in meaningful and self-directed activity. To make sure we nurture and develop our future generations of thinkers, play is

---

2   See e.g. pictures above the section concerning fees.

an essential component of a quality early childhood educational experience. (*Educational Curriculum*)

This focus on learning through play may imply that what is supposed to be learned is learned through habituation rather than through instruction. This relates to the concept of practical reasoning, which develops through experience rather than instruction. The playful activities that enhance learning are characterized as "self-directed activity." There is no reference to how the children learn through adapting to others, negotiating their worldviews or resolving conflicts in groups. The playful learning described here is therefore something different from practical reasoning. The concept of practical reasoning as developed by Aristotle enables us to place more emphasis on the knowledge and experience which we need in order to decide what to choose in some practical situations of choice.

The metaphor of learning as a journey is also relevant for how knowledge is conceptualized in this document. The journey the children are to undergo seems largely to be an individual one. The kindergarten claims to have a commitment to: "[…] the possibilities, aspirations and dreams for each child's learning journey." (*Our Philosophy*) What counts as learning is not described in detail, since it is described in the kindergarten's curriculum. However, the document mentions some concrete skills connected with mathematics and language: "Through interactions and every day experiences children develop and foster an understanding of numeracy, literacy and language which is displayed when children play." (*Our Philosophy*) So, while the learning journey is an individual journey with many possibilities, there are also some concrete outcomes expected from this journey. These outcomes are functional skills needed for participation in society, and not intellectual or moral virtues guiding such participation. The knowledge which this document explicitly mentions therefore has more instrumental characteristics. This may be because the intellectual virtue of *phronesis* is harder to make explicit than skills that develop from instructional learning and which can more easily be measured. In a similar vein, the knowledge developed in collective processes, which is also important for civic participation, is not discussed explicitly.

5. Discussion

By analyzing the kindergarten's role in the community, the arguments derived from character construction, and the role of practical reason, different and partly conflicting discourses have been identified. Both individual and community perspectives are present in the document, illustrating the broad mandate kindergartens can have in a society. My reading has shown that collective learning processes are less emphasised than individual ones, and that communities are not negotiated through deliberation. Conflicting views in situations of choice call for deliberation, and children can be guided through such processes. I would claim that reflecting on such practices in public documents presenting kindergartens may be beneficial, since it provides parents with a better picture of the actual practices in the kindergarten and a better understanding of how the educational and civic goals are realized. This may in turn strengthen parental participation in the kindergarten's effort to enhance learning, play and community together with the children.

My intention in this article has not been to undertake a complete reading of this complex document or a complete presentation of the Aristotelian conceptualization of rhetoric and citizenship. Instead it has been to illustrate what aspects of a document such a reading can illuminate. I would claim that rhetorical citizenship is a fruitful analytical tool when it comes to analyzing how an institution presents itself publicly, and that Aristotelian perspectives are well suited when we want to find out what argumentative implications certain formulations can have within a civic art of rhetoric. Such a reading can show us how the rhetorical use of language has ethical and political implications without being political or persuasive. When it comes to educational institutions, and given their goals for educating future citizens, the concept of rhetorical citizenship is relevant because it calls for a focus on how to involve children in decision-making concerning common resources in society through practical reason and credible arguments.

This reading has revealed different ways in which learning – and thus knowledge – are conceptualized. In the studied document, the many references to the wider community and the overall goals for the kindergarten are not concretized into deliberations concerning learning and knowledge. This may be due to fact that such an enterprise demands more space than it is possible to offer, and is therefore more salient in other documents. Nevertheless, it would be interesting to see some attempts in this direction. Such efforts could include considerations of how character can be constructed, how the general goals guiding the institution are applied in concrete situations of choice, and how diversity in the past and present can be negotiated within a common framework. Deliberation is characterized by the use of examples and practical arguments, and the civic art of rhetoric unfolds itself in the tension between what is unconditionally good (*haplōs*) and what is good under certain circumstances (*tinî*). (Garver 1994, p. 58) This means that descriptions of the particularities of life in a kindergarten would make it easier to materialize the concept of rhetorical citizenship in an ECEC context. This would also imply the need for giving more weight to deliberation than to epidictic discourse and, thus, more weight to discussions involving credible arguments built on character in concrete situations of choice.

6. Conclusion

Aristotle himself did not look upon children as citizens with *phronesis*. According to Aristotle, this intellectual virtue is acquired through the experience of being ruled. Today, it is legitimate to broaden the concept of the citizen but still adhere to the Aristotelian view that citizenship is an activity and not primarily a right or a state of being. Let us remember what Aristotle says: "What counts as living together [...] is sharing conversation and thought [...] and not pasturing in the same place as in the case of grazing animals (NE IX.9.1170b12–13)." (Garver 2011, p. 42) It is this sharing of conversations, thoughts and arguments that constitutes rhetorical citizenship and gives it its characteristics. We would therefore gain a better understanding of rhetorical citizenship in an ECEC context if we studied the actual interactions and not only the formulations in a prospectus. On the other hand, it is also possible to integrate children's language and thoughts to a greater extent in documents like this. This could strengthen the citizenship aspects of the kindergarten, since such public documents provide an opportunity for the kindergarten to present itself within the wider community. I would therefore claim that introducing the concept of rhetorical citizenship in this institutional context could help kindergartens to better show how they participate in society and contribute towards forming connections between language, morals and intellectual virtues in citizens.

References

Australian Government Department of Education, Employment and Workplace Relations: *Belonging, Being and Becoming: the Early Years Learning Framework for Australia*. Commonwealth of Australia: Canberra; retrieved from http://www.deewr.gov.au/Earlychildhood/Policy_Agenda/Quality/Documents/Final%20EYLF%20F ramework%20Report%20-%20WEB.pdf 2009.

Garver, Eugene: *Aristotle's Politics: Living Well and Living Together*. University of Chicago Press: Chicago 2011.

Garver, Eugene: *Confronting Aristotle's Ethics: Ancient and Modern Morality*. University of Chicago Press: Chicago 2006.

Garver, Eugene: *Aristotle's Rhetoric: An Art of Character*. University of Chicago Press: Chicago 1994.

Kock, Christian/ Villadsen, Lisa S.: *Rhetorical Citizenship and Public Deliberation*. Pennsylvania State University Press: University Park, PA 2012.

MCEECDYA (Ministerial Council for Education, Early Childhood Development and Youth Affairs) 2008. *Melbourne Declaration on Educational Goals for Young*

Australians. Retrieved from http://www.curriculum.edu.au/verve/_resources/National_Declaration_on_the_Educational_Goals_for_Young_Australians.pdf.

Sandgate Kindergarten: *Sandgate Kindergarten Prospectus 2015*, retrieved 6.5.2015 from http://sandgatekids.com.au/wp-content/uploads/2014/07/Kindy-Prospectus-20151.pdf.

Anne E. Porter

Providence College

'Responsibilizing' the youth: The rhetoric of civic participation in the World Bank's 2009 climate change essay competition

1. Introduction

Rhetorical analysis concerns itself with the investigation of communicative practices that are essential to deliberative democracy and "rhetorical citizenship." (Kock, Christian/ Villadsen, Lisa: "Introduction, Citizenship as a Rhetorical Practice". In: Kock, Christian/ Villadsen, Lisa (eds.). *Rhetorical Citizenship and Public Deliberation*. Pennsylvania State University Press: University Park, PA 2012, p. 1) In contemporary society, complicated issues like climate change require the involvement of multiple stakeholders. Because of the international, as well as intergenerational, dimensions of climate change, the views of global youth are especially vital in discussions of this issue – and, in recent years, major transnational actors have conducted various kinds of knowledge-making activities to promote and/or frame environmental awareness among global youth. Among these activities, essay contests often figure prominently under the broader umbrella of youth participation or civic engagement, but the rhetorical mechanisms of such contests have rarely been scrutinized. In this chapter, I examine the ways in which the rhetoric of youth civic engagement operated in the World Bank's 2009 youth climate change essay competition. Using the tools of rhetorical analysis, I examine documents published by the World Bank during its "Knowledge for Development era," (Enns, Charis: "Knowledges in Competition, Knowledge Discourse at the World Bank during the Knowledge for Development Era". *Global Social Policy* 15 (1), 2015, p. 61) as well as the prompt and one of the top essays in the 2009 contest, to show how these everyday knowledge-making activities may have conflated a message of youth civic participation with a message of "responsibilization" (Rose, Nikolas: *Powers of Freedom, Reframing Political Thought*. Cambridge University Press: Cambridge 1999, p. 174) in relation to climate change. Moreover, I suggest some broader implications of this observation about the uses of "civic participation" for rhetorical critics of neoliberal globalization.

2. Rhetorical citizenship

Rhetorical critics who concern themselves with questions of deliberative democracy consider questions of civic discourse. They attend to questions not only having to do with public affairs and policy making, but also the ways in which community participation, "rhetorical citizenship," and civic virtue, are defined. Our attention, as rhetorical critics, to questions of a civic nature can be traced to Aristotle, who believed, as Michael Sandel puts it, that "only by…participating in politics do we fully realize our nature as human beings." (Sandel, Michael: *Justice, What's the Right Thing to Do?* Farrar, Strauss and Giroux: New York 2010, p. 195) Active participation and deliberation about matters of the common good are part of our human nature, from an Aristotelian perspective.

Contemporary rhetorical criticism takes this Aristotelian insight seriously by focusing not only on the speeches of major historical figures, formal policy debates, and the contributions of individuals believed to represent model citizenship, but also on the everyday practices of people who engage in a range of often overlooked, rhetorically agentive activities. As Asen suggests, a "discourse theory of citizenship" regards multiple modes of engagement as "enactments of citizenship." (Asen, Robert: "A Discourse Theory of Citizenship". *Quarterly Journal of Speech* 90 (2), 2004, p. 207) Such a view of citizenship requires that we acknowledge as civic discourse the quotidian activities undertaken by groups and individuals not accorded the legal status of citizen as well as those who influence decision-making through unconventional means. This kind of everyday civic engagement can be seen, for example, in the use of bumper stickers to convey a message, such as the one that circulated in the city of Austin, TX as a reminder to "Keep Austin Weird," (Edbauer, Jenny: "Unframing Models of Public Distribution: From Rhetorical Situation to Rhetorical Ecologies." *Rhetoric Society Quarterly* 35 (4), 2005, pp. 5–24) or the graffiti that appeared in downtown Phoenix, AZ after the passage of anti-immigrant legislation in the state Senate in 2010. (Oliver, Veronica: "Civic Disobedience: Anti-SB 1070 Graffiti, Marginalized Voices, and Citizenship in a Politically Privatized Public Sphere". *Community Literacy Journal* 9 (1), 2014, pp. 62–76) Attention to such everyday enactments invites rhetorical critics to think more broadly about the kinds of practices, performances, and processes that participatory engagement might entail, even as it tends to stimulate questions about differential access to participatory processes.

Questions about access and agency are raised by the editors of the 2012 collection titled *Rhetorical Citizenship and Public Deliberation*, Christian Kock and Lisa S. Villadsen, who invite rhetorical scholars to broaden our thinking about participatory engagement. They, like Asen, suggest that "to become an active agent in …democracy, the citizen must be a deliberative rhetor," (Kock/ Villadsen 2012, p. 5) but they additionally raise the following questions: "[W]hat forms of participation does a particular discursive phenomenon encourage – and by whom? How are speaking positions allotted and organized? What discursive norms inform a particular forum?" (Kock/ Villadsen 2012, p. 7) Such questions reflect the concerns of rhetorical scholars who consider the degree to which those who are party to any type of civic discourse are at liberty to engage. They encourage us to consider the mechanisms by which civic actors' "rhetorical agency" (Campbell, Karlyn Kohrs: "Agency, Promiscuous and Protean". *Communication and Critical/ Cultural Studies* 2 (1), 2005, pp. 1–19; Geisler, Cheryl: "How Ought we to Understand the Concept of Rhetorical Agency?" *Rhetoric Society Quarterly* 34 (3), 2004, pp. 9–17; Miller, Carolyn R.: "What Can Automation Tell Us about Agency?" *Rhetoric Society Quarterly* 37 (2), 2007, pp. 137–57) is enabled and constrained. This concept of "rhetorical agency," which has been defined by Campbell as the "competence to speak or write in a way that will be recognized or heeded by others," (Campbell 2005, p. 3) has become a central concern of rhetorical scholars in recent years, and it is one of the central preoccupations of rhetorical scholars who analyze everyday civic discourses involving disenfranchised and/or marginalized populations. In this chapter, I consider how the discourse of youth civic participation was deployed in an essay contest sponsored by a major international agency and probe some of the implications of that discourse in relation to questions of "rhetorical agency" in the neoliberal age. That is, I consider the "discursive norms" that governed this quotidian discourse practice as a forum for youth civic participation in 2009.

3. Youth civic participation

Initiatives involving youth frequently claim to promote their civic empowerment, proclaiming that they allow the voices of young people to be heard. According to Mitra, Serriere and Kirshner (Mitra, Dana/ Serriere, Stephanie/ Kirshner, Ben: "Youth Participation in U.S. Contexts, Student Voice without a National Mandate". *Children and Society* 28, 2014, pp. 292–304), most European countries have taken active measures to increase youth participation, encouraged to do so by their ratification of the 1989 United Nations Convention on the Rights of the Child. These measures, which Mitra, Serriere and Kirshner say occasionally may be merely "tokenistic or symbolic," (2014, p. 293) are nonetheless often taken at the national level – an approach, incidentally, that stands in marked contrast to the less systematic manner of approaching youth initiatives in the U.S. (which, along with Somalia, has not yet ratified the UN agreement). For example, the

European Commission (EU) has developed an "EU Youth Strategy" to direct funding towards initiatives that target education, job training and employment, as well as youth participation, health, social inclusion, volunteerism and cultural programming. (*EU Youth Report 2012*) According to a report published by the EU in 2012, these have included initiatives to promote "entrepreneurship in sustainable development" (*EU Youth Report 2012*, p. 51) and activities that are "youth-led." (*EU Youth Report 2012*, p. 50) This coordinated effort at the level of policy has encouraged specific countries to adopt national policies for youth engagement.

Moreover, in recent years, the European concern with youth participation at the level of national policy has influenced global discourses. This influence can be seen, for example, in recent publications and policy initiatives set forth by major transnational agencies like the World Bank. According to Sukarieh and Tannock (Sukarieh, Mayssoun/ Tannock, Stuart: "In the Best Interests of Youth or Neoliberalism? The World Bank and the New Global Youth Empowerment Project". *Journal of Youth Studies* 11 (3), 2008, pp. 301–312), youth empowerment discourse was clearly visible in key organizational documents such as the *Bank's World Development Report* in 2007, but, according to these researchers, the youth empowerment discourse in that document could more aptly be described as advancing other interests. These researchers claim that the Bank's 2007 development report, in fact, tended to frame the interests of the world's youth and the business sector as "one and the same." (Sukarieh/ Tannock 2008, p. 301) Their analysis suggests that the potential tendency for sponsoring agencies to prematurely determine the nature of youth involvement and/or to equate the goals of the sponsoring agency with the goals of youth suggests the need for ongoing analysis of the ways in which the rhetoric of youth civic participation is deployed.

Researchers who have studied successful youth empowerment initiatives emphasize that young people's involvement with the sponsoring organization or group must be authentic. Efforts that purport to engage youth but that then fail to follow through on those claims run the risk of alienating youth instead of engaging them more fully in societal activities. (Bessant, Judith: "Mixed Messages, Youth Participation and Democratic Practice". *Australian Journal of Political Science* 39 (2), 2004, pp. 387–404) According to researchers, genuine youth involvement necessarily implies fostering their critical capacity, (Jennings, Louise B. et al: "Toward a Critical Social Theory of Youth Empowerment". *Journal of Community Practice* 14 (1–2), 2006, pp. 31–55) and young people involved in participatory efforts must be allowed to set the agenda, and not merely to respond. (Bessant 2004) Researchers who study successful youth initiatives have determined that youth must be treated as active and critical – rather than passive and unwitting – participants in the projects they undertake. Jennings et al. (2006) list the following attributes of successful programs: (1) a welcoming, safe environment, (2) meaningful participation and engagement, (3) equitable power sharing between youth and adults, (4) engagement in critical reflection on interpersonal and sociopolitical processes, (5) participation in sociopolitical processes to affect change, and (6) integrated individual- and community-level empowerment." (Jennings et al. 2006, p. 32) Unfortunately, efforts to encourage youth engagement often fall short of fulfilling criteria like these.

Bessant (2004) lists several reasons for these shortcomings, which she finds to be endemic among efforts to promote youth engagement, generally. These include inattention to the significant obstacles that young people face; a "failure to think through what democratic practice requires," (Bessant 2004, p. 387) and a tendency for sponsoring agents to usurp participatory processes. This tendency on the part of sponsoring organizations to undermine youth participation by usurping the process need not be conscious to be problematic. In this chapter, I analyze the ways in which the rhetoric of youth civic participation was deployed in the World Bank's 2009 Youth Essay Competition, an international contest that invited submissions on the topic of climate change – and assert that this contest may have undermined its stated goal of youth engagement by encouraging not the authentic participation of youth but rather their "responsibilization." (Rose 1999, p. 174)

3.1 "Responsibilization"

According to Rose, "responsibilization" occurs when agencies of government redirect responsibility for solving problems away from the state and from public institutions towards private organizations and/or individuals. Rose suggests that such a move could be seen in the policies of former British Prime Minister Margaret Thatcher, who, in 1979, proclaimed that, "the first principle of this government…is to revive a sense of individual responsibility." (cited in Rose, p. 139) Individual (or personal) responsibility has since become a rallying cry for various administrations committed to a neoliberal ideology. It is often championed by economists, politicians, and governmental actors who promote policies of market deregulation and privatization. But, according to Rose, "responsibilization" actually constitutes a disavowal of responsibility by state (and other governmental) actors, whose moves to diminish the social safety net merely shift those responsibilities to others. To be "responsibilized" in this way is, on the one hand, to be deemed responsible – which, for some might seem like receiving recognition for a job well done or a vote of confidence – but, at the same time, to be the object of this verb also calls to mind other less favorable ways of being hailed. Other verbs that end in "ize," just as the nominalized form of "to responsiblize" does, include "individualize" (to separate from community or familial structures) – for example – or to traumatize or globalize. Verbs like these connote the stunning impact that policies based on neoliberal "responsibilization" may imply.

Thus the usefulness of Rose's term is that it manages to relay the emphasis on "individual responsibility" while at the same time subtly communicating the undercurrent of detachment and violence that the action potentially describes. Rose additionally suggests that "responsibilization" discourse and policies are characteristic of political systems that he terms "advanced liberal," (Rose 1999, p. 137) and others would call "neoliberal" or "new capitalist". (Fairclough, Norman: *Analyzing Discourse: Textual Analysis for Social Research*. Routledge: New York 2003, p. 174) In the following section, I use the tools of rhetorical analysis to examine the ways in which "responsibilization" was conflated with calls for civic participation by a major "new capitalist" player in the field of international development. In doing so, I focus on how these contradictory discourses played themselves out over the question of climate change during a period when neoliberal economics prevailed at the Bank.

4. The World Bank and the knowledge society

The World Bank is a multilateral development organization that was created after World War II to lend financial assistance to governments in poor countries. In many ways, it seems an unlikely sponsor for an essay contest, but – during what Enns has called the "Knowledge for Development era" (2015, p. 61) – the Bank embarked on an ambitious project to make the distribution of knowledge "products" (Kramarz, Teresa/ Momani, Bessma: "The World Bank as a Knowledge Bank, Acknowledging the Limits of a Legitimate Knowledge Actor". *Review of Policy Research* 30 (4), 2013, pp. 409–431) even more central to its mission. This heightened emphasis on spreading ideas signaled a shift that aided the Bank over the last two decades in disseminating its economistic worldview to the farthest reaches of the globe. Under the leadership of Wolfensohn from 1995–2005, and then again under Zoellick from 2007–2011, 20–30% of the Bank's budget (Enns 2015) was targeted towards knowledge-making efforts that would advance a distinctly neoliberal take on development. At the same time, according to Jones, (Jones, Phillip W.: "The World Bank and the Literacy Question, Orthodoxy, Heresy, and Ideology". *International Review of Education* 43 (3), 2005, pp. 367–75) the Bank was becoming a major investor in global education, surpassing other international agencies that specialize in matters of education and human development, including the United Nations Educational, Scientific and Cultural Organization (UNESCO), the United Nations Children's Fund (UNICEF), and the United Nations Development

Program (UNDP). The World Bank's involvement in sponsoring an annual, online essay contest can therefore be seen in light of its advancing role in the "Knowledge Economy" (The World Bank: "Education") and in the context of the dominant neoliberal priorities set by the Bank at the time.

To support the Bank's burgeoning "knowledge" infrastructure, a range of digital and print technologies were brought to bear. These included hundreds of publications per year, such as the Bank's annual development report, a sizeable volume resembling a textbook that is made available to readers in poor countries, often at low or no cost. According to Goldman, (Goldman, Michael: *Imperial Nature, the World Bank and Struggles for Social Justice in the Age of Globalization*. Yale University Press: New Haven, CT 2005) many of the Bank's publications, including its development report, are "cited considerably more often than the average economics or business journal article in the Social Science Citation Index," (Goldman 2005, p. 102) even though they are rarely peer-reviewed – and today, web seminars, sponsored blogs, library e-portals, and online learning modules have been added to the mix. But, in 2009, the Bank was still experimenting with the affordances of digital technologies and the Internet, and a range of hybrid technologies that mixed traditional and online modes of publication were being utilized. In 2009, one of the early technologies for the Bank's global knowledge-making enterprise was the Bank's annual online youth essay contest. Like its print forebears, this contest engaged its participants in a writing task largely framed by the sponsoring organization. But, unlike earlier, exclusively print-based essay contests, the online version proved a particularly efficient mechanism for spreading ideas, especially among young people in the global south.

The analysis that follows investigates the use of the online essay contest as a quotidian discourse practice in the neoliberal age – an age in which the affordances of the Internet serve a wide array of interests but do not always call attention to their ideological leanings. In this case, I suggest that the discourse of civic participation in the World Bank's 2009 youth essay contest, in effect, drew attention away from an ideological move towards "responsibilization," and, in so doing, implicitly appointed young people, especially those in poor countries, the responsible party for solving a problem that the rest of the world had deemed unsolvable and largely chosen to ignore.

4.1 The World Bank's 2009 youth essay competition

In 2009, the World Bank invited essay submissions on the topic of "The Next Generation of Green Entrepreneurs" for its annual, online youth essay competition. The topic reflected the emphasis that the Bank was placing at the time on environmental issues, following the publication of the *Stern Review* in 2006, which sparked the attention of economists by urging attention to the economic effects of climate change. Young people from all over the world, ages 18–25, were invited to submit essays over the web in English, French, or Spanish in response to the following questions: "How does climate change affect you?" and "How can you tackle climate change through youth-led solutions?" These two questions invited essayists to document the impacts of climate change in their communities and to offer an original proposal for addressing the problem. All of the winning and finalist essays documented the effects of climate change in the essayists' home communities and offered solutions ranging from "green" schools to bio-intensive farming to "green" investment portfolios. Additionally, thousands of other college-age participants who did not win but submitted essays also were invited to engage the problematic posed by the prompt. According to a report prepared by a Consultant for External Affairs at the Bank, there were 57, 000 unique monthly visitors to the contest website leading up to the contest deadline. Blogs with names like "Young Global Pinoys" even made a point of advertising its occurrence, a fact which suggests that the contest enjoyed some degree of digital circulation initiated by the youth. Figure 13.1. shows an announcement for the World Bank's 2009 International Essay Competition.

Figure 13.1: World Bank International Essay Competition 2009 www.essaycompetition.org

The contest appeared to have a global youth following. According to Kuznicka's report, nearly 2,500 young people from over 150 countries participated in the 2009 contest, and 95% of these hailed from so-called "developing countries." (Kuznicka, Anna: *Report on the 2009 International Essay Competition*. World Bank: London Office 2009, p. 4) The top winners were awarded $3,000 for first place, $2,000 for second and $1,000 for third. They, along with five other finalists, hailed from Australia, Mexico, Ghana, Cameroon, the Philippines, India, and Indonesia. Moreover, it is clear that the appeal to youth was an intentional feature of this Bank-sponsored literacy initiative. Not only was the contest targeted at 18–25 year-old writers, but organizational partners who were involved in youth leadership initiatives were recruited to do the judging. According to Kuznicka's report, the panel of judges was comprised of one representative of the World Bank, another from the National Autonomous University in Mexico, and six representatives of international non-governmental organizations (NGO's) focused on youth leadership and development.

The stated goal of the series of annual competitions, which ran from 2004–2011 (and of which this contest was an installment), was to engage young people in problem-solving about large scale issues related to poverty reduction. According to materials available on the World Bank website, the annual contest was intended "to provide an opportunity for youth around the world to share their ideas on critical development issues." ("The World Bank") Topics from past years had dealt with an array of development-related themes, such as "Building a Secure Future," fighting corruption, "shaping the city of [their] dreams," and addressing youth migration. All of these were issues that the Bank and its co-sponsoring organizations had decided to highlight in any given year, and the contest became a forum for engaging youth in these matters of national and international interest.

The language of civic engagement and of youth participation was integral to these contests and frequently employed in contest materials to describe the competition's raison d'etre. The report on the 2009 contest emphasizes, for example, that the youth perspective is crucial in international affairs, given the fact that "the majority of the developing world's poor are children and youth....Youths are key agents of change, but too often the nature and impact of their projects are not recognized or documented sufficiently." (Kuznicka 2009, p. 3) The report employs the rhetoric of civic participation to demonstrate that the coordinators of the contest recognize that "youth face difficulties being heard and engaging more directly in civic life" (Kuznicka 2003, p. 3) and insists that the contest represents one of the means by which young people might increase their involvement. But even though the language of the report suggests that the aims of the contest were primarily civic in nature and oriented to securing the participation of youth, a critical reading of the contest prompt, as well as testimony from one of the top essays, suggests that the contest potentially masked a discursive move towards neoliberal "responsibilization" – that is, a shifting of responsibility for climate solutions away from the state onto other (more vulnerable) actors.

4.2 Analyzing "responsibilization" as a discourse strategy

An implicit move towards "responsibilization" was contained in an expanded version of the essay prompt that essayists could access on the website. This version of the prompt ends with the question: "How can youth contribute?" This open-ended question seems admirably to position the 18–25 year-old respondent as a young person with ideas to share. At the same time, however, it may also have had the (perhaps unintended) effect of blaming the victim. That is to say, it seems to charge young people (in poor countries) with the task of accepting responsibility for the complex problem of climate change. This interpretation is consistent with the language used by one of the finalists, Jean-Paul Affana, from Cameroon, to describe his experience. Affana, in his essay, reports on the spike in climate-related deaths caused by water-borne illnesses linked to torrential rains and landslides in his home community. In a section titled, "How Can I Contribute To Controlling Climate Change in My City?", the writer adopts a confessional tone in blaming himself for contributing to climate change, explaining the harmful health and the environmental effects of "zoa-zoa fuel, a mixture of gas and oil" (cited in Kuznicka 2009, p. 57) that is purchased inexpensively on the black market. This writer describes the strong sense of guilt that he carries about having engaged in this practice. As a taxi driver who has resorted to the use of this fuel, he tells of how he first "came upon the map of global warming on the Internet....The accompanying testimony sent shivers up my spine. I realized the extent to which I am utterly vulnerable to climate *change and the extent to which I bear responsibility for it....* Since that time, I promised myself that if I could *acknowledge my culpability*, then I could also reverse the trend." (cited in Kuznicka 2009, p. 58, emphasis mine) The striking sense of responsibility – even "culpability"– that this writer expresses may have been exacerbated by the use of the second person address in question number two of the prompt, *"How can you tackle climate change through youth-led solutions?"* This essayist's words suggest that he may have perceived the second person address in this question as implying responsibility or blame.

The potential for young people from the poorest countries to accept this ascription of blame is especially troubling from the perspective of the climate justice movement, which calls attention to the fact that the countries that have contributed least to climate change are those most affected by it and that rich countries should bear the greatest responsibility for climate action. Indigenous and marginalized groups – and, more recently, Pope Francis, the head of the Catholic Church (Pope Francis: *Laudato Si', On Care for our Common Home.* Our Sunday Visitor Publishing Division: Huntington, IN 2015, p. 105) – have been particularly vocal in denouncing attempts to saddle future generations with the planet's environmental woes. Seen, therefore, from the perspective of these climate justice advocates, the discourse of "youth participation" in the 2009 contest was especially problematic because it seemed to shift responsibility for solving the climate crisis away from state and transnational agencies onto the shoulders of the poor and of youth – and to redirect attention away from the rhetorical move towards "responsibilization" embedded within it.

Additional evidence to support this critical reading of the contest could be found in the fact that "responsiblization" discourse was also present in the Bank's organizational mission statement at the time. That mission statement read: "The World Bank Group aims to fight poverty with passion and professionalism for lasting results - to *help people help themselves* and their environments by providing resources, sharing knowledge, building capacity, and forging partnerships in the public and private sectors." (The World Bank: "Vision," emphasis mine) Here, the idea of helping people helping themselves is read not as empowerment discourse but rather as expressing a sentiment in keeping with the guiding neoliberal dictum of personal responsibility mentioned before. This statement implies that people should not rely on government to solve problems like climate change but that they should look instead at what they can do outside of government, perhaps through public-private partnerships, to decrease their reliance on the public sector. In this mission statement, the message of self-reliance also extends to the environment: note the addition of helping themselves "and their environments." In general, the mission statement couches privatization and "responsibilization" rhetoric inside of language that confounds it – a rhetoric of empowerment that emphasizes instead positive actions like "building capacity."

The fact that this "responsibilization" qua empowerment discourse appears in a document as important as the organizational mission statement suggests, moreover, that these potentially contradictory ideas were at the very heart of the Bank's communications at the time. And, even though, in 2013, this mission statement was changed to the more simply stated goals of ending extreme poverty within a generation, (The World Bank: "The World Bank Group Goals") the idea of people helping themselves – couched in the language of youth empowerment or participation – was present in a range of Bank materials in 2009.

This linking of "responsibilization" to climate change could also be seen in the Bank's major publication on the issue, the *2010 World Bank Development Report on Development and Climate Change*. Chapter headings in this textbook-length report, which was distributed widely throughout the world, similarly call to mind "responsibilization" discourse. Consider, for example, the heading for Chapter Two, "Reducing Human Vulnerability: Helping People Help Themselves," (The World Bank: *World Development Report 2010, Development and Climate Change*. The World Bank: Washington D.C 2010, p. 87) and a sub-heading for Chapter Eight, "Harnessing individuals' behavioral change." (The World Bank: *World Development Report 2010*, p. 322) These headings and topics emphasize the idea that people should accept individual responsibility for climate change, even as this emphasis conflicts with other parts of the report that call for "Bringing the State Back In." The upshot of this analysis is that the presence of "responsibilization" discourse in these various Bank documents reveals not only how the affordances of the so-called knowledge society were used to promote a neoliberal perspective on climate-change problem-solving in 2009, but also how the potential conflation of the discourses of "responsibilization" and civic participation may represent a broader neoliberal strategy that rhetorical critics should be watchful for.

5. Conclusion

With its 188 member countries and about 9,000 employees, the Bank (now called The World Bank Group) is a large and exceedingly complex organization. As a result, it would be erroneous to conclude that "responsibilization" as a rhetorical strategy represents a coherent system or diehard characteristic of all Bank discourse. In fact, as Benjamin observes, the Bank is best understood not as "a reified abstraction of global capitalism." (Benjamin, Bret: *Invested Interests, Capital, Culture, and the World Bank*. University of Minnesota Press: Minneapolis 2007, p. xxvi) but rather as "a powerful but mutable agent, perpetually transforming itself in reaction to critique and crisis." (Benjamin 2007, p. xxvi) Indeed, there seems to be a marked change in tone in some of the Bank's more recent communications, since it came under the leadership in 2012 of the Harvard-trained medical doctor and academic anthropologist, Jim Yong Kim, who, in interviews with the media, (Cunningham, Lillian: "Trying to Change the World Bank." *The Washington Post*, April 10, 2014) has signaled his intentions to foster a culture of change there. Nonetheless, it is possible to conclude from these instances of the Bank's discourse during its "Knowledge for Development Era" (Enns 2015) that there may be a troubling tendency on the part of neoliberal regimes to exploit the language of civic participation for other purposes. And, since the rhetoric of civic participation pervades so many academic and social institutions, it is important for educators and rhetorical scholars to be aware of its potential for misuse.

The "responsibilizing" discourse of the 2009 contest constituted one such instance of misuse because it undermined the message of youth empowerment by displacing responsibility for the climate crisis onto the shoulders of the poor and of youth. And, as advocates of climate justice suggest, such a displacement fails to address "the underlying causes of climate change, which are seen as rooted in unjust economic relations at all levels and in unsustainable patterns of consumption by the [global] North and by Southern elites." (Pettit, Jethro: "Climate Justice: A New Social Movement for Atmospheric Rights". *IDS Bulletin* 35 (3), 2009, p. 104) Additionally, as Pope Francis suggests, generational justice demands that older generations recognize their responsibility for the problems they are handing down to their children and grandchildren. From the perspective of these climate justice advocates, such a rhetorical move to "responsibilize" the poor and the youth, therefore, does not equate to authentic youth empowerment. Empowering young people, from a climate justice perspective, would require real and long-lasting commitments from the countries with the greatest carbon emissions, as well as economic, political and regulatory action on the part of powerful, international bodies. It would require, moreover, the capacity for youth to help set the environmental agenda and not merely to respond to it. Elsewhere, I have argued that the prompt's emphasis on "green entrepreneurial" solutions in the 2009 contest placed limits on the kind of environmentalism it was suitable for the essayists to express. (Porter, Anne: "Sponsoring 'Green' Subjects, The World Bank's 2009 Youth Essay Contest". In: Bazeman, Charles et al. (eds.) *International Advances in Writing Research: Cultures, Places, Measures. Perspectives on Writing.* The WAC Clearinghouse and Parlor Press: Fort Collins, Colorado 2012, pp. 251–266) Those in a position to foster youth literacy and civic engagement must take considerations like these into account.

The rhetoric, therefore, of civic participation, as it applies to youth involvement in major issues like climate change, is too important to be misunderstood or misappropriated by other actors. In this chapter, I have shown how, during the World Bank's "Knowledge for Development Era," (Enns 2015) the Bank's confounding rhetoric of "youth participation" may have blurred or obscured its concurrent message of "responsibilization," and I have argued that, in an era of neoliberal globalization, this conflation of discourses is one to which rhetorical critics should attend. Urgent environmental dilemmas like climate change demand the involvement of all stakeholders, including the full participation of global youth in defining and promoting their best interests, and, by teasing apart discrepant discourses such as these, rhetorical criticism can play a vital role in expanding opportunities for genuine civic action in the knowledge society.

References

Asen, Robert: "A Discourse Theory of Citizenship". *Quarterly Journal of Speech* 90 (2), 2004, pp. 189–211.

Benjamin, Bret: *Invested Interests, Capital, Culture, and the World Bank*. University of Minnesota Press: Minneapolis 2007.

Bessant, Judith: "Mixed Messages, Youth Participation and Democratic Practice." *Australian Journal of Political Science* 39 (2), 2004, pp. 387–404, retrieved 9.25.2015, from DOI: 10.1080/1036114042000238573.

Campbell, Karlyn Kohrs: "Agency, Promiscuous and Protean". *Communication and Critical/ Cultural Studies* 2 (1), 2005, pp. 1–19.

Cunningham, Lillian: "Trying to Change the World Bank." *The Washington Post*, April 10, 2014, retrieved 9.27.15 from https://www.washingtonpost.com/news/on-leadership/wp/2014/04/10/trying-to-change-the-world-bank/.

Edbauer, Jenny: "Unframing Models of Public Distribution: From Rhetorical Situation to Rhetorical Ecologies". *Rhetoric Society Quarterly* 35 (4), 2005, pp. 5–24.

Enns, Charis: "Knowledges in Competition, Knowledge Discourse at the World Bank during the Knowledge for Development Era." *Global Social Policy* 15 (1), 2015, pp. 61–80, retrieved 6.17.2015 from DOI: 10.1177/1468018113516968.

EU Youth Report 2012, retrieved 6.17.2015 from http://ec.europa.eu/youth/library/reports/eu-youth-report-2012_en.pdf.

Fairclough, Norman: *Analyzing Discourse: Textual Analysis for Social Research*. Routledge: New York 2003.

Geisler, Cheryl: "How Ought We to Understand the Concept of Rhetorical Agency?" *Rhetoric Society Quarterly* 34 (3), 2004, pp. 9–17.

Goldman, Michael: *Imperial Nature, the World Bank and Struggles for Social Justice in the Age of Globalization*. Yale University Press: New Haven, CT 2005.

Jennings, Louise B. et al: "Toward a Critical Social Theory of Youth Empowerment". *Journal of Community Practice* 14 (1–2), 2006, pp. 31–55, retrieved 9.25.2015, from http://dx.doi.org/10.1300/J125v14n01_03.

Jones, Phillip W.: "The World Bank and the Literacy Question, Orthodoxy, Heresy, and Ideology." *International Review of Education* 43 (3), 2005, pp. 367–75.

Kock, Christian/ Villadsen, Lisa: "Introduction, Citizenship as a Rhetorical Practice". In: Kock, Christian/ Villadsen, Lisa (eds.). *Rhetorical Citizenship and Public Deliberation*. Pennsylvania State University Press: University Park, PA 2012.

Kramarz, Teresa/ Momani, Bessma: "The World Bank as a Knowledge Bank, Acknowledging the Limits of a Legitimate Knowledge Actor". *Review of Policy Research* 30 (4), 2013, pp. 409–431.

Kuznicka, Anna: *Report on the 2009 International Essay Competition*. World Bank: London Office, 2009, retrieved 8.9.2011, from www.essaycompetition.org.

Miller, Carolyn R.: "What Can Automation Tell us about Agency?" *Rhetoric Society Quarterly* 37 (2), 2007, pp. 137–57.

Mitra, Dana/ Serriere, Stephanie/ Kirshner, Ben: "Youth Participation in U.S. Contexts, Student Voice without a National Mandate". *Children and Society* 28, 2014, pp. 292–304, retrieved 9.25.2015, from DOI:10.1111/chso.12005.

Oliver, Veronica: "Civic Disobedience: Anti-SB 1070 Graffiti, Marginalized Voices, and Citizenship in a Politically Privatized Public Sphere". *Community Literacy Journal* 9 (1), 2014, pp. 62–76.

Pettit, Jethro: "Climate Justice: A New Social Movement for Atmospheric Rights". *IDS Bulletin*. 35 (3), 2009, pp. 102–106.

Pope Francis: *Laudato Si', On Care for our Common Home*. Our Sunday Visitor Publishing Division: Huntington, IN 2015.

Porter, Anne: "Sponsoring 'Green' Subjects, The World Bank's 2009 Youth Essay Contest". In: Bazeman, Charles et al. (eds.) *International Advances in Writing Research: Cultures, Places, Measures. Perspectives on Writing*. The WAC Clearinghouse and Parlor Press: Fort Collins, Colorado 2012, pp. 251–266.

Rose, Nikolas: *Powers of Freedom, Reframing Political Thought*. Cambridge University Press: Cambridge 1999.

Sandel, Michael: *Justice, What's the Right Thing to Do?* Farrar, Strauss and Giroux: New York 2010.

Stern, Nicholas Sir: *The Economics of Climate Change, The Stern Review*. Cambridge University Press: Cambridge 2007.

Sukarieh, Mayssoun/ Tannock, Stuart: "In the Best Interests of Youth or Neoliberalism? The World Bank and the New Global Youth Empowerment Project". *Journal of Youth Studies* 11 (3), 2008, pp. 301–312, retrieved 9.25.2015, from DOI: 10.1080/13676260801946431.

The World Bank: *World Development Report 2010, Development and Climate Change*. The World Bank: Washington D.C 2010.

The World Bank: "Education/ "Education for the Knowledge Economy," retrieved 11.6.2011, from http://web.worldbank.org.

The World Bank: "The World Bank", retrieved 7.2.2013, from www.theworldbank.org.

The World Bank: "The World Bank Group Goals", retrieved 6.17.2015, from www.theworldbank.org.

The World Bank: "Topic", retrieved 3.14.10, from www.essaycompetition.org/contentm09_1_.

The World Bank: "Vision", retrieved 7.202013, from http://go.worldbank.org.

Young Global Pinons: "2009 World Bank Essay Competition" retrieved 9.27.15, from http://youngglobalpinoys.blogspot.com/2009/02/2009-worldbank-international-essay.html.

Contributors

Ludmilla A'Beckett (PhD) is research fellow at the Unit for Language Facilitation and Empowerment of University of the Free State, South Africa. Her main research fields are cognitive linguistics and discourse analysis. She analyses Post-Soviet discourse and intercultural communication between former Soviet Republics. Multimodality, linguistic approaches to literature and language policy are also among her research interests. E-mail: berchonok@gmail.com

Bas Andeweg (PhD) is assistant professor at the Centre for Languages and Academic Skills at Delft University of Technology in The Netherlands. He is an active researcher on various aspects of oral communication. E-mail: b.a.andeweg@tudelft.nl

Ove Bergersen is associate professor at the University of Stavanger, Norway. His main research interests are early childhood education and care, child language, multilingualism, rhetoric and rhetorical citizenship, including rhetorical perspectives on children's language acquisition. http://www.uis.no/om-uis/kontakt-oss/finn-ansatt/bergersen-ove-article74471-11198.html; E-mail: ove.bergersen@uis.no

Maureen Daly Goggin works at Arizona State University, USA. Her research can be divided into four strands: history of rhetoric; visual rhetoric and material culture; discursively constructed racial, gendered, and sexual identities; and writing pedagogy held together by a common scholarly interest in the ways in which discursive practices are created, circulated, taught, and learned, and the interdynamic roles they play in creating personal, social, political, economic, and cultural identities. E-mail: maureen.goggin@asu.edu

Markus Gottschling received his M.A. in German Literature, English Literature and Rhetoric in 2011. Since then he has been a member of the Presentation Research Center at the Department of General Rhetoric, University of Tuebingen, Germany, and focused on research and training for the nationwide youth science competition and school development program "Jugend präsentiert" ('Youth Presents'). His research includes media theory and media rhetoric, rhetoric of presentation as well as spatial theory and narratology. E-mail: markus.gottschling@uni-tuebingen.de

Christine Isager (PhD) is associate professor at University of Copenhagen, Denmark. Her research interests include imitation in rhetorical practice and portrayals of writing and writers in journalism as well as in popular film. E-mail: isager@hum.ku.dk

David Isaksen from University College of Southeast Norway, is interested in the impact rhetoric has on group deliberations and the contributions it can make to deliberative democracy. Other interests include rhetoric of science, rhetoric and aesthetics, rhetorical criticism, and textual analysis. E-mail: d.e.isaksen@tcu.edu

Jaap de Jong (PhD) is full professor at the Faculty of Humanities of Leiden University in The Netherlands. His research interests are modern rhetoric, stylistics and rhetorical and stylistic analysis of journalism. He is editor of *Onze Taal* and co-author of publications including *Bending Opinion* (2012), *Visual Language* (2012) and *Beïnvloeden met emoties: pathos en retorica* (2015). E-mail: j.c.de.jong@hum.leidenuniv.nl

Agnieszka Kampka (PhD in Sociology and MA in Philology and History of Art) is assistant professor at the Faculty of Social Sciences at the Warsaw University of Life Sciences (SGGW) and a member of the Rhetoric Society of Poland. Her research interests include the sociology of politics, visual sociology, rhetoric and social semiotics. She authored *Perswazja w języku polityki* [Persuasion in the language of politics] (2009) and *Debata publiczna. Zmiany społecznych norm komunikacji* [Public debate: Changes of social communication rules] (2014). She co-edits the international open access journal *Res Rhetorica*. E-mail: agnieszka_kampka@sggw.pl

Katarzyna Molek-Kozakowska (PhD) is assistant professor at the Institute of English, Opole University, Poland. Trained as a linguist, she specializes in discourse analysis and media studies. She has published articles and chapters on various aspects of mass-mediated political discourse, rhetorical and stylistic properties of journalistic discourse, methodology of critical discourse analysis and critical media literacy. She authored a monograph *Discursive Exponents of the Ideology of Counterculture* (2011). She co-edits the international open access journal *Res Rhetorica*. E-mail: molekk@uni.opole.pl

Cezar M. Ornatowski is professor of Rhetoric and Writing Studies at San Diego State University, USA, and associate faculty in the Master of Science program in Homeland Security. His main research interests are political rhetoric, rhetoric and political transformation (esp. in Central/Eastern Europe), totalitarian and extremist rhetoric, and visual rhetoric. His recent publications include an anthology *Rhetorics of 1989: Rhetorical Archaeologies of Political Transition* (2015). More information: http://rhetoric.sdsu.edu/faculty_staff/profiles/cezar_ornatowski.htm; E-mail: ornat@mail.sdsu.edu

Anne E. Porter works at Providence College, USA. Her research interests include composition, rhetoric, and literacy. She has published in *International Advances in Writing Research: Cultures, Places, Measures* and *Assessing Writing*. E-mail: aporter1@providence.edu

Gabriela Scripnic (PhD) is professor at the Faculty of Letters, "Dunărea de Jos" University of Galați, Romania, where she lectures on French phonetics, phonology and morphosyntax. As a member of the Argumentation-Rhetoric-Communication group, her research focuses on rhetorical devices in political, media or ordinary discourses. She explored the use of knowledge source indicators within the framework provided by the pragma-dialectical approach to argumentation. She authored *Communication, argumentation et médiativité. Aspects de l'évidentialité en français et en roumain* (2012) and *Langue française contemporaine. Phonétique et phonologie* (2011), several handbooks and numerous articles on argumentation, rhetoric and discourse analysis. E-mail: Gabriela.Scripnic@ugal.ro

Louise Therese Schou Therkildsen is a PhD-student at Uppsala University, Sweden. Her main research interests include migration and identity. Theoretical and conceptual interests are, among others, constitutive rhetoric, narrative theory, rhetorical citizenship and nation building. E-mail: louise.therkildsen@littvet.uu.se

Hilde van Belle is associate professor at KU Leuven Campus Antwerp, Belgium. Her main research interests are rhetoric and argumentation, narrative and persuasive aspects in the media, non-fiction and new journalism, literary translation and style. She teaches text analysis in the Masters in Translation and in Journalism. In her publications on Dutch literature, narrative journalism and rhetoric, both literary and critical analyses are performed. Her recent publications include volumes *Let's Talk Politics: New Essays on Deliberative Rhetoric* (2014) and *Verbal and Visual Rhetoric in a Media World* (2013). E-mail: Hilde.VanBelle@kuleuven.be

Martijn Wackers is a lecturer in communicative skills at the Centre for Languages and Academic Skills at Delft University of Technology in The Netherlands. He received Master's degrees in Rhetoric & Argumentation and Journalism from

Leiden University. His current PhD research at Leiden University focuses on the influence of rhetorical techniques on the audience's information retention. He is co-author of a textbook containing evidence based presentation advice (*Presenteren: wat werkt echt en wat echt niet?* 2012). E-mail: m.j.y.wackers@tudelft.nl

List of figures

Fig. 2.1	André Skupin. "In Terms of Geography". 2005 (Courtesy of André Skupin, San Diego State University, San Diego, CA. Reproduced by permission of the author)	32
Fig. 4.1–4.6:	JR One Year of Turning the World Inside Out	66
Fig. 4.7–4.12	Putting Time in Perspective by 'Prezi Jedi'	68
Fig. 5.1	Overview of the most frequently mentioned advised retention techniques in the public speaking textbooks from the period 1980–2009, broken down into the English-language and Dutch-language textbooks. The frequency of the technique is expressed in the number of books in which it is mentioned, compared to the total number of books in that sub corpus (= 40).	80
Fig. 5.2	Overview of the most important characteristics of the analyzed speech/presentation corpora.	82
Fig. 5.3	The definitions of the rhetorical retention techniques focused on structure/organization of the speech used in the analysis (research presentations and political speeches).	84
Fig. 5.4	Overview of the use of structural retention the techniques per data set and overall. The frequency of the upper four techniques is expressed in the percentage of the total amount of speeches in the corpus (they can only occur once every text); the frequency of the explicit transition and question figures is expressed in occurrences per speech and per 1000 words of the (sub)corpus.	86
Fig. 7.1	Front page of pamphlet issued by Science and Philosophy Group of the California Labor School. Illustrations by Giancomo Patri.	121
Fig. 11.1	The metaphorical mapping of acquisition and participation metaphors	193
Fig. 11.2	Photo-essay and critical reflection assignment	201
Fig. 11.3	Multimodal research essay assignment	204
Fig. 11.4	Multimodal research group proposal	205
Fig. 11.5	Research assignment for multimodal project	206
Fig. 11.6	Individual critical reflection for multimodal project	206
Fig. 13.1	World Bank International Essay Competition 2009 www.essaycompetition.org	230

Index

A
agon 150, 151, 164
allusion 168, 169, 171, 175–177, 182
argument 11, 12, 15, 16, 111, 113, 115, 122, 124, 125, 139, 140, 152, 159–162, 178, 211–213, 219–221
argumentation 15, 16, 57, 58, 99, 125, 135, 152, 155, 160, 161, 164, 213
audience 11, 14, 43, 46, 51, 57–70, 76, 77, 81, 83, 85, 88–90, 110, 116, 119, 123, 131, 136, 138–146, 154, 162, 163, 167, 172, 177–179, 182, 195
authority 16, 28, 43, 111, 117, 123, 125, 126, 140, 141, 158–160, 163, 165

B
Big Data 30, 34, 38, 39

C
citizenship 13, 16, 19, 93–97, 105, 106, 164, 209–213, 220, 221, 224
civic participation 211, 216, 223, 225–228, 231, 234, 235
close reading 94, 96, 97, 106
constitutive rhetoric 94, 96, 97, 99, 107

D
debate 13, 82, 110, 123–125, 133–135, 145, 150, 154-156, 164, 224
deliberation 10, 11, 13, 17, 20, 21, 94, 131. 133, 134, 145, 150, 211, 212, 216, 220, 224
discourse 20, 57, 63, 134, 137, 140, 141, 144, 150, 151, 158, 161, 164, 167, 170, 171, 174, 182, 198

dissensus 20, 150–152, 155, 161, 164, 165

E
education 16, 21, 126, 190–195, 209–211, 218, 228
emotion 20, 115, 119, 134–138, 140, 142–146, 153, 168
enérgeia 60, 62, 64, 211
eristic 15, 150
ethos 12, 48, 51, 90, 119, 138, 140, 144, 168, 212, 213, 216, 218
evidentia 18, 58, 60–66, 69, 70

J
journalist 43, 154, 155, 158, 160, 161, 163–165, 169, 172–175, 183

K
knowledge (knowledge creation, knowledge process) 10, 13, 15, 17, 18, 21, 27–31, 34–37, 39, 40, 44, 50, 59–64, 69, 70, 75, 76, 83, 90, 91, 94, 105, 106, 110, 112, 116, 120, 124, 131, 140, 143, 149, 154, 189–196, 217–220, 223, 228, 229, 233
knowledge society 9, 10, 16, 22, 57, 75, 76, 91, 94, 110, 125, 167, 189, 190, 194, 228

L
logos 12, 136, 150, 168, 212

M
media 11, 13, 14, 20, 59, 63, 64, 75, 149, 153–156, 159–161, 163, 164, 168, 169, 172, 178, 181

memory 19, 76, 77, 79–81, 84
metaphor 9, 19, 21, 28, 39, 46–48, 60, 61, 80, 81, 90, 97–100, 118, 168–171, 175, 192–194, 216, 219
multimodal 10–12, 197, 198

O

orator 14, 44, 59, 60, 64, 136

P

partitio 80, 83, 86, 87, 89, 90
pathos 9, 119, 131, 134, 136, 137, 141, 143, 153, 168
performance 44, 46, 47, 63, 167, 168, 224
persuasion 9, 14, 18, 20, 44, 58, 136, 140, 141, 143, 151
phronesis 17, 21, 210, 213, 219, 221
polemics 149, 150, 152–154, 161–164
professional speaker 75, 77, 78, 89, 90
public speaking 19, 46, 77–83, 85, 89, 90
public sphere 10–15, 17, 20, 131–135, 145, 146, 150–152, 212

R

rationality 21, 112, 150, 152, 153, 163, 164, 177, 210, 212
reasoning 14, 15, 99, 116, 122, 219
retention 19, 77–83, 87–90
retention techniques 18, 19, 79–81, 83–86, 89–91
rhetor 45, 46, 109, 225
rhetorical action 17, 44, 54, 55

rhetorical agency 43–45, 47, 50, 51, 53, 54, 225
rhetorical analysis 9, 19, 81–84, 89, 90, 95, 109, 167, 169, 209, 223, 228
rhetorical citizenship 21, 209, 212–218, 220–224
rhetorical performance 47, 167, 168
rhetorical practice 43, 75, 211
rhetorical situation 12, 21, 46, 58–60
rhetorical strategies/rhetorical strategy 19, 20, 131, 136, 142, 153, 234
rhetorical technique 77, 79, 89, 90

S

scientific community 109, 110, 123, 126
seeing 34, 60, 63–65
society 27, 94, 98, 101, 104–106, 118, 131, 138, 149, 154, 155, 163, 168, 177, 190, 213–216, 219
surveillance 28–40
symbol 35, 40, 94, 109, 162

T

telos 210, 213
textbook 19, 76–80, 83, 89, 90, 93–98, 101–106
topoi/topic 33, 88, 137, 138, 143, 146, 152–154, 160, 171, 175, 181, 182, 198, 227, 229, 231, 234

V

visualization 12, 17, 18, 27, 30–33, 57, 58, 61–69, 76, 80, 89, 90

Studies in Language, Culture and Society

Edited by Łucja Biel, Andrzej Kątny and Piotr Ruszkiewicz

The editors of this series invite books addressing the nexus between language, culture and society. Contrastive studies are welcome in particular, whether of a synchronic or diachronic orientation. Various perspectives on language / communication are of interest: grammatical, pragmatic, sociolinguistic, discursive and semiotic. A wide range of theoretical and methodological positions is accepted: cognitive / anthropological / corpus linguistics, as well as pragmatics, interactional sociolinguistics, (specialized) genre analysis, and critical discourse studies.

The cutting edge of the series is to publish innovative research elucidating the processes of *inter-* and *intra-*language variation and change, and – at the same time – relating them to flows *in* and *across* cognate categories of culture, community and society.

The series publishes monographs and edited volumes reporting on data-driven research that carries a potential for application in translation studies, language teaching, multilingual (multicultural) education, and interdisciplinary critical discourse studies.

The languages of publication are English and German, yet book proposals in other major languages will also be considered, if centrally contributive to the main aim of the series.

Vol. 1   Ewa Kucelman: Self-based Anaphora in Early Modern English. 2013.

Vol. 2   Łucja Biel: Lost in the Eurofog: The Textual Fit of Translated Law. 2014.

Vol. 3   Marek Kuźniak / Agnieszka Libura / Michał Szawerna (eds.): From Conceptual Metaphor Theory to Cognitive Ethnolinguistics. Patterns of Imagery in Language. 2014.

Vol. 4   Grzegorz Kowalski: Claim-making and Claim-challenging in English and Polish Linguistic Discourses. 2015.

Vol. 5   Małgorzata Tryuk: On Ethics and Interpreters. 2015.

Vol. 6   Anna Duszak / Grzegorz Kowalski (eds.): Academic (Inter)genres: between Texts, Contexts and Identities. 2015.

Vol. 7   Alicja Witalisz: English Loan Translations in Polish. Word-formation Patterns, Lexicalization, Idiomaticity and Institutionalization. 2015.

Vol. 8   Agnieszka Kampka / Katarzyna Molek-Kozakowska (eds.): Rhetoric, Knowledge and the Public Sphere. 2016.

www.peterlang.com

www.ingramcontent.com/pod-product-compliance
Ingram Content Group UK Ltd.
Pitfield, Milton Keynes, MK11 3LW, UK
UKHW041923210426
5322IPUK00002B/30